The Essence of Software Engineering

Volker Gruhn • Rüdiger Striemer

Editors

The Essence of Software Engineering

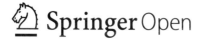 Springer Open

Editors

Volker Gruhn
The Ruhr Institute for Software Technology
University of Duisburg-Essen
Essen, Germany

Rüdiger Striemer
adesso AG
Berlin, Germany

ISBN 978-3-030-08880-4   ISBN 978-3-319-73897-0   (eBook)
https://doi.org/10.1007/978-3-319-73897-0

Preface

Software is key to effective business processes in many industries. As a result, software engineering is an important area in modern societies. Software processes are becoming increasingly reliable and effective, but they are different in nature from production processes.

Software engineering research is all about understanding the nature of software processes, finding appropriate architectures of software systems, and identifying the essential and value-creating activities in software development. There is an urgent need for concise solutions to these issues, which are key to industrial software development. That is why, software engineering research and high-end software development in practice go hand in hand.

adesso was founded 20 years ago in exactly this spirit: to merge scientific cognition with solution approaches from software development in practice. During the last 20 years, adesso has significantly benefited from very close ties with internationally renowned chairs and research facilities in software engineering. At the same time, adesso did not only achieve custom software development. Participation in research projects was always a cornerstone of the company's strategy, mostly to return practical experience to the scientific community.

Today, adesso employs more than 2700 people in distinguished software engineering projects. And the company's growth persists, as in the world of ever-increasing digitalization, software also becomes increasingly relevant. Today, people are literally surrounded by software in any conceivable situation. This leads to entirely new challenges, which we aim to master in the tradition of our long-lasting cooperation with international partners from software engineering.

Thus, this volume about the essence of software engineering shall not only highlight its status quo. It also dares to catch a glimpse of potential future developments in the area. We are very grateful for all the contributions that have been written especially for this volume by authors from scientific and business backgrounds. They make this book very unique! We also highly appreciate those authors who cordially accepted our invitation to speak at the twentieth anniversary of our conference. More than 200 guests joined the conference on November 16,

2017, at the UNESCO World Heritage Site "Zeche Zollverein" and were entertained by world-class speeches.

Finally, special thanks go to Isabell Ehnert, who was responsible for the book's contributors, and Niklas Spitczok von Brisinski, who took the lead in the organization of the highly acclaimed conference.

Essen, Germany   Volker Gruhn
Berlin, Germany   Rüdiger Striemer

Contents

List of Contributors

Alfred Bröckers joined adesso AG in 1998 where he worked as a consultant and project manager mainly in software projects for the insurance industry. Currently, he is managing director of adesso insurance solutions GmbH, an adesso subsidiary.

Alfred Bröckers holds a diploma in computer science from the University of Dortmund, Germany, and received his PhD in computer science from the University of Kaiserslautern, Germany, in 1996.

Manfred Broy served as the Founding Dean of the Department of Mathematics and Information Systems at the University of Passau in 1983 and as the Founding Dean of the Department of Informatics at the Technical University of Munich in 1992, where he had been holding the Chair of Software and Systems Engineering since 1989. The research groups under his direction addressed the application of techniques derived from mathematics to software and systems engineering. Broy founded the "fortiss" research institute and currently serves as the Founding President of the Zentrum Digitalisierung.Bayern.

Angela Carell holds a doctorate in education and is working in the IT context since 2002. At adesso, she is responsible for the adesso research division. She also conducts design thinking workshops and coaches design thinking trainers. Since 2015, she has been lecturing at the University of Hannover on design thinking.

Schahram Dustdar is full professor of computer science and head of the Distributed Systems Group at TU Wien, Austria. He is recipient of the ACM Distinguished Scientist award (2009), the IBM Faculty Award (2012), an elected member of the Academia Europaea: The Academy of Europe, where he is chairman of the Informatics Section, and an IEEE Fellow (2016).

Carlo Ghezzi is an ACM fellow (1999), an IEEE fellow (2005), and a member of the European Academy of Sciences and the Italian Academy of Sciences. He received the ACM SIGSOFT Outstanding Research Award (2015) and the Distinguished Service Award (2006). He has been President of Informatics Europe. He has been a member of the program committee of flagship conferences in the software engineering field, such as the ICSE and ESEC/FSE, for which he also served as Program and General Chair. Ghezzi's research has been mostly focused on different aspects of software engineering. He has coauthored over 200 papers and eight books. He coordinated several national and international research projects. He has been the recipient of an ERC Advanced Grant.

Harald Gall is Dean of the Faculty of Business, Economics, and Informatics at the University of Zurich (UZH). He is professor of software engineering in the Department of Informatics at UZH. Prior to that, he was associate professor at the Technical University of Vienna in the Distributed Systems Group (TUV), where he also received his PhD (Dr. techn.) and master's degree (Dipl.-Ing.) in informatics.

He held visiting positions at Microsoft Research in Redmond, USA, and University of Washington in Seattle, USA.

His research interests are in software engineering with focus on software evolution, software architecture, software quality analysis, mining software repositories, and cloud-based software engineering.

He is probably best known for his work on software evolution analysis and mining software archives. Since 1997, he has worked on devising ways in which mining these repositories can help to better understand software development, to devise predictions about quality attributes, and to exploit this knowledge in software analysis tools such as Evolizer, ChangeDistiller, and SOFAS.

Wilhelm Hasselbring is professor of software engineering at Kiel University, Germany. In the competence cluster Software Systems Engineering (KoSSE), he coordinates technology transfer projects with industry. In the excellence cluster Future Ocean, a large-scale collaborative project of Kiel University and the GEOMAR Helmholtz Centre for Ocean Research Kiel, he is principal investigator and coordinator of the research area Digital Ocean.

Ivar Jacobson is a father of Software Engineering with contributions such as component architecture, use cases, Unified Modelling Language, and Rational Unified Process.

Since 2005, he has been working on how to deal with methods and tools in a smart, superlight, and agile way, resulting in the Essence standard kernel and language. He is the principal author of seven influential and bestselling books.

Kim Lauenroth is chief requirements engineer at adesso in Germany and first Chair of the International Requirements Engineering Board (IREB) e.V. Kim has more than 15 years of experience in software and requirements engineering in different domains and in various roles, including requirements engineer, project manager, and consultant. As chief requirements engineer at adesso, he is responsible for the overall quality of Requirements Engineering methods and helps his customers to develop effective and pragmatic methodological cultures for software development. Kim received his PhD in the field of requirements engineering and studied computer science, business administration, and psychology.

Andreas Metzger is senior academic councillor at the University of Duisburg-Essen and head of adaptive systems and big data applications at paluno (The Ruhr Institute for Software Technology). He is deputy secretary general of the European Big Data Value Association (BDVA), vice chair of the steering committee of the European Technology Platform NESSI (Networked European Software and Services Initiative), and technical coordinator of the European big data lighthouse project TransformingTransport.

Stefan Nastic is a postdoctoral research assistant at the Distributed Systems Group at TU Wien, Austria. His research interests include: Internet of Things and Edge Computing, Cloud Computing, Big Data Analytics, and Smart Cities. Nastic has been involved in several EU-funded research projects such as SMART-FI, U-Test and SM4ALL, as well as, large industrial projects such as Pacific Controls Cloud Computing Lab (PC3L).

Leon Osterweil is pursuing research on defining, analyzing, and improving medical, election, software, and other processes. Osterweil received ACM SIGSOFT Lifetime Achievement Awards for Research (2003), Education (2010), and Service (2014). He was General Chair of ICSE 2006 and an editor of IEEE TSE and ACM TOSEM. He was Dean of Sciences at the University of Massachusetts. He is a fellow of the ACM.

Dirk Platz studied computer science at the University of Dortmund and received his doctorate in computer science at the University of Siegen. He has been working for adesso AG since 1999 and currently leads the software development in Business Line Insurance Services with more than 120 software developers. His passion is project management. He is responsible for the education program for project managers at adesso and is active in large projects. Currently, he is the main project manager in the implementation of the policy administration system for life insurance, PSLife, at one of the largest German life insurance companies.

Klaus Pohl is full professor for Software Systems Engineering at the University of Duisburg-Essen and director of paluno (The Ruhr Institute for Software Technology). From 2005 to 2007, he was scientific founding director of lero (The Irish Software Engineering Research Centre). He is member of the board of the European Technology Platform NESSI (Networked European Software and Services Initiative) and member of the steering committee of the German innovation alliance SPES (Software Platform for Embedded Systems).

Manfred Reichert is a full professor at Ulm University, where he is director of the Institute of Databases and Information Systems. His research interests include business process management, service-oriented computing, and mobile services. Manfred was PC Co-Chair of the BPM'08, CoopIS'11, and EDOC'13 conferences. Furthermore, he served as General Chair of the BPM'09 and EDOC'14 conferences as well as the BPM'15 workshops. Recently, he has coauthored a Springer book on process flexibility and obtained the BPM Test of Time Award at the BPM 2013 conference.

Richard N. Taylor is pursuing research on software architecture and design—issues, techniques, and agents involved in creating and evolving software artifacts and processes. His current work is directed at developing the Computational REST style for computational exchange on the Internet.

Bernhard Rumpe heads the Software Engineering Department at the RWTH Aachen University, Germany (one of the top three universities in CS as well as Mechanical Engineering). Earlier he had positions at INRIA/IRISA, Rennes, Colorado State University, TU Braunschweig, Vanderbilt University, Nashville, and TU Munich.

His main interests are rigorous and practical software and system development methods based on adequate modeling techniques. This includes agile development methods like XP and SCRUM as well as model engineering based on UML-like notations and domain-specific languages. He has many modeling techniques to his credit, including the UML standardization. He also applies modeling, e.g., to autonomous cars, human brain simulation, BIM energy management, juristical contract digitalization, production automation, cloud, and many more. In his projects, he intensively collaborates with all large German car manufacturers, energy companies, insurance and banking companies, a major aircraft company, a space company, as well as innovative start-ups in the IT-related domains.

He is author and editor of ten books and Editor-in-Chief of the Springer International Journal on Software and Systems Modeling (www.sosym.org). His newest books Agile Modeling with the UML and Engineering Modeling Languages: Turning Domain Knowledge into Tools were published in 2016 and 2017.

The Leading Role of Software and Systems Architecture in the Age of Digitization

Manfred Broy

1 Introduction: Software Is Eating the World

The age of digitization can be characterized by the fact that digital technology is more and more closely integrated with business models. It provides key support of everyday life both in business and the private. In economy, more and more enterprises directly depend on their abilities to combine all the potentials of digital technology with their business models and their possibilities in the market generating customer experience and customer journeys. Here, it is absolutely clear that software is the most important part of digital technology since, in the end, it determines the functionality of digital systems and plays a decisive role (see [1]). For companies, it becomes a key capability to understand how software can be used to create innovative products, innovative processes, and instruments to reach the customer. As a consequence, more and more software platform companies are typical for software technology with platforms which can guarantee a short time to market, high quality, and low costs with respect to maintenance and evolution. For platform companies and generally for software-intensive systems, architectural issues become most decisive (see [2]).

Quite hard to understand, programming languages to a large extent are still in the infant state of computer hardware of the 1960s. Most programming languages including object-oriented languages, in principle, follow a conventional von Neumann-style programming paradigm where sequential execution without any considerations of real-time properties, concurrency, parallelism, and continuous interaction are the foundational concepts. This is surprising in a world which is full of network systems, software that is embedded in physical devices and interacts over

M. Broy (✉)

Institut für Informatik, Technische Universität München, München, Germany
e-mail: broy@in.tum.de

© The Author(s) 2018
V. Gruhn, R. Striemer (eds.), *The Essence of Software Engineering*,
https://doi.org/10.1007/978-3-319-73897-0_1

powerful communication networks. For such systems, paradigms are needed that provide support for distribution, interaction, parallelism, and real-time properties. However, we cannot wait until appropriate programming languages are available. Today, we have to build software systems using the programming technology which is around.

Nevertheless, there are options to deal with the important aspects at the level of architecture.

2   Structuring Architecture: Future Reference Architecture

Following the ideas of platform-dependent and platform-independent views onto software systems, a software architecture has to be structured basically into the following three views.

Functional Service Architecture Here we describe for software systems all the functionalities that are offered by the software systems to the outside world. Since today software systems like smartphones or cars offer a large number of services, it is important to structure those services into an architecture of services and to describe both their interface behavior which is the functionality provided to the outside their mutual relationships which define their functional dependencies, often called feature interactions. Therefore, we need description techniques capturing both interface behaviors, their structuring, and their dependencies (see [3]). In fact, specifications of interfaces might also rely on assumptions about their context.

Platform-Independent Component Architecture To realize software systems, we structure and decompose them into a set of components. From the viewpoint of architecture, these components have to be described by their roles, captured by the services they offer in terms of their interfaces including their interface behavior. The description of the components is independent of any execution platform, but, nevertheless, in the interfaces we have to be able to specify parallel behavior, real-time behavior, and also probabilistic behavior (see [4]).

Platform-Dependent Software and Hardware Architecture In the end, the abstract system described in terms of the functional service architecture and the platform-independent component architecture has to be implemented on a well-chosen hardware platform. This means that we have to define the deployment of the software components and their scheduling. Here, it is important that the components of the component-oriented architectures are independent deployable units that are only related to their environments only by their interfaces.

For all these approaches, we need an appropriate concept of interface, of interface behavior, and of system composition in terms of interfaces as well as techniques for their specification.

Finally, we have to be able to describe the context of software systems and assumptions about and its behavior. A well-understood way to describe the properties of the context that are relevant for the systems is assumptions in terms of interface assertions (see [5, 6]). Therefore, the core of the whole approach from its foundations is an approach to describe interfaces and the concept of composition including assumptions formulated by assertions (see [5]).

3   On Systems, Their Interfaces and Properties

In the following, we use the term system in a specific way. We address discrete systems, more precisely discrete real-time system models with input and output. For us, a system is an entity that shows some specific behavior by interacting with its operational context. A system has a boundary, which determines what is inside and what is outside the system. Inside the system there is an encapsulated internal structure called component architecture. The set of actions and events that may occur in the interaction of the system with its operational context at its border determines the syntactic ("static") interface of the system. At its interface, a system shows some *interface behavior*.

From the behavioral point of view, we distinguish between:

- The *syntactic interface* of a system that describes which input and output actions may be executed at the interface and which kind of information is exchanged by these actions across the system border
- The *semantic interface* (also called *interface behavior*) which describes the behavior evolving over the system border in terms of the specific information exchanged in the process of interaction by actions according to the syntactic interface

For specifying predicates there are further properties that we expect. We require that system behaviors fulfill properties such as causality and realizability (see [7]). However, not all interface assertions guarantee these properties.

3.1   *About Architecture*

Architecture of systems and also of software systems is about the structuring of systems. There are many different aspects of structuring systems and therefore of architecture. Examples are functional feature architectures which structure systems in terms of their offered services—also called functional features. We speak of a *functional architecture* or of a *service feature architecture* (see [3]). Another very basic concept of architecture is the decomposition of a larger system into a number of subsystems that are composed and provide this way the behavior of the overall system. We speak of a *subsystem* or of a *component architecture* (see [5]).

This shows that architecture is the structuring of a system into smaller elements, a description of how these elements are connected and behave in relationship to each other. A key concept of architecture is the notion of element and interface. An interface shows at the border of a system how the system interacts with its operational context.

3.2   On the Essence of Architecture: Architecture Design Is Architecture Specification

Architecture is not what is represented and finally implemented in code but a description of architectural structures and rules which are required by the design for implementations leading to code that is correct w.r.t. the specified architecture. The rules, structure, and therefore the principles of architecture usually cannot be reengineered from the code but provide an additional design frame that is documented in the architecture specification. An architecture design consists of the specification of the system's structures, rules, and principles.

Implemented systems realize architectures, more precisely architecture designs described by specifications. Architectures define the overall structure of systems. Consequently, architectures have to be specified. Designs of subsystem architectures are specifications of the sets of subsystems, relevant properties of their interfaces including their interface behavior, and the way the interfaces are connected. This defines the way the subsystems are composed as described by the design of an architecture in terms of their interfaces that follow the rules and principles of the architectural design.

3.3   Logical Subsystem Architectures

Logical subsystem architectures including service-oriented architectures are execution platform independent. They consist of the following ingredients:

- A set of elements called subsystems or components, each equipped with a set of interfaces
- An architectural structure connecting these interfaces

This shows that a key issue in architectural design is the specification of interfaces including their interface behavior and the description of the architectural structure.

4   Interfaces Everywhere

As can be seen from the description of architectures and their concepts, interfaces are a key issue. In our terminology, interface comprises both a syntactic interface and an interface behavior. Interfaces are used to describe the functions of sub-components. Interfaces are used to describe the functionality of systems and their structuring into sub-services that again can be described by interfaces. This shows that the notion of an interface is essential in architectural design. Thus, interfaces occur everywhere, in the functional service architecture, in the logical subsystems or components architecture, and in the technical architecture as well.

There are several ways to describe interfaces. Specifying interfaces can be done by assertions. Assertions can be formulated quite formally or rather informally. We refer to a fully formalized notion of interface and interface behavior that is powerful enough to support specification and that is modular for parallel composition. Although fully formalized, it can nevertheless be used in an informal or as well as in a semiformal way.

4.1   Property-Oriented Specification of Interfaces of Systems

Since the components have to run in parallel and systems, in general, have to run in parallel, since they are distributed and they have to communicate and to interact in order to be part of networks, the interface concept has to be chosen appropriately. We chose an interface concept which is able to describe services that are interactive, run in parallel in a property-oriented way.

We denote a syntactic interface by $(I \triangleright O)$, where I denotes the set of input channels of the interface and O denotes the set of output channels. A fully formalized instance of a theory of interfaces is found in the appendix. This interface theory includes the specification of real-time properties and can be extended to a probabilistic view (see [4]). It supports the description of probabilistic interface properties.

Channels allow us, in addition, the structuring of interfaces. Interfaces consist of channels where each channel has a data type indicating which data are communicated.

An important aspect in structuring interfaces is the separation of the set of channels of the interface into input and output channels. This has semantic consequences. We require causality which is a notion similar to monotonicity in a domain theoretic approach. Causality for an interface consists of a set of input channels and output channels where the input and output are timed streams indicating the asymmetry between input and output. Causality basically says that the output produced till time t does only depend on input received before time t. The reverse does not hold. Input generated at time t can be arbitrary and does not have to depend on the output produced till time t.

Given a syntactic interface ($I \blacktriangleright O$), we write F: ($I \blacktriangleright O$) for an interface behavior F for the syntactic interface ($I \blacktriangleright O$). An interface assertion Q for the syntactic interface ($I \blacktriangleright O$) is used to specify properties for interface behaviors F: ($I \blacktriangleright O$). We write $F \in Q$ to express that behavior F fulfills the specification Q (note that Q specifies a set of interface behaviors).

Given syntactic interface ($I \blacktriangleright O$) we call the syntactic interface ($O \blacktriangleright I$) then *inverse* interface. It is denoted by $(I \blacktriangleright O)^{-1}$.

4.2 Composition

Given two systems S_1 and S_2 with syntactic interfaces ($I_n \blacktriangleright O_n$) and interface specifications Q_1 and Q_2, and corresponding sub-interfaces ($I'_n \blacktriangleright O'_n$) such that $(I'_1 \blacktriangleright O'_1) = (I'_2 \blacktriangleright O'_2)^{-1}$ and where the $(I_n \blacktriangleright O_n) \backslash (I'_n \blacktriangleright O'_n)$ are disjoint for $n = 1, 2$, we may compose S_1 and S_2 over their corresponding sub-interfaces and get a system with syntactic interface

$$(I_1 \blacktriangleright O_1) \backslash (I'_1 \blacktriangleright O'_1) \cup (I_2 \blacktriangleright O_2) \backslash (I'_2 \blacktriangleright O'_2)$$

and interface assertion (here $H = I'_1 \cup O'_1 \cup I'_2 \cup O'_2$ denotes the internal channels that connect the two systems and $G = (I_1 \cup O_1 \cup I_2 \cup O_2) \backslash H$ denotes the external channels of the composite system):

$$\exists H : Q_1 \wedge Q_2$$

This shows a modular composition of systems over their corresponding sub-interfaces. We can also specify the property of the connector H of the two systems:

$$\exists G \backslash H : Q_1 \wedge Q_2$$

This property of the connector can be used to formulate a watchdog like an assert statement in object-oriented programming.

This form of composition is beautiful in the sense that it reflects two major concepts of architecture, namely, parallel composition and channel hiding, by two key concepts of logic, namely, logical "and" reflecting parallel composition and existential quantification reflecting hiding. In fact, this relationship between architectural concepts and logic is not only of interest from an aesthetic point of view. It is also very helpful that we can map architectural concepts one-to-one onto such basic logical concepts.

4.3   Structuring Interfaces

Another important point is that we have to be able to structure interfaces. A system, in particular a large system, has a very large interface with a huge interface behavior, impossible to describe in a monolithic form. Therefore, it is important to introduce a concept of interface *decomposition*, which allows us to decompose and structure an interface into a number of services. Since these services may be not independent, we also have to be able to model the dependency between these services.

A syntactic interface can be structured into a set of sub-interfaces. Given a syntactic interface $(I \blacktriangleright O)$, we write $(I' \blacktriangleright O') \subseteq (I \blacktriangleright O)$ to express that $(I' \blacktriangleright O')$ is a sub-interface of $(I \blacktriangleright O)$. If there is a set of sub-interfaces $S_1, \ldots, S_k$ that are disjoint with union $(I \blacktriangleright O)$, we speak of a decomposition of $(I \blacktriangleright O)$.

Given interface assertions $Q_1, \ldots, Q_k$ for interfaces $S_1, \ldots, S_k$, we speak of a *faithful* decomposition for interface $(I \blacktriangleright O)$ with Q if (see [3])

$$Q \equiv Q_1 \wedge \cdots \wedge Q_k$$

Often such a faithful decomposition does not exist. Then we need an auxiliary syntactic interface H for the exchange of mode messages between the sub-interfaces and we have to include the rule of feature interactions in the assertions Q_i such that

$$Q \equiv \exists H : Q_1 \wedge \cdots \wedge Q_k$$

Such a decomposition is both useful for the functional service architecture and, in particular, leads to functional service architecture but it is also useful for using systems as components in platform-independent component architecture where a component offers a set of sub-interfaces which are used to compose these components with others.

5   Composition: Interfaces in Architectures

Given specifications of IF1 and IF2 by interface assertions P_1 and P_2, we define the interaction assertion

$$P_1 \wedge P_2$$

which specifies the interaction between the subsystems that are connected via their interfaces. Note that here we did not add the concept of channel hiding.

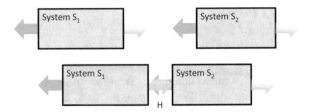

Fig. 1 Connecting subsystem $S1$ with subsystem $S2$ via their matching interfaces

5.1 Interaction Assertions

Given a set of systems with interface assertions, we may compose them into an architecture, provided the semantic interfaces fit together. We call the architecture *well-formed*, if all assumptions are implied by the interface assertions the interfaces they are composed with (see [8]).

For each pair of connected interfaces, we speak of a *connector*, we derive an *interaction assertion* which describes the properties of the data streams that are communicated over this connector (see the internal channels in H of the composition shown in Fig. 1).

5.2 Using Different Types of Interfaces Side by Side

We distinguish the following three types of interfaces:

- *Export interfaces*: they describe services offered by the system to its outside world.
- *Import interfaces*: they describe services required by the system from its outside world.
- *Assumption/commitment interfaces*: they describe assumptions about the behavior of the outside world and the commitment of the system under the condition that the assumption holds.

We consider the following cases of composing systems via their interfaces:

- Connecting export and import interfaces: Given an export interface of one system described by interface assertion P and an import interface of another system described by interface assertion Q which fit together syntactically, we speak of a sound connection if

$$P \Rightarrow Q$$

- Connecting two export interfaces: Given two export interfaces with interface assertions P and Q that fit together syntactically, we speak of a sound connection annotated by

$$P \wedge Q$$

- Connecting two assumption/commitment interfaces: Given two assumption/commitment interfaces with assumptions A_1 and A_2 and commitments P_1 and P_2 that fit together syntactically and where

$$(A_2 \Rightarrow P_2) \Rightarrow A_1$$

$$(A_1 \Rightarrow P_1) \Rightarrow A_2$$

we speak of a sound connection; the connection is annotated by the assertion

$$P_1 \wedge P_2$$

The case of connecting an export interface with an assumption/commitment interface is considered as a special case of connecting two assumption/commitment interfaces where one assumption is true.

5.3 Layered Architectures

A layer in a layered architecture (see [9]) the interface looks as shown in Fig. 2. Its interface specification reads as follows:

$$A \Rightarrow P$$

Layered architectures have many advantages. In many applications, therefore layered architectures are used.

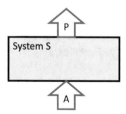

Fig. 2 Interface of a layer

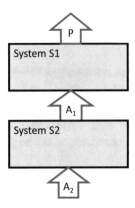

Fig. 3 Composition of two layers

In a layered architecture as shown in Fig. 3, the key idea is that system $S2$ offers some service that does not include any assumptions about the way it is used. Therefore, we describe the service by some interface assertion A_2. The interface P of system $S1$ can be arbitrary. However, the specification of the interface Q of $S1$ reads as follows:

$$Q = [A_1 \Rightarrow P]$$

and P is an interface specification for the reverse interface; then the interface can only be used in a meaningful way if the assumption is fulfilled by system $S1$. Note that $S2$ does not rely in any way on the behavior of $S1$—it is supposed only to offer export interface A.

Figure 3 shows the composition of layer $S2$ providing service A_1 with system $S1$ requiring this service. We get

$$(A_1 \Rightarrow P) \wedge (A_2 \Rightarrow A_1)$$

which hiding interface A_1 results in the interface assertion

$$A_2 \Rightarrow P$$

If we replace the component $S2$ with the interface assertion A_2 by the component $S2'$ with interface assertion $A_2 \Rightarrow B$ where

$$B \Rightarrow A_1$$

then the arguments work as well. $S2'$ is a refinement of $S2$ and we get for the composition

$$(A_2 \Rightarrow B) \wedge (B \Rightarrow A_1)$$

which results the hiding interface B again into

$$A_2 \Rightarrow P$$

The subsystems of a layered architecture are partitioned in layers. The set of layers is in a linear order and subsystems of layer k are only connected to layer $k - 1$ or $k + 1$.

However, this definition is not sufficient. The key idea of a layered architecture is that layer k offers services to layer $k + 1$ but does not assume anything about layer $k + 1$. Layer k may use services offered by layer $k - 1$ but has to know nothing more about layer $k - 1$. In other terms, a layer imports a number of services (from layer $k - 1$) and exports a number of services (for layer $k + 1$). The only relationship between the layers is by the services that are exported to the next layer.

The idea of layered architecture thus is therefore not captured by data flow (by the idea that data may only flow from lower to higher layers or vice versa) nor by control flow (by the idea that calls may only be issued by higher to lower layers) but by the "design flow." Lower layers can be designed without any knowledge of the higher layers—only knowing the services that are requested at the higher layer.

6   On the Asset of Foundations

A powerful approach to architectural design needs a formal foundation provided by a model for the types of interfaces that are used, which has all the properties that are needed for designing systems. These are in particular abstraction, modularity of composition, and property-oriented specification. This way, we are able to understand all of the principal properties of the approach.

It is important, however, that we are not forced always to describe architectures and their elements such as functional services and components in full formality. It is important that we offer an approach which gives the freedom to the developer to be as formal as needed.

6.1   Not Formal Methods but Formal Foundation

Our introduced concept to deal with architectures provides a purely functional and logical approach to architectures. We considered the value of this approach not so much in the fact that we can use it in the sense of formal methods by giving formal specifications of architectures and computing the results of compositions and even doing computer-based formal verification. This is certainly one way to make use of it. But what we consider much more important is to provide a scientific foundation for forming architectures. What we get is a complete understanding of what the properties of architectures are that are relevant and of the logical properties we can express by that. So, we get a scientific underpinning of the notion of an architecture which can be used as a guideline in many more practical approaches, for instance, when trying to understand what approaches like UML and SysML are trying to do. This architectural logical framework gives a comprehensive and complete scientific foundation which allows us to justify all kinds of practical issues like diagrams to describe architecture's rules, to do verification and analysis with architectures as well as the verification of design patterns or the description of architectural styles like layered architectures. What we get is a foundation of architectures.

Now this foundation follows the principle of Occam's razor. It keeps everything as simple as possible. As can be seen from the appendix, the whole theory to describe architectures can be written down with only a few pages. It does not use very difficult mathematics. We have taught this approach of architectures to engineers in many different companies, and they never faced difficulties in understanding the whole approach and understanding what it gives to them.

6.2   Flexibility and Universality of the Presented Approach

The approach is powerful enough to describe not only the classical components of digital systems and their interfaces. It can also describe all kinds of particular additional elements such as protocols, sensors, and actuators, man-machine interaction, and many more aspects. It finally leads into a universal modeling instrument. When being interested in adapting the whole approach to the physical, it is possible to generalize it to physical systems. Then, in addition to the discrete interface concepts, we have to introduce continuous interface concepts where we replace discrete streams by continuous ones generalizing the whole approach in the direction of control theory.

6.3   System Components as Schedulable and Deployable Units

The notion of component is described in detail in Szyperski's work (see [10]). What he considered important is a component that is independently deployable and independently schedulable. This should also apply to our notion of components.

In principle, we could also see physical units, in particular cyber-physical systems as components, but when reduced in the view to study only software components, we stick to the concept of Szyperski that a component should be independently deployable and independently schedulable. In particular, components should be designed in the way that they run in parallel and can be connected also by real-time properties over their interfaces.

6.4   Modularity

A key idea in the approach of components is the idea that components can be described to the outside world only by their interfaces. Interfaces are as described highly parallel, allowing the description of the real-time properties, and supporting the formulation of components contracts.

It is decisive that the specification of components can be exclusively done by describing their interface properties following the idea of Jeff Bezos of a truly service-oriented architecture. This also supports the classical idea of modularity. In this approach, a component concept is modular if we can derive all the relevant interface properties of a composed component by the specifications of their components given the architecture of the components.

6.5   Strict Property Orientation: Architecture Designs by Specifications

In a strict property orientation, we describe interfaces by property-oriented specifications. When we compose interfaces, we get communication links for those interfaces for which we can describe the histories of the data streams communication over those communication links again in terms of property-oriented specifications. As a result, we get a perfect property-oriented view onto architectures (see [6]).

An additional issue is the fact that often in systems and their interfaces we need assumptions about their context that are required with respect to be able to guarantee certain commitments. Other assumptions can be seen purely as properties and so finally we get also a property-oriented view onto assumptions.

When designing architecture following our lines of thought, we describe the components of systems, their interfaces, and the interface behavior in terms of their properties by interface assertions. These properties are specifications. Implementation of architecture may introduce additional properties beyond those required in the architectural design.

6.6   Real Time and Probability: Functional Quality Properties

There is a long debate in the literature about functional and nonfunctional properties. However, there is not a clear definition of what functional properties are and what nonfunctional properties are. Following our concept, we call all properties functional that can be expressed in terms of interface properties.

If we introduce the notion of interfaces with talks about real time, then real-time properties are functional properties and this is, in contrast to IEEE standards, the more adequate view. If we are interested in using functions where real time is an issue, it is essential that real-time properties are part of our functional requirements.

However, we could go even one step further. Based on the concept of interfaces as we have introduced it, it is, at least from a conceptual point of view, an easy step to generalize interfaces to probabilistic properties. Formally, our interfaces are described in terms of functions that map real-time input data streams onto a set of allowed real-time output data streams. It is a straightforward idea to introduce a probability distribution over the set of real-time data output streams (see [4]). This way, we can assign a probability to sets of behaviors. Having done so, we are even able to specify concepts like reliability, availability, safety, and many more (see [11]). A large amount of the classical quality properties that are considered in the old style of looking at systems as nonfunctional properties are then functional properties, and this is correct if we are interested in the reliability of a system. Then, it is absolutely clear that we understand reliability as a required functional property.

7   Concluding Remarks

Following the idea as introduced and explained, we get an extended view onto architecture of systems. Looking at the architecture of systems, we see all the required things that are necessary. We see the functional service architecture with the set of services and functions offered to the outside; we see the relationship in terms of feature interactions between those functions which give a comprehensive structure description of the functionality of a system including functional properties such as real time and also probabilistic properties such as reliability or safety if needed.

It uses the same techniques to describe the decomposition of a system into a set of components that are connected over their interfaces and provide the required functionality.

It is a straightforward step to introduce also concepts of classes and instantiations into the approach being able to define and describe dynamic architectures, and another extension would be to go into continuous data streams and also to introduce control theory. Finally, we get along that lines a comprehensive foundational model of architecture and system behavior in terms of interaction which also to do a comprehensive documentation of state-of-the-art software systems and also of cyber-physical systems.

When looking at software families and product lines, architecture becomes even more significant, because it determines the possibilities and options of variability and reusability (see [12]). With this in mind, it is a key issue to have an appropriate methodology with a calculus for the design of architectures. This includes a number of ingredients:

- A key concept for *subsystems*, also called components, as building blocks of architectures: this means that we have to determine what the concept of a subsystem is and, in particular, what the concept of an *interface* and *interface behavior* is. Interfaces are the most significant concept for architectures. Subsystems are composed and connected via their interfaces.

- The second ingredient is *composition*. We have to be able to compose systems by composition via their interfaces. Composition has to reflect parallel execution.
- This requires that interfaces of subsystems can be structured into a *family* of sub-interfaces, which are then the basis for the composition of subsystems, more precisely the composition of sub-interfaces of subsystems with other sub-interfaces of subsystems. For this we need a syntactic notion and a notion of behavior interface.
- In addition, we are interested in options to *specify properties* of *interface behaviors* in detail.
- Moreover, we have to be able to deal with *interface types* and *subsystem types*. These concepts allow us to introduce a notion of subsystems and their types, called *system classes* as in object-oriented programs, and these can also be used to introduce types of interfaces, properties of assumptions of the interfaces of subsystems which we compose.
- As a result, we also talk about the concept of refinement of systems and their interfaces as a basis of inheritance.

A key is the ability to specify properties of subsystems in terms of their interfaces and to compose interface specifications in a modular way.

We introduce a logical calculus to deal with interfaces and show how we can use it to define subsystems via properties of their interface assumptions also be able to deal with architectural patterns such as layered architectures.

Appendix: A Formal Model of Interfaces

The key to software and system design are interface specifications where we do not only describe syntactic interfaces but also specify interface behavior.

Data Models

System exchange messages. Messages are exchange between systems and their operational context and also between subsystems. Systems have states. States are composed of attributes. In principle, we can therefore work out the data model for a service-oriented architecture which consists, just as an object orientation, of all the attributes which are part of the local states of the subsystems which consists of the description of the data which are communicated over the interfaces between the subsystems.

Syntactic Interfaces and Interface Behavior

We choose a very general notion of interface where the key is the concept of a channel. A channel is a directed typed communication line on which data of the specified type are transmitted. As part of an interface, a channel is a possibility to provide input or output to a system. Therefore, we speak about input channels and output channels.

Syntactic Interfaces

An interface defines the way a system interacts with its context. Syntactically an interface is specified by a set C of channels where each channel has a data type assigned that defines the set of messages, events, or signals that are transmitted over that channel.

In this section, we briefly introduce syntactic and semantic notions of discrete models of *systems* and their *interfaces*. This theoretical framework is in line with [13] called the FOCUS approach. Systems own input and output channels over which streams of messages are exchanged. In the following, we denote the universe of all messages by IM.

Let I be a syntactic interface of typed input channels and O be a syntactic interface of typed output channels that characterize the syntactic interface of a system. $(I \blacktriangleright O)$ denotes this *syntactic interface*. Figure 4 shows system F with its syntactic interface in a graphical representation as a data flow node.

System Interaction: Timed Data Streams

Let IN denote the natural numbers (including 0) and IN^+ denote the strictly positive natural numbers.

The system model is based on the concept of a global clock. The system model can be described as time synchronous and message asynchronous. We work with streams that include discrete timing information. Such streams represent histories of

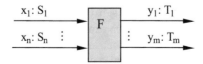

Fig. 4 Graphical representation of a system F as a data flow node with its syntactic interface consisting of the input channels $x_1, \ldots, x_n$ of types $S_1, \ldots, S_n$ and the output channels $y_1, \ldots, y_m$ of types $T_1, \ldots, T_m$, resp.

communications of data messages transmitted within a time frame. By this model of discrete time, time is structured into an infinite sequence of finite time intervals of equal length. We use the natural numbers IN^+ to number the time intervals.

Definition Timed Streams

Given a message set $M \subseteq IM$ of data elements of type T, we represent a *timed stream s* of type T by a function

$$s : IN^+ \to M^*$$

In a timed stream s, a sequence of messages $s(t)$ is given for each time interval $t \in IN^+$; $s(t) = \varepsilon$ indicates that in time interval t no message is communicated. By $(M^*)^\infty$ we denote the set of timed streams. ☐

A *channel history* (also called *channel valuation*) for a set C of typed channels (which is a set of typed identifiers) assigns to each channel $c \in C$ a timed stream of messages communicated over that channel. Let C be a set of typed channels; a (total) *channel history x* is a mapping

$$x : C \to \left(IN^+ \to M^*\right)$$

such that $x(c)$ is a timed stream of type $Type(c)$ for each channel $c \in C$. We denote the set of all channel histories for the channel set C by $\vec{C}$. A finite (partial) channel history is a mapping

$$x : C \to \left(\{1, \ldots, t\} \to M^*\right)$$

with some number $t \in IN$ such that $x(c)$ respects the channel type of c. ☐

As for streams, for every history $z \in \vec{C}$ and every time $t \in IN$, the expression $z \downarrow t$ denotes the partial history (the communication on the channels in the first t time intervals) of z until time t. $z \downarrow t$ yields a finite history for each of the channels in C represented by a mapping of the type $C \to (\{1, \ldots, t\} \to IM^*)$. $z \downarrow 0$ denotes the history with the empty sequence associated with all its channels.

Interface Behavior

For a given syntactic interface $(I \blacktriangleright O)$, a relation that relates the input histories in $\vec{I}$ with output histories in $\vec{O}$ defines its behavior. It is called *system interface behavior* (see [2]). We represent the relation by a set-valued function. In the following, we write $\wp(M)$ for the power set over M.

Definition Interface Behavior and Causal Interface Behavior A function

$$F : \vec{I} \to \wp\left(\vec{O}\right)$$

is called *I/O behavior*; F is called *causal in input x* if (for all times $t \in \mathrm{IN}$ and input histories $x, z \in \overrightarrow{I}$)

$$x \downarrow t = z \downarrow t \Rightarrow \{y \downarrow t : y \in F(x)\} = \{y \downarrow t : y \in F(z)\}$$

F is called *strongly causal* if (for all times $t \in \mathrm{IN}$ and input histories $x, z \in \overrightarrow{I}$)

$$x \downarrow t = z \downarrow t \Rightarrow \{y \downarrow t + 1 : y \in F(x)\} = \{y \downarrow t + 1 : y \in F(z)\} \qquad \square$$

Causality indicates consistent time flow between input and output histories (for an extended discussion of causality, see [1]).

Interface Assertions

The interface behavior of systems can be specified in a descriptive logical style using interface assertions.

Definition Interface Assertion
 Given a syntactic interface $(I \blacktriangleright O)$ with a set I of typed input channels and a set O of typed output channels, an *interface assertion* is a formula in predicate logic with channel identifiers from I and O as free logical variables which denote streams of the respective types. $\qquad \square$

We specify the behavior F_S for a system with name S with syntactic interface $(I \blacktriangleright O)$ and an *interface assertion* Q by a scheme:

spec S
in I
out O
Q

Q is an assertion containing the input and the output channels as free variables for channels. We also write $q(x, y)$ with $x \in \overrightarrow{I}$ and $y \in \overrightarrow{O}$ for interface assertions. This is only another way to represent interface assertions which is equivalent to the formula $Q[x(x_1)/x_1, \ldots x(x_n)/x_n), y(y_1)/y_1, \ldots y(y_m)/y_m]$.

Definition Meaning of Specifications and Interface Assertions
 An interface behavior F fulfills the specification S with interface assertion $q(x, y)$ if

$$\forall x \in \overrightarrow{I}, y \in \overrightarrow{O} : y \in F(x) \Rightarrow q(x, y)$$

S and $q(x, y)$ are called *(strongly) realizable* if there exists a "realization" which is a strongly causal function $f : \overrightarrow{I} \to \overrightarrow{O}$ that fulfills S. $\qquad \square$

The purpose of a specification and an interface assertion is to specify systems.

Composing Interfaces

Finally, we describe how to compose systems from subsystems described by their interface behavior. Syntactic interfaces $(I_k \blacktriangleright O_k)$ with $k = 1, 2$ are called *composable*, if their channel types are consistent and $O_1 \cap O_2 = \varnothing$, $I_1 \cap O_1 = \varnothing$, $I_2 \cap O_2 = \varnothing$.

Definition Composition of Systems—Glass Box View
Given for $k = 1, 2$ composable interface behaviors $F_k : (I_k \blacktriangleright O_k)$ with composable syntactic interfaces; let $I = I_1 \backslash O_2 \cup I_2 \backslash O_1$, $O = O_1 \cup O_2$, and $C = I_1 \cup I_2 \cup O_1 \cup O_2$; we define the composition $(F_1 \times F_2) : (I \blacktriangleright O)$ by

$$(F_1 \times F_2)(x) = \left\{ y \in \vec{O} : \exists z \in \vec{C} : x = z|I \wedge y \right.$$

$$= z|O \wedge z|O_1 \in F_1(z|I_1) \wedge z|O_2 \in F_2(z|I_2) \}$$

where | denotes the usual restriction operator for mappings.

In the glass box view, the internal channels and their valuations are visible. In the black box view, the internal channels are hidden. From the glass box view, we can derive the black box view of composition.

Definition Composition of Systems—Black Box View—Hiding Internal Channels
Given two composable interface behaviors $F_k : (I_k \blacktriangleright O_k)$ with $k = 1, 2$; let $I = I_1 \backslash O_2 \cup I_2 \backslash O_1$ and $O = O_1 \backslash I_2 \cup O_2 \backslash I_1$ and $C = I_1 \cup I_2 \cup O_1 \cup O_2$

$$(F_1 \otimes F_2)(x) = \left\{ y \in \vec{O} : \exists z \in \vec{C} : y = z|O \wedge z \in (F_1 \times F_2)(x) \right\}$$

Shared channels in $(I_1 \cap O_2) \cup (I_2 \cap O_1)$ are hidden by this composition.

Black box composition is commutative and associative as long as we compose only systems with disjoint sets of input channels.

A specification approach is called *modular* if specifications of composed systems can be constructed from the specification of their components. The property of modularity of composition of two causal interface specifications F_k, $k = 1, 2$, where at least one is strongly causal, is as follows. Given system specifications by specifying assertions P_k:

spec F_1

in I_1
out O_1

P_1

Fig. 5 Composition $F_1 \otimes F_2$

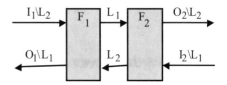

> **spec** F_2
> ---
> **in** I_2
> **out** O_2
> ---
> P_2

we obtain the specification of the composed system $F_1 \otimes F_2$ as a result of the composition of the interface specification F_1 and F_2 as illustrated in Fig. 5; $L_1 \cup L_2$ denotes the set of shared channels:

> **spec** $F_1 \otimes F_2$
> ---
> **in** $I_1 \backslash L_2 \cup I_2 \backslash L_1$
> **out** $O_1 \backslash L_1 \cup O_2 \backslash L_2$
> ---
> $\exists\, L_1, L_2: P_1 \wedge P_2$

The specifying assertion of $F_1 \otimes F_2$ is composed in a modular way from the specifying assertions of its components by logical conjunction and existential quantification over streams denoting internal channels.

In a composed system, the internal channels are used for internal communication.

The composition of strongly causal behaviors yields strongly causal behaviors. The set of systems together with the introduced composition operators form an algebra. For properties of the resulting algebra, we refer to [1, 5]. Since the black box view hides internal communication over shared channels, the black box view provides an abstraction of the glass box composition.

Note that this form of composition works also for instances. Then, however, often it is helpful to use not channels identified by instance identifiers but to connect the channels of classes and to use the instance identifiers to address instances.

Specifying Contracts

Contracts are used in architectures (see [4, 6, 9, 10, 14–17]). In the following, we show how to specify contracts.

Interface Assertions for Assumption/Commitment Contracts

Specifications in terms of assumptions and commitments for a system S with syntactic interface $(I \blacktriangleright O)$ and with input histories $x \in \overrightarrow{I}$ and output histories $y \in \overrightarrow{O}$ are syntactically expressed by interface assertions $asu(x, y)$ and $cmt(x, y)$. We write A/C contracts by the following specification pattern:

$$\begin{aligned} \textbf{assume}: \quad & asu\,(x, y) \\ \textbf{commit}: \quad & cmt\,(x, y) \end{aligned}$$

with interface assertions $asu(x, y)$ and $cmt(x, y)$. In the following section, we explain why, in general, in the assumption not only the input history occurs but also the output history y. We interpret this specification pattern as follows:

- Contracts as context constraints: the assumption $asu(x, y)$ is a specifying assertion for the context with syntactic interface $(I \blacktriangleright O)$.

Understanding the A/C-contract pattern as context constraints leads to the following meaning: if the input x to the system generated by the context on its input y, which is the system output, fulfills the interface assertion given by the assumption $asu(x, y)$, then the system fulfills the promised assertion $cmt(x, y)$. This leads to the specification

$$asu\,(x, y) \Rightarrow cmt\,(x, y)$$

Assertion $asu(x, y)$ is a specification indicating which inputs x are permitted to be generated by context E fulfilling the assumption given the output history y.

Contracts in Architectures

Architectures are blue prints to build and structure systems (a simple example is shown in Fig. 6). Architectures contain descriptions of subsystems and specify how to compose the subsystems. In other words, architectures are described by the sets of subsystems where the subsystems are described by their syntactic interfaces and their interface behavior. Shared channels describe internal communication between the subsystems.

We assume that each system used in an architecture as a component has a unique identifier k.

We get a logical calculus of interface assertions for the composition of systems. Each system is specified by a contract describing its interface behavior in terms of an interface assertion, possibly structured into sub-interfaces and into assumptions and commitments.

Fig. 6 Architecture of a
system with interface
behavior $F = F_1 \otimes F_2 \otimes F_3$

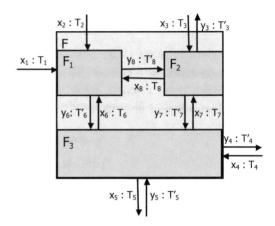

References

1. Andreessen, M.: Why Software Is Eating The World. http://www.wsj.com/articles/SB10001424053111903480904576512250915629460
2. Geisberger, E., Broy, M.: agendaCPS – Integrierte Forschungsagenda Cyber-Physical Systems (acatech STUDIE). Springer, Heidelberg (2012)
3. Broy, M.: Multifunctional software systems: structured modeling and specification of functional requirements. Sci. Comput. Program. **75**, 1193–1214 (2010)
4. Neubeck, P.: A probabilistic theory of interactive systems. Dissertation, Technische Universität München (2012)
5. Broy, M.: A logical basis for component-oriented software and systems engineering. Comput. J. **53**(10), 1758–1782 (2010)
6. Broy, M.: A logical approach to systems engineering artifacts: semantic relationships and dependencies beyond traceability—from requirements to functional and architectural views. Softw. Syst. Model. (2017)
7. Broy, M.: Interaction and realizability, In: van Leeuwen, J., Italiona, G.F., van der Hoek, W., Meinel, C., Sack, H., Plasil, F. (eds.) SOFSEM 2007: Theory and Practice of Computer Science, Lecture Notes in Computer Science 4362, pp. 29–50. Springer (2007)
8. Broy, M.: Theory and methodology of assumption/commitment based system interface specification and architectural contracts. Formal Methods Syst. Design **52**(1), 33–87 (2018)
9. Herzberg, D., Broy, M.: Modeling layered distributed communication systems. Form. Asp. Comput. **17**(1), 1–18 (2005)
10. Szyperski, C.: Component Software: Beyond Object-Oriented Programming, 2nd edn. Addison-Wesley Professional (2002)
11. Broy, M.: System behaviour models with discrete and dense time. In: Chakraborty, S., Eberspächer, J. (eds.) Advances in Real-Time Systems, pp. 3–25. Springer, Berlin (2012)
12. Clements, P., Bachmann, F., Bass, L., Garlan, D., Ivers, J., Little, R., Merson, P., Nord, R., Stafford, J.: Documenting Software Architectures: Views and Beyond, 2nd edn. Addison-Wesley, Boston (2010)
13. Broy, M., Stølen, K.: Specification and Development of Interactive Systems: FOCUS on Streams, Interfaces, and Refinement. Springer (2001)
14. Derler, P., Lee, E.A., Tripakis, S., Törngren, M.: Cyber-physical system design contracts. In: Proceedings of the ACM/IEEE 4th International Conference on Cyber-Physical Systems (ICCPS '13), pp. 109–118. ACM, New York, NY (2013)

15. Soderberg, A., Vedder, B.: Composable safety-critical systems based on pre-certified software components. In: 2012 IEEE 23rd International Symposium on Software Reliability Engineering Workshops (ISSREW), pp. 343–348 (2012)
16. Tripakis, S., Lickly, B., Henzinger, T.A., Lee, E.A.: A theory of synchronous relational interfaces. ACM Trans. Program. Lang. Syst. **33**(4), 14:1–14:41 (2011)
17. Westmann, J.: Specifying safety-critical heterogeneous systems using contracts theory. KTH, Industrial Engineering and Management. Doctoral Thesis Stockholm, Sweden 2016

Formal Methods and Agile Development: Towards a Happy Marriage

Carlo Ghezzi

1 Introduction

Change is connatural to software: no other human artifact shares this characteristic. Its immaterial nature and lack of physical constraints make it perfectly malleable: any change is in principle possible. Through simple textual operations, software engineers can add, delete, or modify functionalities offered by the software and improve its qualities (e.g., its performance). Technically, both the functional and the non-functional properties may be changed. The ability to provide extremely powerful functionalities in a highly flexible and changeable manner has been the key factor that leads to the current software-dominated world.

Change, however, does not come for free. Despite the apparent simplicity of change operations, it is hard to ensure that changes achieve the desired goals. Change operations operate at a very low level (code level), while the requests for change are dictated by higher level goals, such as adding new functionalities, or speeding up execution, or improving usability. Making sure that changes achieve the new goals, while preserving satisfaction of other unchanged goals, is very often extremely hard. This is the reason why software developers often restrain changes.

Change has been a concern since the 1970s, leading to the research work by Parnas [31–34], Belady and Lehman [6, 27], among others, and the recognition of "software maintenance" as a key concern. Traditional software development processes were mainly structured in a phased, rigidly planned manner, ideally intended to lead to robust processes that would eliminate the need for reconsidering and changing previous design decisions.

C. Ghezzi (✉)
DEIB—Politecnico di Milano, Milano, Italy
e-mail: carlo.ghezzi@polimi.it

© The Author(s) 2018
V. Gruhn, R. Striemer (eds.), *The Essence of Software Engineering*,
https://doi.org/10.1007/978-3-319-73897-0_2

Change, however, turned out to be inevitable in most practical cases. Requirements for a given application are often only vaguely known when a new development starts. They become progressively better known as development proceeds, and feedback information starts flowing from customers and from operation. Knowledge about the operational context in which the software will be embedded is often uncertain at development time. Moreover, even if the requirements and the context are known in the initial stages, they are subject to changes, which may, for example, be due to changes in the wider business context where the application is embedded.

Turbulence in requirements leads to devising alternative software process models, which could naturally accommodate change into the process, to support iterative and incremental development and better align software products to evolving requirements. The term *agile software development* has become popular to collectively characterize a number of industrial efforts aimed at reducing the cost of changes in requirements through multiple short development cycles, rather than long monolithic ones. For a presentation of the different proposals and a discussion of pros and cons, the reader can refer to [30].

Software often supports critical functionalities. Hence it needs to undergo a careful assurance process to assess its *dependability* attributes [1]. The main way agile methods address dependability is through testing. Testing has been effectively integrated into agile development life cycles, leading to what is often called *test-driven development*. Test cases are defined before starting implementation of a new application fragment and stand as a kind of specification for the fragment. They are run on the fragment as soon as it is implemented.

Agile methods focus on adding flexibility and supporting change in the development process. They do so through a feedback loop that involves customers and leads to progressive calibration of requirements. The development cycle, however, runs concurrently with operation. The observations and data gathered on the running software may lead to further changes, which need to be designed, implemented, and then deployed and instantiated. The integration of development and operations in an overall agile framework became known as *DevOps* [5].

The work on agile development has been mainly driven by industry, with little contribution from academic research. By and large academic research has focused more on formal methods to support development and verification through formal models. These efforts lead to approaches that some proposers of agile development even deprecated. The divide between the two worlds has unfortunately widened.

This paper argues that time is now mature for reconciliation of the two worlds. Formal methods developed a stage where they can be effectively incorporated into agile methods to give them rigorous engineering foundations and make them systematic and robust. Rather than being deprecated, they can bring added value and industrial strength to agility. This, however, requires researchers in formal modeling and formal verification to revisit the powerful approaches they developed to make them usable by practitioners and fit the agile world. The purpose of this chapter is exactly to provide arguments in support of this thesis. Arguments will be provided by referring to previously published work. Excerpts from previous publications are included in this chapter, where appropriate. For complementary discussions of these issues, the reader may refer to [2, 3, 18, 19, 22].

The paper is organized as follows. Section 2 provides a systematic framework to understand and classify software changes. Section 3 focuses on research results that investigated how change can be self-managed by software to achieve increased autonomy. The key concept here is that models and verification should be kept at run time to support continuous run time monitoring and verification as triggers for self-adaptation. Section 4 discusses how formal modeling and verification can be incorporated in the software process to support agile formal verification. This leads to a unified software development and operation approach (DevOps) that is rooted on formal methods. The unified approach is further discussed in Sect. 5. Finally, Sect. 6 concludes the chapter and calls for the further research efforts needed to make the vision of formal methods marrying agile development become true.

2   Understanding Change

Since change is connatural to software, it is important to understand where it comes from so that we can handle it properly. The foundational work by Zave and Jackson [37] on requirements engineering, which sheds the light on software and change, is briefly summarized in Sect. 2.1. This work leads to a useful distinction between *evolution* and *adaptation*, discussed in Sect. 2.2. We will also argue that adaptation can often be anticipated through careful design, and this can lead to development of *self-adaptive* software.

2.1   The Machine and the World

Engineers design machines to perform intended actions in an automated way. Traditional engineers design machines that are powered by chemical, thermal, or electrical means. Likewise, software engineers develop abstract machines, powered by data and algorithms, to satisfy real-world goals.

In their foundational work on requirements engineering, Jackson and Zave observe that software engineers should carefully distinguish between two main concerns: the *world* and the abstract *machine* to be realized by software. The world (also called the *environment*, or the *domain*) is the portion of the real world affected by the machine. The ultimate purpose of the machine is always to be found in the world: the goals to be met and the *requirements* are ultimately dictated by what has to be achieved in the world.

Requirements should be clearly spelled out before developing a machine. They should be expressed in terms of the phenomena that occur in the real world. Some of these phenomena are *shared* with the machine: they are either controlled by the world and observed by the machine—through sensors—or controlled by the machine and observed by the world—through actuators. The machine is built exactly for the purpose of achieving satisfaction of the requirements in the real world. Requirements *specification* prescribes constraints on *shared phenomena* that must be enforced by the abstract machine to be developed. The goal of the software engineer is to design and implement a machine that is *dependable*, that is, it behaves according to the specification.

To properly understand the requirements and design the software, software engineers need to understand how the affected portion of the world—the embedding environment—behaves (or is expected to behave), because this may affect satisfaction of the requirements. Quoting from [37],

> The primary role of domain knowledge[1] is to bridge the gap between requirements and specifications.

As a simple example, consider the design of a robotized system whose goal is to move boxes from a point A to a point B on a flat surface, assuming that no obstacles are placed between A and B. To satisfy the requirement, the software might instruct an actuator to apply a suitable force in the direction A to B. Kinematics laws express environment knowledge in this example. The relevant law here is that to move the box in a certain direction, we need to apply a force in the same direction, whose magnitude exceeds the friction of the box with the surface. In other terms, there is an *environment property* that ensures satisfaction of the requirement if the software correctly implements the functionality of sending a suitable force command to the actuator (and, of course, assuming that the actuator works properly).

As another example, consider the design of an e-commerce system whose goal is to support user interactions ensuring a given maximum response time. To provide a solution that satisfies the response time requirement, a software engineer needs to make certain *environment assumptions*. For example, she needs to make assumptions about the maximum rate of request submissions from customers. Under a given assumption, she can design a solution that ensures satisfaction of the requirement.

Notice that in the previous discussion we distinguished between environment "properties" and "assumptions." The distinction is crucial, although it is not always obvious. By "property" we mean a statement that cannot be falsified. Typically, it expresses a law of behavior that has been proven by an accepted theory, as in the case of kinematics above. By "assumption" instead we mean a statement that can be falsified. It may express uncertain or changeable knowledge. Very often, it represents partial or uncertain knowledge that we have when the system is being designed, which may only become known when the system will be running. User profiles (like in the previous e-commerce example) are a typical example. They are hard to predict, and they may change over time. Other increasingly common examples of uncertainty about the environment arise in the case of virtualized run time environments (cloud computing, service-oriented computing),

---

[1]The terms environment and domain are used interchangeably.

where the environment has hard-to-predict effects on non-functional requirements like performance or reliability.

The approach described by Jackson and Zave provides a formal conceptual framework to express in mathematical logic what we described informally so far. Let R be a set of logical statements that formalize the requirements, and let S be a set of logical statements that formalize the machine specification; let EP and EA be sets of logical statements that formalize the environment properties and assumptions, respectively. Assuming that S, EP, and EA are all satisfied (i.e., the software is correct with respect to S and the environment satisfies EP and EA) and consistent with each other, the designer's responsibility is ultimately to ensure the following entailment relation:

$$S, EP, EA \models R \tag{1}$$

Equation (1) formalizes the *main dependability argument* that software engineers need to make as part of assurances for their artifacts.

2.2   Evolution and Adaptation

Hereafter we discuss how changes can be classified and how they may affect the dependability argument described by Eq. (1).

Changes may affect environment assumptions. The environment might behave according to a different set of assumptions—say EA'—which may lead to breaking the dependability argument. As we already mentioned, this is a rather common case, since environment assumptions embody uncertain and changeable knowledge. If this happens, and requirements cannot be changed (e.g., weakened), assurance of the dependability argument requires that S should also change, and hence the software implementation. This kind of software change can be called *adaptation*. Changes may also affect the requirements. As mentioned earlier, requirements are highly volatile in practice, and a change of requirements inevitably leads to a change in the software. This kind of software change can be called *evolution*.

Adaptation can often be self-managed by software. Advances in research in the past decade have shown that if the sources of possible environment changes may be anticipated, one may design the software in a way that it monitors changes, analyzes their potential effects, and self-adapts accordingly, if necessary. The main findings of research on self-adaptive software are reported in Sect. 3.

Not all environment changes can be anticipated. Certain phenomena that may affect requirements satisfaction may be initially overlooked and are discovered only later, thus leading to changes in the software. Expert human inspections are required to discover unanticipated dependencies and to plan redesign activities that may lead to a correct solution. Expert human intervention is also needed to elicit and specify requirements changes and then change the software accordingly.

As we discussed earlier, requirements changes are pervasive, from the initial conception throughout all the software lifetime. The need to structure the software lifetime around the notion of change leads to devising agile methods. In the sequel, we will elaborate the notions of change discussed in this section to show how formal methods can be amalgamated with agile methods to engineer dependable software.

3   Achieving Self-adaptive Software

The goal of making software self-adaptable has been a hot research topic in the last decade and many promising results have been proposed. For a broad view of the area, the reader may refer to the series of SEAMS workshops and symposia[2] and the two Dagstuhl reports [11, 13].

Engineering self-adaptive systems calls for specific new approaches to the development and operation of software that guarantee lifelong requirements fulfillment in the presence of environmental changes. A particularly relevant—and perhaps prevailing—case concerns self-adaptation to keep satisfying *non-functional requirements*, such as reliability, performance, and different kinds of cost-related requirements, such as energy consumption. Non-functional requirements are often quite sensitive to environment changes. For example, response time to queries (performance) may depend on traffic assumptions. Likewise, heavy traffic may cause denial of service and thus affect service reliability.

We outline an approach that can (1) predict possible requirements failures caused by changes occurring in the environment and (2) self-adapt by triggering appropriate countermeasures that dynamically reconfigure the running application to prevent breaking the dependability argument. For a further discussion on self-adaptation to preserve satisfaction of non-functional requirements, the reader can refer to [20].

To be self-adaptive, a software system must be able to (1) detect the relevant changes in the external world in which it operates, (2) reason about its own ability to continue to fulfill the requirements as a consequence of the detected changes, and (3) reconfigure itself to guarantee a seamless adaptation to the new external conditions.

Several promising approaches to software self-adaptation rely on the use of *models at run time* [9, 10]. Past work of the author and co-authors fully embraced this view: models are kept alive at run time and updated automatically as changes are dynamically discovered through monitoring (see [14–16, 20, 21]). Formal models are kept at run time to support automatic detection of possible requirements violations. Different kinds of operational models may be kept, each specialized to detecting specific requirements violations. For example, Markovian models can be used to model performance, reliability, and performance, as discussed in [17]. The model's state space can be systematically and exhaustively explored through *on-line model checking* against a formal description of requirements expressed as

---

[2]http://www.self-adaptive.org.

logic statements. The outcome of model checking may trigger proper adaptation strategies to steer system reconfigurations and prevent requirements violations. Conceptually, this framework establishes a *feedback control loop* between models and the running system. At run time, monitored environment data are fed back to generate possible model updates, which are in turn analyzed against requirements. Adaptation thus becomes model driven. This approach reflects and formalizes the *autonomic control loop* advocated in [25].

Whenever verification at run time fails, the currently running application because the environment does not behave according to the current assumptions, the application should try to self-adapt. To make the application self-adaptive, different approaches have been proposed. In the increasingly common case where the application is structured as a service-oriented architecture, dynamic binding to external services may try to solve the problem [23]. It is also possible to address the problem by designing the application as a dynamic software product line [24]. In any case, dynamic reconfiguration must occur while the application is running. Several techniques have been devised to support dynamic software reconfigurations in a completely safe, nondisruptive, and efficient way [4, 26, 36].

To make the approach practical, run time verification must be performed efficiently. If verification is performed by model checking, most mainstream techniques and tools cannot be adopted. Existing techniques, in fact, were originally defined to support off-line (development-time) analysis and are not meant for on-line usage, where they need to comply with strict real-time constraints. Run time verification must in fact support timely adaptation, to avoid unacceptable disruption in service provision. To solve this problem, solutions have been developed to bring model checking to run time.

A possible solution is based on the observation that changes often are not radical and have a local scope. This assumption allows model checking to be made *incremental*. For example, [15] shows how models described as discrete time Markov chains can be incrementally checked in a very efficient way against temporal probabilistic requirements. The approach is based on the hypothesis that uncertain and changeable assumptions about the environment can be encoded as model parameters (specifically, as unknown probabilities associated with transitions), which can then be estimated at run time through monitoring.

In conclusion, self-adaptation to changes in the environment can be achieved under the following assumptions:

1. During design, it is possible to identify the possible sources of uncertainty.
2. A parametric model can be produced for the system where parameters encode environmental conditions that may change and become known during operation. This allows computing simple verification conditions that must be evaluated at run time.
3. Environmental data can be collected at run time to provide the actual values of model parameters, which can be fed into the verification conditions.
4. The application is structured in a way that it can be reconfigured dynamically in order to accommodate run time parameter variability.

4   Supporting Dependable Evolution

Agile methods support software development in an iterative and incremental manner to accommodate continuous change. In the initial phases of a new project, requirements must be progressively calibrated and exploration of different design alternatives must be supported. Subsequently, as soon as a version of software is deployed and running, concurrent development activities produce new versions, which may, for example, improve satisfaction of non-functional requirements, meet additional requirements, or deal with environment changes that were not anticipated and not supported by self-adapting policies of the current operational versions.

Current state-of-the-art practices in agile development mainly address the organizational aspects involved in iterative and incremental development. To support product quality assurance, they advocate *test-driven development—TDD*. In essence, TDD prescribes that each product increment should be initially specified by designing the test cases the implementation should run successfully, and then relies on automation of test case execution. Although this emphasis on continuous quality assurance is commendable, more can and should be done to achieve dependability.

Advances in formal modeling and formal verification have led to results that may be incorporated in the practice of software development. To achieve this, however, more software engineering research is needed to align formal methods to the needs of practitioners. To support explorative design, verification should be possible also on incomplete (partial) formal models. It is also necessary to provide techniques to formally verify models in face of their evolution [22, 35].

In an agile approach, software development is structured through frequent iterations: an incomplete specification evolves into a complete one once the unknown or uncertain aspects become known. In addition, parts of the system can be deliberately left incomplete at a given stage, and their completion is postponed to a later stage. Suppose that model checking is used to verify the various iterations. To do so, we need a model-checking procedure that can support both *reusability* and *incrementality* [28]. Reusability matters because changes to a model may have a local impact, and thus redoing the whole verification after any change, as several existing model-checking approaches require, would be very inefficient and would become a bottleneck in practice. Furthermore, often software is designed through an iterative decomposition, to support prioritization of different parts and separate developments. This requires that it should be possible to complete a specification incrementally. It would thus be useful to be able to check if an incomplete specification meets the specified requirements. In the likely case that satisfaction of the global property depends on the missing components, it would be desirable to know under which constraints the missing parts would satisfy it. Verification of these constraints would be later performed by analyzing only the added parts.

To tackle these problems, the incremental approach presented in [29] allows state models to include *black-box* states, that is, states that encapsulate an unspecified behavior, whose design is deferred to a later stage. The verification procedure checks the incomplete design against a formal property in temporal logic, expressing a global system requirement. The outcome of verification can be *OK*, if the model satisfies the property of *KO* if it does not. The outcome can also be *MAYBE*, if there is a possible refinement of the black box that may lead to a violation. In this last case, the verification procedure also synthesizes a formal property (called *proof obligation*) that expresses a constraint on the unspecified part to be met in order to satisfy the global requirement.

Another relevant line of research has focused on making analysis incremental. Incrementality is a necessary feature to be supported if one wishes to make formal verification practically usable. Since iterative development is based on continuous relatively small changes, the ability to verify if changes keep satisfying requirements is of paramount importance. An incremental verification approach reuses the results of previous analysis to verify an artifact after change, and tries to minimize the portion of new analysis to be performed. It may explain the outcomes of analysis in terms of the changes. It has expected benefits over a non-incremental approach in terms of speed. It also has benefits since it helps focusing analysis on the scope of a change. The principle of incrementality can be applied to verification of any artifact, for example, both models [7] and code [8].

5 Towards a Unified View of Development and Operation

Agility emerged as an important principle in the software industry. Development and operation are viewed as iterative, interacting processes that may lead to quality products that better satisfy customer needs. We argued that software engineering research on formal models and verification, rather than being an obstacle to agility, can help to make a substantial step forward in making agile methods more rigorously founded and ultimately more robust.

By marrying agile and formal methods, we can envision the process shown in Fig. 1. The process is *model and verification driven* and is based on rigorous mathematical foundations. The design phase is an iterative process (1) in which models for the requirements, the environment, and the software are progressively developed and formally verified. Requirements are progressively refined, along with the specification of environment properties and assumptions. The software models designed by engineers are continuously verified against requirements. The models are transformed into an executable implementation, which is then deployed in the target environment. The running application monitors the environment and provides actual data that can be used to update the assumptions on which the current model is based. Verification at run time can lead to self-adaptation. The run time self-adaptive loop (2) may fail and require intervention by the software engineer. This is represented by the feedback loop (3).

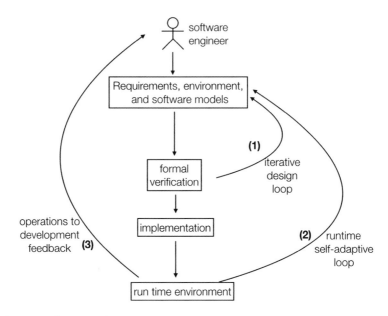

Fig. 1 The development and operation process

6   Concluding Remarks

Progress in software engineering has been remarkable in many directions. Agile methods acknowledged that change has to be handled as a primary concern and recommended iterative processes to cover development and operation in a seamless fashion. Progress has also been remarkable in formal modeling and verification. Software engineers, like engineers in other fields, can now design and analyze models of their artifacts before implementing them. Model-driven engineering has developed automated tools to support derivation of implementations from models [12]. Models and verification can be kept at run time to support self-adaptation.

It is now time to reconcile agility and formal methods. The demand for agility coming from the practitioners' world can be empowered by the rigorous and systematic foundations provided by formal methods. To make this view possible, further research is needed to adapt modeling and verification to fit into the iterative nature of agile processes. Here we reviewed some of the current research efforts moving in this direction, but more remains to be done. This chapter can be viewed as a call for a collective effort that encompasses both researchers and practitioners.

References

1. Avizienis, A., Laprie, J.-C., Randell, B., Landwehr, C.: Basic concepts and taxonomy of dependable and secure computing. IEEE Trans. Dependable Secure Comput. **1**, 11–33 (2004)
2. Baresi, L., Ghezzi, C.: The disappearing boundary between development-time and run-time. In: Proceedings of the FSE/SDP Workshop on Future of Software Engineering Research, FoSER '10, pp. 17–22 (2010)
3. Baresi, L., Di Nitto, E., Ghezzi, C.: Toward open-world software: issue and challenges. IEEE Comput. **39**(12), 36–43 (2006)
4. Baresi, L., Ghezzi, C., Ma, X., Panzica La Manna, V.: Efficient dynamic updates of distributed components through version consistency. IEEE Trans. Softw. Eng. **43**(4), 340–358 (2017)
5. Bass, L., Weber, I., Zhu, L.: DevOps: A Software Architect's Perspective. Addison-Wesley Professional, Reading (2015)
6. Belady, L.A., Lehman, M.M.: A model of large program development. IBM Syst. J. **15**(3), 225–252 (1976)
7. Bianculli, D., Filieri, A., Ghezzi, C., Mandrioli, D.: Incremental syntactic-semantic reliability analysis of evolving structured workflows. In: International Symposium on Leveraging Applications of Formal Methods, Verification and Validation, pp. 41–55 (2014)
8. Bianculli, D., Filieri, A., Ghezzi, C., Mandrioli, D., Rizzi, A.M.: Syntax-driven program verification of matching logic properties. In: Proceedings of FME Workshop on Formal Methods in Software Engineering (2015)
9. Blair, G., Bencomo, N., France, R.B.: Models @ run time. IEEE Comput. **42**(10), 22–27 (2009)
10. Calinescu, R., Ghezzi, C., Kwiatkowska, M., Mirandola, R.: Self-adaptive software needs quantitative verification at runtime. Commun. ACM **55**(9), 69–77 (2012)
11. Cheng, B., et al.: Software engineering for self-adaptive systems: a research roadmap. In: Software Engineering for Self-adaptive Systems, pp. 1–26. Springer, Berlin (2009)
12. Combemale, B., France, R., Jézéquel, J.M., Rumpe, B., Steel, J., Vojtisek, D.: Engineering Modeling Languages: Turning Domain Knowledge into Tools. CRC Press, Boca Raton (2016)
13. De Lemos, R., et al.: Software engineering for self-adaptive systems: a second research roadmap. In: Software Engineering for Self-adaptive Systems II, pp. 1–32. Springer, Berlin (2013)
14. Epifani, I., Ghezzi, C., Mirandola, R., Tamburrelli, G.: Model evolution by run-time parameter adaptation. In: IEEE 31st International Conference on Software Engineering, pp. 111–121 (2009)
15. Filieri, A., Ghezzi, C., Tamburrelli, G.: Run-time efficient probabilistic model checking. In: Proceedings of the 33rd International Conference on Software Engineering, pp. 341–350 (2011)
16. Filieri, A., Ghezzi, C., Tamburrelli, G.: A formal approach to adaptive software: continuous assurance of non-functional requirements. Form. Asp. Comput. **24**(2), 163–186 (2012)
17. Filieri, A., Tamburrelli, G., Ghezzi, C.: Supporting self-adaptation via quantitative verification and sensitivity analysis at run time. IEEE Trans. Softw. Eng. **42**(1), 75–99 (2016)
18. Ghezzi, C.: Dependability of adaptable and evolvable distributed systems. In: Bernardo, M., De Nicola, R., Hillston, J. (eds.) Formal Methods for the Quantitative Evaluation of Collective Adaptive Systems: 16th International School on Formal Methods for the Design of Computer, Communication, and Software Systems, SFM 2016, Bertinoro, June 20–24, 2016, pp. 36–60. Springer, Berlin (2016)
19. Ghezzi, C.: Of software and change. J. Softw. Evol. Process **29**, 1–14 (2017)
20. Ghezzi, C., Tamburrelli, G.: Reasoning on non-functional requirements for integrated services. In: Proceedings of 17th IEEE International Requirements Engineering Conference, pp. 69–78 (2009)
21. Ghezzi, C., Pinto Sales, L., Spoletini, P., Tamburrelli, G.: Managing non-functional uncertainty via model-driven adaptivity. In: Proceedings of the 2013 International Conference on Software Engineering, pp. 33–42 (2013)

22. Ghezzi, C., Sharifloo Molzam, A., Menghi, C.: Towards agile verification. In: Münch, J., Schmid, K. (eds.) Perspectives on the Future of Software Engineering: Essays in Honor of Dieter Rombach, pp. 31–47. Springer, Berlin (2013)
23. Ghezzi, C., Panzica La Manna, V., Motta, A., Tamburrelli, G.: Performance-driven dynamic service selection. Concurr. Comput. Pract. Exp. **27**(3), 633–650 (2015)
24. Hallsteinsen, S., Hinchey, M., Sooyong P., Schmid, K.: Dynamic software product lines. IEEE Comput. **41**(4), 93–95 (2008)
25. Kephart, J.O., Chess, D.M.: The vision of autonomic computing. IEEE Comput. **36**(1), 41–50 (2003)
26. Kramer, J., Magee, J.: The evolving philosophers problem: dynamic change management. IEEE Trans. Softw. Eng. **16**(11), 1293–1306 (1990)
27. Lehman, M.M., Belady, L.A.: Program Evolution: Processes of Software Change. Academic Press Professional, Inc., San Diego (1985)
28. Menghi, C.: Verifying incomplete and evolving specifications. In: Companion Proceedings of the 36th International Conference on Software Engineering, pp. 670–673 (2014)
29. Menghi, C., Spoletini, P., Ghezzi, C.: Dealing with incompleteness in automata-based model checking. In: FM 2016: Formal Methods - 21st International Symposium, Limassol, November 9–11, 2016, Proceedings, pp. 531–550 (2016)
30. Meyer, B.: Agile!: The Good, the Hype and the Ugly. Springer Science, Berlin (2014)
31. Parnas, D.L.: On the criteria to be used in decomposing systems into modules. Commun. ACM **15**(12), 1053–1058 (1972)
32. Parnas, D.L.: On the design and development of program families. IEEE Trans. Softw. Eng. **2**(1), 1–9 (1976)
33. Parnas, D.L.: A rational design process: How and why to fake it. IEEE Trans. Softw. Eng. **12**(2), 251–257 (1986)
34. Parnas, D.L.: Software aging. In: Proceedings of the 16th International Conference on Software Engineering, pp. 279–287 (1994)
35. Uchitel, S., Alrajeh, D., Ben-David, S., Braberman, V., Chechik, M., De Caso, G., D'Ippolito, N., Fischbein, D., Garbervetsky, D., Kramer, J., Russo, A., Sibay, G.: Supporting incremental behaviour model elaboration. Comput. Sci. Res. Dev. **28**(4), 279–293 (2013)
36. Vandewoude, Y., Ebraert, P., Berbers, Y., D'Hondt, T.: Tranquility: a low disruptive alternative to quiescence for ensuring safe dynamic updates. IEEE Trans. Softw. Eng. **33**(12), 856–868 (2007)
37. Zave, P., Jackson, M.: Four dark corners of requirements engineering. ACM Trans. Softw. Eng. Methodol. **6**(1), 1–30 (1997)

Escaping Method Prison – On the Road to Real Software Engineering

Ivar Jacobson and Roly Stimson

Background

The world has developed software for more than 50 years. Software has changed virtually every aspect of our lives so we cannot live without it. Thus, the software industry as a whole has been very successful. We could choose to be happy and continue doing what we are doing. However, under the surface it is not as beautiful as it seams: too many failed endeavors, quality in all areas is generally too low, costs are too high, speed is too low, etc. Obviously, we need to have better ways of working or - which is the same - we need better methods.

In this article a method provides guidance for all the things you need to do when developing software. These things are technical, such as work with requirements, work with code and conduct testing, or people related, such as work setting up a well-collaborating team and an efficient project, as well as improving the capability of the people and collecting metrics. The interesting discovery we made in 2003 was that even if the number of methods in the world is huge it seemed that all these methods were just compositions of a much smaller collection of 'mini-methods', maybe a few hundred of such

(continued)

I. Jacobson (✉) · R. Stimson
Ivar Jacobson International, London, UK

© The Author(s) 2017
V. Gruhn, R. Striemer (eds.), *The Essence of Software Engineering*,
https://doi.org/10.1007/978-3-319-73897-0_3

'mini-methods' in total. These distinct 'mini-methods' are what people in general call practices.

In this paper the term method also stands for related terms such as process, methodology, method framework, even if these terms strictly speaking have a different meaning.

This is not a new observation. Over all these 50+ years we have been searching for a better method. In some ways our methods of developing software have dramatically changed over time, in other ways they have stayed much the same. As an industry we have followed a zig-zag path moving from paradigm to paradigm and from method to method, changing very much like the fashion industry inspires wardrobe changes. Every new method adoption is generally a very expensive, demoralizing affair. It is expensive because it means retraining the software developers, the teams and their leaders. In some cases existing software may even have to be rewritten in order to work more efficiently with new software. It is demoralizing because the more experienced developers feel they have to relearn what they already know.

Companies, especially larger ones, realize that having a great method provides a competitive advantage – even if it is not the only thing you need to have. They also realize that their method must be explained and explicit so that it can be applied consistently across the organization. And, they realize that one size doesn't fit for all they do – they need a multitude of methods.

1   Typical Methods and Their Problems

Let's take a look at four of the most well-known methods (called method frameworks) for scaling agile: The Scaled Agile Framework (SAFe), Scaled Professional Scrum (SPS), Disciplined Agile Delivery (DAD) and Large Scale Scrum (LeSS).

They are all popular and used by organizations around the world. They deliver value to their user organizations in both overlapping ways and in specific ways. Overlapping means that they include some practices that are the same, specific means they have some special practices that makes the difference. If an organization applies one of these methods its users usually don't know anything about the other alternatives; the reason usually is that the other alternatives are described in different ways with partly different terminology.

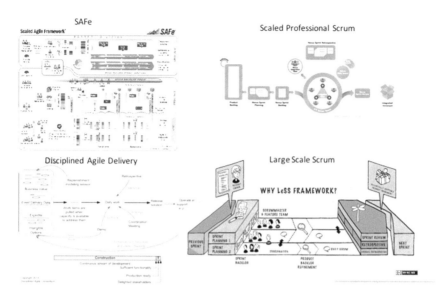

Fig. 1 Big pictures of four well-known scaled agile methods

A method can be tacit – in the heads of people - or explicit – described at different levels of detail. A lot of software in the world is developed using tacit methods. Organizations using a tacit method are generally not aware of the problem with method prisons. This is because they have a hard time to change their methods so they stay with what they have for a very long time. Indeed they are caught in their method prison.

What are then the problems?

1. *They are all monolithic – non-modular.*

    Most methods (not just the four ones discussed here) are monolithic meaning they are not designed in a modular way. This means that you can't easily exchange one module with another one and keep the other practices intact.

    Instead, what we want is a library of reusable modules, which is being updated as users learn more and more. Since every method is just a composition of practices, we want reusable practices. Teams and teams-of-teams should be able to easily agree on their own method by mixing and matching the practices they want to use from the library and compose them together.

2. *They have their own individual presentation style.*

    Every method has its individual specific structure, and uses its own style and terminology to describe its selected practices. The owners of the method have decided about these important aspects for themselves without following any standard. As a result, its practices are incompatible with practices from other methods.

3. *They have a lot in common – but it is hidden.*

   Moreover, though every method has some unique practices, it has a lot more in common with others. Every method "borrows" practices from other methods and "improves" them. So, commonalities are hidden behind new terms and "new" features. We use quotation marks to indicate that it is not really exactly "borrowing" that happens, and it is not always "improving", but due to misunderstanding or reinterpretation of the original practice, it often becomes a perversion or confusion of the original. Likewise the "new" features are typically not completely new at all, but new name for an evolution or variation of a previously existing practices ("new bottles for old wine").

4. *Every method is controlled by a warden – the guru*

   The guru has decided which practices should be combined into his or her method, and in some cases extended the method with practices "borrowed" and "improved" from other methods. The method reflects the particular perspectives, prejudices and experiences of its guru, and not to what we as a development community have collectively learned. Methods should reuse what the team or organization considers the best practices for their specific challenges and purposes, and not those selected by one single guru independent of these considerations.

5. *Every method is branded and often trademarked and copyrighted.*

   Other gurus are now, if its users like practices from other methods, forced to "borrow" these practices and "improve" what could have been re-used. This way of working doesn't stimulate collaboration with other gurus, on the contrary. Given the investment in time and capital by the gurus of these other methods, they must defend their turf with feverish determination, resulting in method wars.

2   Method Prisons

As a consequence, adopting a method – published or homegrown – means that you are stuck with a monolith, presented with its individual style, using many practices that are common but you don't know it, guarded by a guru who has branded his method making it difficult to reuse. Your method cannot easily reuse practices from a global practice library. Instead, you are in a *method prison*. You are stuck with how the guru of your method has decided how practices are described and how things are done while working with his/her method. To be clear here, we are not suggesting that gurus consciously try to put you in a method prison; they just continue do what we as an industry have done since our origin, because we didn't know anything better.

Thus, once you have adopted a method, you are in a method prison controlled by the guru of that method. Ivar Jacobson, one of the authors of this paper, was once one of the gurus governing the Unified Process prison. He realized that this was "the most foolish thing in the world" (of course the software world) and it was unworthy of any industry and in particular of such a huge industry as the software industry. Recently similar ideas have been expressed by others, e.g. see [0].

We as software professionals need to put a stop to this ridiculous development. We want people with creative practice ideas to collaborate and together provide libraries of reusable practices to the world. We want them to serve the whole industry and not be forced to create branded methods.

As a summary, you are most likely in a method prison if your method (framework) is:

1) Branded and controlled by a guru (or several gurus).
2) Presented in a way that you cannot mix and match practices from it with practices from other methods.
3) Described using a homegrown structure, vocabulary, style instead of using an international standard such as Essence.

Many organizations don't realize they are in a method prison. It is easy to understand why not. They have not identified any problems because they haven't seen how it could be different than today. The problems are too abstract without a solution to them. Once upon a time users didn't know that software should be built using components, e.g. java beans. Similarly, they didn't know they needed use cases or user stories to capture requirements. And so on. However, once they got it, and started to use it, they saw the value. Similarly, once they see that they can have access to a global library of practices, which are continuously improved, and from which they can select their own method, they won't go back to what we have today.

It is easy to understand that branded methods put you in a method prison. However, the situation for in-house developed methods is not different, just not so visible. What about agile methods? Most agile methods are today light in description. However, they also suffer from the same problem of not supporting reuse, mixing and matching practices, building a practice library, etc. We also advocate very light descriptions focusing on the essentials, but with the ability to extend with details when desirable.

3 A History of Methods and Method Prison

Since we started to develop software and adopted published methods we have had method prisons. Moreover, method prisons have some side effects that we also need to eliminate, the three most negative ones are the reliance on gurus, the method war and the zig-zag path. Our history will focus on how methods have created method prisons and their side effects. We will do that from two perspectives: lifecycles and practices.

3.1 Gurus, Method Wars and Zig-Zag Paths

Why is the *reliance on a guru* bad?

1. We all understand that relying on a single method/guru is risky. Big companies cannot accept the risk that individuals outside their domain of control should play such a vital role in their way of satisfying their clients. No single method can possibly effectively contemplate the endless variables that arise from the variety of working environments, industries, individual companies and their employees.
2. You effectively ransom your organization's own future competitiveness and ability to adapt, survive and thrive. In the future the method guru decides if and how the method prison is changed over time. And if you don't like it, or it doesn't match your strategic direction of travel and associated needs, there is nothing you can do, because you are stuck inside this method prison, unless you want to suffer the cost and pain of moving to yet another different method prison.

> Of course, many people, executives and developers, but not all, realize that the method they adopt is not the whole truth, so they only adopt part of it. Still, for political reasons, they want to tell the world that they use this particular method, to justify the money they have spent in adoption, and if the method is popular it attracts new people to the company. This was true once for RUP, and it is true for the moment with some other currently popular methods. But history tells us that none of these fashions lasts for very long.

There is a *method war* going on out there. It started 50 years ago and it still goes on – jokingly we can call it the Fifty Year's War, which has been even longer than the Thirty Year's War in Europe early 1600 (which was also a "religious war", incidentally). There are no signs that this will stop by itself.

It is a war because, as the situation has been and still is today, it is very hard to compare methods. We have not had a common ground to work as shared reference. Methods use different terminology, terms that could be synonyms have been adorned by some small differences and these differences are overemphasized, and terms that are nearly homonyms, but not quite, make any comparison very hard to do. Gurus and their followers talk about their method in religious terms, with a lot of passion and zealotry, which makes reasoned comparison and evaluation much harder. Not standing on a standard platform makes it impossible to compare methods and have a rational discussion on methods.

Once upon a time we had a large number of different notations to describe elements in software engineering. Then we got the Unified Modeling Language (UML) standard in 1997 and all these different notations were replaced by one single standard – the notation war was over. Notations are only one aspect of methods, so we need a similar standard for all other aspects of methods, a standard that allow for all the diversity needed from methods.

The software industry has followed a *zig-zag path* from paradigm to paradigm and from method to method.

1. With every major paradigm shift, such as the shift from Structured Methods to Object Methods in the 1980-90's and from the latter to the Agile Methods in the 2000's-now, basically the industry throw out almost all they know about software development and started all over again, with new terminology with little relation to the old one. Old practices are dismissed as garbage, and new practices hyped. To make this transition from the old to the new is extremely costly to the software industry in the form of training, coaching and tooling.
2. With every major new technical trend, for instance service-oriented architecture, big data, cloud computing, internet of things, the method authors also 'reinvent the wheel'. They create new terminology and new practices even if they could have reused what was already in place. The costs are not as huge as in the previous point, since some of the changes are not fundamental across everything we do and thus the impact is limited to, for instance, cloud development, but there is still significant and foolish waste.

Within every such trend there are many competing methods. For instance, back early 1990 there were about 30 competing object-oriented methods. The issue is that all these methods suffer from the five problems resulting in method prisons. This is of course to the advantage of method authors whose method is selected, even if this was not their conscious intention.

We need to eliminate the need for a continued zig-zag path.

3.2 Lifecycles and Method Prisons

From the ad hoc approach used in the early years of computing, came the waterfall methods. There were hundreds of them published. Some of the most popular were Structured Analysis and Design Technique (SADT), Structured Analysis / Structured Design (SA/SD) and Information Engineering (IE). They had their greatness from 1960 to year 2000.

The waterfall methods were heavily influenced by the practices of construction project management – the mantra was "find ways to build software like civil engineers build bridges". They described a software development project as going through a number of phases such as requirements, design, implementation (coding), and verification (i.e. testing and bug-fixing).

Around the year 2000 they were more and more replaced by iterative methods originally introduced by Barry Boehm's Spiral Model of Software Development and Enhancement, and methods such as RUP and DSDM, and later simplified and further popularized by agile practices such as XP and Scrum. All the four methods introduced earlier, SAFe, SPS, DAD and LeSS, apply an iterative lifecycle.

Of course, all different methods were accompanied by method prisons, and we relied on gurus and perpetuated the method wars.

3.3   Practices and Method Prisons

Since the beginning of software development we have struggled with how to do the right things in our projects. Originally, we struggled with programming because writing code was what we obviously had to do. The other things we needed to do were ad hoc. We had no real guidelines for how to do requirements, testing, configuration management and many of these other important things.

We have had three major eras in software engineering (years are just approximate):

- 1960-1980: The Structured Methods Era,
- 1980-2000: The Object Methods Era, and
- 2000 – now: The Agile Methods Era,

resulting in the zig-zag path from era to era. We don't want any more eras and no zig-zag path in future.

The Structured Methods Era

In this era the most popular methods, such as (e.g. SADT, SA/DT, IE), all separated functional process logic from data design. They did this for what were good reasons at the time - because computers at that time were designed exactly like that - with separate program logic and data storage structures. They were used for all kinds of software development – including both "Data Processing" and "Real-Time" systems, following the common parlance of the time. The value of the function/data approach was of course that what was designed was close to the realization – to the machine – you wrote the program separate from the way you designed your data. The systems were hard to develop and even harder to change safely and that became the "Achilles heel" for this generation of methods.

The Object Methods Era

The next paradigm shift came in the early 1980s, inspired by a new programming metaphor - object-oriented programming, triggered by a new programming language Smalltalk. The key ideas behind Smalltalk were much older, being already supported by Simula in 1967. Around 1990, a complement to the idea of objects came to widespread acceptance. Components with well-defined interfaces, which could be connected to build systems, became a new widely accepted architectural style. Components are still the dominating metaphor behind most modern methods.

With objects and components a completely new family of methods evolved. The old methods and their practices were considered to be out of fashion and thrown out. What came in was in many cases similar practices with some significant differences but with new terminology, so it was almost impossible to track back to their ancestors. A new fashion was born. In the early 1990s, as we already have said, about 30 different object-oriented methods were published. They had a lot in common but it was almost impossible to find the commonalities since each method author created his/her own terminology and iconography.

In the second half of 1990s the Object Management Group (OMG - see omg.org) felt that it was time to at least standardize on how to represent drawings about software – notations used to develop software. This led to a task force being created to drive the development of this new standard. The work resulted in the Unified Modeling Language (UML). This basically killed all other methods than the Unified Process (marketed under the name Rational Unified Process (RUP)); the Unified Process dominated the software development world around year 2000. Again a sad step, because many of the other methods had very interesting and valuable practices that could have been made available in addition to some of the Unified Process practices. However, the Unified Process became in fashion and everything else was considered out of fashion and more or less thrown out. Yes, this is how foolish we were.

The Agile Methods Era

The agile movement – often referred to just as "agile" - is now the most popular trend in software development and embraced by the whole world. The Agile movement changed the emphasis away from the technical practices, placing the team, the work and the people front and center.

As strange as it may sound, the methods employed in the previous eras did not pay much attention to the human factors. Everyone understood of course that software was developed by people, but very few books were written about how to get people motivated and empowered in developing great software. The most successful method books were quite silent on the topic. It was basically assumed that one way or the other this was the task of management. With agile many new people practices came into play, for instance self-organizing teams, pair programming, daily standups.

Given the impact agile has had on the empowerment of the programmers, it is easy to understand that agile has become very popular and the latest trend. Moreover, given the positive impact agile has had on our development of software there is no doubt it has deserved to become the latest trend. And, while some agile practices will be replaced by other, better, practices, agile as a philosophy and attitude is not a fad that will pass away. It will stay with us for the foreseeable future.

To summarize

Though the different eras have contributed knowledge and experience, and a lot of it is specific for each era, they all resulted in a continuation of the method war controlled by a few gurus.

4   What to do to Escape Method Prisons

It took us a while to understand what was wrong with how we have dealt with software development methods (see [1] and [2]). However, once we had seen the "most foolish thing in the world", it didn't require a genius to figure out that the key to put an end to it was to find a common language with a common terminology or in one word *a common ground*, which we can use when talking about and using practices and methods. Thus in 2009 the SEMAT community was founded with the mission to "re-found software engineering... [1] include a kernel of widely agreed elements that would be extensible for specific uses" [3].

We need to find a common ground

Most methods include (or imply) a lifecycle, technical practices and people practices. Thus there is something we have in common. However this is hidden and not easy to discover, because different gurus describe these things using different vocabulary and language. Thus the common ground we are searching for includes a vocabulary and a language. We called the vocabulary the *kernel* and the language the *kernel language*.

Common Ground = Kernel + Language = Essence

Starting with the kernel

Given that the kernel is intended to help describing methods and practices, it needs to contain "things" that are or should be perceived as always prevalent in any method. In essence, what are the things we always have, always do and always produce when developing software[2]? We, the team of SEMAT volunteers (about 20 people from around the world), working with the kernel, agreed that these things called the *universals* should be "applicable no matter the size or scale of the software under development, nor the size, scale or style of the team involved in the development". "In essence it provides a practice independent framework for thinking and reasoning about the practices we have and the practices we need. The goal of the kernel is to establish a shared understanding of what is at the heart of software development."

As an input to the work on finding the kernel in 2010, the three founders of SEMAT (Ivar Jacobson, Bertrand Meyer and Richard Soley) wrote a vision statement [4]. The three of us understood that finding the kernel needed to be guided by criteria and principles. We first agreed on some *criteria for inclusion* of elements in the kernel (see [4] for more complete description of the criteria).

Elements should be: *universal, significant, relevant, defined precisely, actionable, assessable and comprehensive. Relevant* was explained as "available for application by all software engineers, regardless of background, and methodological camp (if any)" and *comprehensive* as "applies to the collection of the kernel elements; together, they must capture the essence of software engineering, providing

---

[1]We use the to denote that we have removed some non-important words from the original quote.
[2]https://sematblog.wordpress.com/2009/12/07/establishing-a-kernel/

a map that supports the crucial practices, patterns and methods of software engineering teams".

We also identified the following general principles deemed as essential to finding a kernel (also in [4]): *Quality, simplicity, theory, realism and scalability, justification, falsifiability, forward-looking perspective, modularity and self-improvement. Theory* meant "the kernel shall rest on a solid, rigorous theoretical basis", *realism and scalability* "the kernel shall be applicable by practical projects, including large projects, and based where possible on proven techniques", *self-improvement* "the kernel shall be accompanied by mechanisms enabling its own evolution".

Moreover, the vision statement [4] also formulated what features the kernel should have: *Practice independence, lifecycle independence, language independence, concise, scalable, extensible and formally specified. Scalable* was explained as the kernel must support the very smallest of projects – one person developing one system for one customer – it must also support the largest of projects, in which there may be systems-of-systems, teams-of-teams and projects-of-projects. *Extensible* meant the kernel needs to possess the ability to add practices, details and coverage, and to add lifecycle management and to tailor the kernel itself to be domain-specific or to integrate the software development work into a larger endeavor.

With these criteria, principles and features the SEMAT team set out to find the kernel.

Followed by the language

To explain the universals in the kernel and also practices and methods we need a language. Using just English is not precise enough so we need to have a formal language with syntax and semantics.

The language must be designed for its principal users who are professional software developers participating in a software development endeavor. The language must also allow competent practitioners to create and improve practices without having to learn an advanced language.

The language should support four principal applications: Describing, simulating, applying and assessing. From [4]: "The concept of state is likely to play an important role in the kernel language, to represent work progress."

The same vision statement gave rather specific requirements on the language. For example "The language should be designed for the developer community (not just process engineers and academics)", which is an important requirement asking for a more intuitive and more engaging user experience in working with methods than what has been available today. Another example of a requirement is that the language must provide "validation mechanisms, so that it is possible to assess whether a project that claims to apply a given method element ... actually does, and is not just paying lip service to it."

We need more than a kernel – we need practices and methods

The role of the kernel and the kernel language is to be used to describe practices and methods with a common ground. To get there, a useful common ground had to be applied in describing a large number of methods. We needed to agree on what a practice and a pattern is [4]. We said for example: "A practice is a separate concern of a method. Examples are ... iterative development, component-based development", "every practice, unless explicitly defined as a continuous activity, has a clear beginning and an end" and "every practice brings defined value to its stakeholders".

With these principles, values and requirements in the baggage the SEMAT team had got a good idea of WHAT was needed to escape the method prison.

5   How to Escape the Method Prison

From idea to tangible result is a long way. We first had to get a common ground.

5.1   Essence - the common ground of software engineering

As a response to "the most foolish thing in the world", the work on an escape route from method prison started in 2006 in Ivar Jacobson International (IJI). In 2009 the SEMAT community was founded and in 2011 the work was transferred to OMG, which eventually gave rise to a standard common ground in software engineering called Essence [5]. Essence became an adopted standard in 2014. Thus Essence didn't come like a flash from "the brow of Zeus", but was carefully designed based on the vision statement [4].

We were also inspired by Michelangelo: "In every block of marble I see a statue as plain as though it stood before me, shaped and perfect in attitude and action. I have only to hew away the rough walls that imprison the lovely apparition to reveal it to the other eyes as mine see it." We felt that we from all this mass of methods had to find the essence so we paraphrased it: *"We are liberating the essence from the burden of the whole."*

And by Antoine de Saint-Exupéry: "You have achieved perfection not when there is nothing left to add, but when there is nothing left to take away." We took a very conservative approach in deciding what should be in the kernel and what should be outside the kernel. It is easier to add new elements to the kernel than to take them away.

5.2   Using Essence

Instead of giving the whole theory behind Essence, we will show its usage by presenting a practice described on top of Essence – using Essence as a platform to present the practice.

We have selected to describe User Story as an example of an Essence practice – calling it here User Story Essentials. Figure 2 below shows (not to be read in detail) the set of 14 cards that represent the headline essentials of the practice.

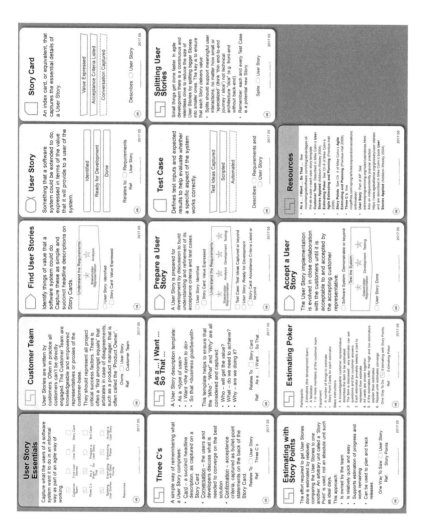

Fig. 2 The User Story practice as an example of an Essentialized Practice

It is not our intention to here describe the entire practice but to give you a good understanding of what an essentialized practice look like.

An Essentialized practice/method is described using Essence and it focuses the description on what is essential. It doesn't mean changing the intent of the practice or the method. Essentialization provides significant value. We as a community can create libraries of practices coming from many different methods. Teams can mix and match practices from many methods to get a method they want. If you have an idea for a new practice, you can just focus on essentializing that practice and add it to a practice library for others to select; you don't need to "reinvent the wheel" to create your own method. This liberates that practice from monolithic methods, and it will open up the method prisons and let companies and teams get out to an open world.

Thus, we have selected a representative set of cards being briefly described next.

User Story Essentials (Overview Card) – gives an overview of the practice in terms of:

- A brief description that gives an insight into why (benefits) and when (applicability) we might use the practice
- A contents listing – showing named practice element icons for all the elements within the practice (each of which is described with its own card).

Note that the color coding gives an immediate visual indication as to the scope of application of the practice – in this case we see that the practice is:

- Mainly Yellow cards – the Essence color coding for the Solution area of concern – telling us that this practice is concerned with the software system we are building and/or its requirements.
- One Green card – the Essence color coding for the Customer area of concern – telling us that the practice also concerns itself with how we interact with business / customer area concerns such as the Opportunity and the Stakeholders.
- Zero Blue cards – Essence has three areas of concerns, the third color coded in blue standing for the Endeavor area of concern. The User Story Essentials practice has no cards in this area.

Note also that in this case there is a strong separation of concerns between the Solution and Customer concerns that User Story Essentials addresses and the Endeavor space, which includes concerns such as the Team and how we manage the Work. The practical impact is that this practice can be used with any number of different management practices that mainly operate in the blue Endeavor space, such as a timeboxed, Scrum-style approach to work management or a continuous flow, Kanban-style approach.

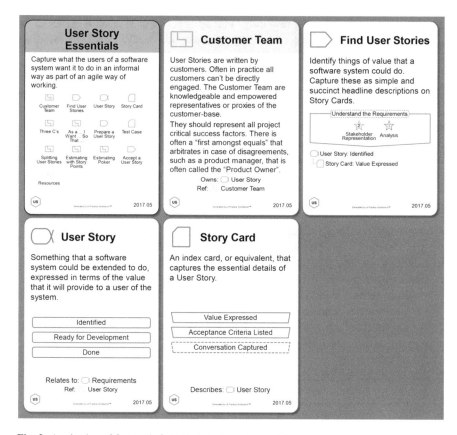

Fig. 3 A selection of five cards form the User Story Essentials practice

Customer Team (Pattern Card) – patterns give supporting guidance relating to other elements and/or how these relate to each other, in terms of (in this case):

- Textual description – encapsulating the critical aspects of the guidance that the pattern provides.
- Named associations – showing which other element or elements the pattern relates to primarily – in this case the User Story element.
- A Reference Link – to a named Reference on the Resources card – which in turn provides one or more pointers to sources of more guidance or information. The Resources card is one of the 14 cards in Figure 2 describing the practice.

Essentialized practices can de described at different levels of detail. The cards in this practice don't attempt to provide all the information for example that a novice team would need to successfully apply the practice. If history has taught us anything it is:

- No amount of written process enables novices to succeed without expert support.
- The more words there are the less likely that any of them will be read.

- Instead of "borrowing and rewriting" other people's words when it comes to the more voluminous detailed supporting guidance, it is better to simply reference the original sources of this guidance.

Essentialized practices such as this one work on the principle that novice teams need support from expert coaches to be successful. The cards become a tool for expert coaches to use to help teams to adopt, adapt and assess their team practices, or for expert teams to use in the same way.

Finally note that, when presented electronically as browsable HTML images, the association and reference links can all be navigated electronically, as can other link elements on other cards.

Find User Stories (Activity Card) – gives guidance to a team on what they should actually do, in terms of (in this case):

- A description of the activity.
- An indication of the Competencies and Competency Levels that we need for the activity to be executed successfully. For instance the card requires Stakeholder Representative competency at level 2 and Analysis competency at level 1 (all of which is defined in the Essence kernel, and can be immediately drilled into from the electronic browsable HTML and cards)
- An indication of the space that the Activity operates in – i.e. what "kind of thing it helps us do" (the generic kernel "Activity Space" – in this case "Understand the Requirements")
- An indication of the purpose of the activity expressed as the end-state that it achieves – in this case a User Story is Identified and a physical Story Card produced that expresses the value associated with the User Story.

Note that activities are critical because without them nothing actually ever gets done - it is remarkable how many traditional methods inundate readers with posturing and theorizing, without actually giving them what they need, which is clear advice on what they should actually do!

User Story (Alpha) – a key thing that we work with, that we need to progress, and the progression of which is a key trackable status indicator for the project – you can think of Alphas as the things that you expect to see flowing across Kanban boards, described here in terms of:

- A brief description that makes clear what this thing is and what it is used for.
- A sequence of States that the item is progressed through – in this case from being Identified through being Ready for Development through to being Done. (Think of these as candidate columns on a Kanban Board – although teams may want to represent other interim states as well depending on their local working practices).
- The "parent" (kernel) Alpha that the multiple User Stories all relate to (the Requirements in this case).

Story Card (Work Product Card) – gives guidance on the real physical things that we should produce to make the essential information visible – in this case a key defining (though often forgotten) feature of the User Story approach is that we use something of very limited "real-estate" (an index card or electronic equivalent) as the mechanism for capturing the headline information about what we want to build into the Software System. The Work Product is defined here on the card in terms of:

- A brief description.
- The Levels of Detail that we progressively elaborate – in this case indicating that initially we ensure that we have captured and communicated the associated value, and that we also need to continue on at some stage to list the acceptance criteria – the dotted outline of the third level of detail indicating that we may or may not capture associated conversations – for example in an electronic tool if we are a distributed team.
- The Alpha that the Work Product describes – a User Story in this case.

Putting it all together

We have now described a representative subset of the different types of card which are used in the User Story Essentials practice, so we will not describe the other cards because the story will rapidly become familiar and repetitious (which is part of the value of using a simple, standard language to express all our practice guidance).

Now we understand what all the cards mean, we also need to understand at a high level how the whole practice works. The cards themselves give us all the clues we need as to how the elements fit together to provide an end-to-end story – which activities progress and produce which elements, but it is also here useful to tell the joined-up story in terms of end-to-end flow through the different activities.

- First we need to Find User Stories. This brings one or more User Stories into existence in the initial Identified state, each documented by a Story Card with just enough information to ensure that the User Story has its Value Expressed.
- On a Story-by-Story basis, we will select a User Story that we wish to get done next, and use the Prepare a User Story activity to progress the User Story to be Ready for Development, which involves ensuring that we have the Acceptance Criteria Listed on the Story Card, and during which we may also get any supporting Conversation Captured. As part of this same activity we also fully elaborate the associated Test Cases.
- The final activity that this practice describes is how we work to Accept a User Story, the successful completion of which moves the User Story to the Done state.

Notice that this "chaining" of Activities primarily via the state of the things that they progress does not over-constrain the overall flow. It does not, for example, imply a single-pass, strictly sequential flow. We might, for example, iterate around the different activities for different User Stories in different ways. Exactly how may be further constrained as part of adopting other practices. For example, if we use the User Story practice in conjunction with Scrum, as is very common, we may agree the following general rules as a team:

- Do the Find User Stories before we start our First Sprint, but also allow this to happen on an ad hoc basis ongoing.

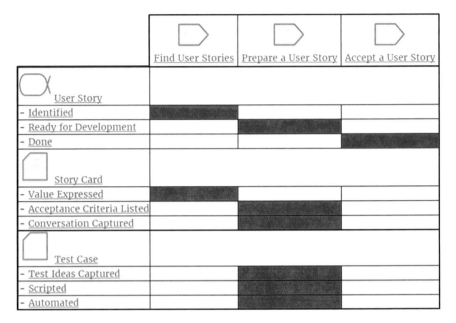

Fig. 4 State Progression Matrix showing end-to-end flow through the Activities

- Do the Prepare a User Story activity before the first Sprint and then during each Sprint for the User Stories for the next Sprint, in time for Sprint Planning.
- Aim to Accept a User Story as soon as it is done, to get all the User Stories selected for the Sprint Done before the end of Sprint Review.

To summarize the general rules and principles illustrated here:

Essence distinguishes between elements of health and progress versus elements of documentation. The former is known as *alphas* while the latter is known as *work products*. Each alpha has a lifecycle moving from one *alpha state* to another. *Work products* are the tangible things that describe an alpha and give evidence to its alpha states; they are what practitioners produce when conducting software engineering activities, such as requirement specifications, design models, code, and so on. An *Activity* is required to achieve anything, including progressing Alphas and producing or updating a Work Product. *Activity spaces* organize activities. To conduct an activity requires specific *Competencies. Patterns* are solutions to typical problems. An example of a pattern is a role, which is a solution to the problem of outlining work responsibilities.

(continued)

Essence in defining only the generic standard "common ground" defines no work products, activities or patterns, since these are all practice-dependent. It defines 7 alphas with its states, 15 activity spaces and 6 competencies, which are all practice-agnostic. Practices defined on top of Essence introduce new elements or subtypes of the standard kernel element types.

Key features and benefits

Some of the key features and benefits of essentialized practices as illustrated by this one example are:

- The practice is tightly scoped – it tells us how to do one thing well, and does not constrain or limit any of our other choice when it comes to other practices we want to use in other spaces (Scrum, Kanban, etc.).
- The practice is VERY concisely expressed – it's a little compressed in the above graphic, but when "life-size" the cards in the practice together represent roughly the equivalent of a side of A4.
- The practice is accessible and can be interacted with – the cards are used in all kinds of ways – including making an annotated team way of working instantly visible, self-assessing the adequacy of local practices and prioritizing improvement areas.
- The practice is expressed in a simple, standard way – now you understand these 4 cards from User Essentials, there are no barriers to understanding any other Essence practice from any other source - just because you like this User Story practice, you aren't now captive in its method prison – you are free to roam the open market to select any other practices from any other sources.
- The practice "plugs into" the Essence standard kernel, thus ensuring it interoperates in well-defined ways with any other essentialized practices.
- This same fact enables scope and coverage of any practice to be instantly assessed (our practice adds activities into the Essence kernel activity spaces "Understand the Requirements" and "Test the System", but adds nothing to the other 13 activity spaces outlined by the Essence kernel ("Implement the System", "Deploy the System", . . .) – so if this is the only practice we adopt, it is clear that we have no agreed or defined way of doing these other things (which may or may not be a problem, but *is* a clearly visible fact . . .).
- It contains all the essentials – you may or may not be doing many other things, but if you are not doing this set of things in this kind of way (or locally modified equivalent things, or possibly explicitly NOT doing one particular aspect for a clearly understood and well-articulated reason) then can you reasonably claim to be doing "User Stories" at all?

5.3 *Reflection*

In section 5.2 we presented the User Story practice essentialized without first presenting the Essence kernel and language. We presented the practice with "Essence in Stealth Mode", to coin an expression we have got from Paul McMahon. However, underneath the essentialized practice we rely heavily on Essence. In our example User Story is a sub-alpha related to the *Requirements* kernel alpha. The "Find User Stories" activity is allocated to the "Understand the Requirements" activity space and so is the activity "Prepare a User Story", while the "Accept a User Story" belongs to the activity space "Test the System".

We have attempted to show that practices are easily understood even without first giving a long and, too many people, boring introduction to Essence. This has been done in many other papers and books already, see [6] - [10]. Thus, here we will just mention some important things you may need to take away.

When the SEMAT volunteers designed Essence as a response to HOW to escape the method prison, particular attention was paid to the "simplicity clause" that "the kernel shall only include essential concepts", which the team interpreted as the guidelines for a method or practice should focus on the essentials.

- The experience is that developers rarely have the time or interest to read detailed methods or practices. Starting to learn the essentials gets teams ready to start working significantly earlier than if they first have to learn "all" there is to say about the subject.
- The essentials were defined as a rule of thumb being about 5% of what an expert knows about the subject.
- Some teams and organizations need more than the essentials, so different levels of detail must be made optional.

The SEMAT team also knew we had to come up with a new user experience to teach practices. The current way of doing it through books and web sites didn't help during actual work – books are dead descriptions and not active guides. We searched for a more engaging way of working and found inspiration in modern work on gamification. We used cards, as you have seen.

We also consistently applied the principle of 'Separation of Concerns' in many different contexts (for general discussion see http://en.wikipedia.org/wiki/Separation_of_concerns). Practices are separate concerns, which can be composed into methods through a merge operation, known in Essence as "composition". The kernel is also a separate, more abstract, concern, on top of which practices can be composed, also merged.

In summary, Essence enables us to escape from method prisons because it sets out a description of what all methods have in common, and a standard language for talking about this common ground and about all our practices. This means we are free to select essentialized practices from any source we choose, including from our own organization as well as external sources, and free to mix-and-match them with practices from other sources, in order to get the best from all worlds, without being locked in to any of them.

6   Out of the Method Prison

Many companies are now in the process of essentializing their existing methods. For instance, in the words of Tata Consulting Services (TCS): "TCS has engaged with all of its core industry partners like SAP, Oracle, Microsoft and others and also the clients of TCS and is working with the core methodology teams of those companies to help foster the collaborative adoption of the Essence standard and turn this de-jure standard into a de facto standard."

These companies get reusable practices available in a practice library. Teams and organizations are able to mix and match practices from different methods and create their own ways of working. Today, we believe that there are around hundred practices described on top of Essence. Ivar Jacobson International has developed about 50 practices and made 25 of them available in a practice library at https://practicelibrary.ivarjacobson.com.

Those companies are getting out of their method prisons. They don't rely on gurus anymore. They won't follow a zig-zag path, but they expect a sustainable evolution. The method war is over for them. However, getting out of method prisons is not all they are expecting. They have much higher ambitions. They are on a path to industrial-scale agile – moving software development from primarily being a craft to primarily being an engineering discipline, but still being agile in both software development and in working with methods.

To be successful we still will rely on the craftsmanship of our empowered teams, but this will be underpinned with a shared base of codified engineering practices that can be reused in different permutations and combinations across different technical domains and project types. This will enable us to maintain high levels of craftsmanship consistently across all our projects, and to sustain this indefinitely through future challenges and changes.

We also need a supporting organization with a learning culture open to new ideas and comfortable with experimentation. Discussing this is out of scope for this paper, but we refer to papers already published (see [8]-[10]).

Essence is also making inroads in the academic world. Universities around the world are teaching Essence to a varying degree. Here a quote from Professor Pekka Abrahamsson, "At one of the largest technical universities in Scandinavia, Norwegian University of Science and Technology in Trondheim, in the Spring of 2017, we have successfully taught Essence in Software Engineering course to 460 students. Essence empowered students to gain control of their project, work methods and practices. We have finally moved beyond Scrum and Kanban. ... Data and results convinced me and thus my Software Engineering education in the future will be driven by Essence."

Maybe this move to Essence is "the smartest thing in the world" to these companies and universities.

References

0. Hastle S., Linders B., McIntosh S., Ferreira R.M., Smith C. "Opinion: What 2017 Has in Store for Culture & Methods", https://www.infoq.com/news/2017/01/2017--culture-methods, InfoQ, 2017.
1. Jacobson I., Meyer B. Methods need theory. Dr. Dobb's Journal, 2009.
2. Jacobson I, Spence I. 2009. Why we need a theory for software engineering. Dr. Dobb's Journal, 2009.
3. Jacobson I., Meyer B., Soley R. 2009. Call for Action: The Semat Initiative. Dr. Dobb's Journal, 2009.
4. Ivar Jacobson, Bertrand Meyer, Richard Soley. "Software Engineering Method and Theory – a Vision Statement", Feb 2010.
5. Object Management Group, "Essence - Kernel And Language For Software Engineering Methods", November 2014. (http://www.omg.org/spec/Essence/).
6. Ivar Jacobson, Pan-Wei Ng, Paul E. McMahon, Ian Spence and Svante Lidman, "The Essence of Software Engineering: The SEMAT Kernel," Communications of the ACM, Volume 55, Issue 12, December 2012.
7. Ivar Jacobson, Pan-Wei Ng, Paul E. McMahon, Ian Spence and Svante Lidman, "The Essence of Software Engineering: Applying the SEMAT Kernel", Addison-Wesley, 2013
8. Ivar Jacobson, Ian Spence and Pan-Wei Ng. "Agile and SEMAT: Perfect Partners", Communications of the ACM, Volume 11, Issue 9, Oct. 2013
9. Ivar Jacobson and Ed Seidewitz, "A New Software Engineering," Communications of the ACM, Volume 57, Issue 12, Pages 49-54. December 2014.
10. Ivar Jacobson, Ian Spence, Ed Seidewitz. "Industrial-scale agile: from craft to engineering", Communications of the ACM: Volume 59 Issue 12, December 2016.

What is software?

The Role of Empirical Methods in Answering the Question

Leon J. Osterweil

The main addition that this paper makes to the previous version is to note a potentially key contribution that Empirical Methods could make to these understandings. In the paper we argue that the understanding of an object (physical or non-physical) is greatly enhanced by the ability to measure that object. Indeed, Lord Kelvin suggested, over 100 years ago that

> *...when you can measure what you are speaking about, and express it in numbers, you know something about it; but when you cannot measure it, when you cannot express it in numbers, your knowledge is of a meagre and unsatisfactory kind; it may be the beginning of knowledge, but you have scarcely in your thoughts advanced to the state of Science, whatever the matter may be.*

That being the case, Empirical Methods research should be viewed as being essential to gaining knowledge and establishing the science of the nature of software, in that it addresses issues of how to measure various aspects of software. This paper focuses as a case in point on how to define one particular basic measure of software, namely its size. This would seem to be a basic measure and yet we note that no such satisfactory measure of software size seems to exist. Grappling with this and related questions has been a focus of the Empirical Methods community. The community's success in understanding how to establish such measures of computer software is clearly important to progress in being more effective in computer software engineering, but might indeed also have important ramifications

---

This article by Leon Osterweil had already been published in 2008 in the Journal "Automated Software Engineering, Issue 3–4, 2008" (https://link.springer.com/journal/10515/15/3/page/1). Copyright © Springer Science+Business Media, LLC 2008. Republished as Open Access with Permission.

L. J. Osterweil (✉)
Laboratory for Advanced Software Engineering Research, School of Computer Science, University of Massachusetts, Amherst, MA, USA
e-mail: ljo@cs.umass.edu

© The Author(s) 2018
V. Gruhn, R. Striemer (eds.), *The Essence of Software Engineering*,
https://doi.org/10.1007/978-3-319-73897-0_4

for improvements in the engineering of other kinds of software, such as processes and laws as well. For that reason the ongoing efforts of the Empirical Methods research community should be viewed by the entire "software" community as being of fundamental importance.

1 Apologia

When the words "software" and "engineering" were first put together [Naur and Randell 1968] it was not clear exactly what the marriage of the two into the newly minted term really meant. Some people understood that the term would probably come to be defined by what our community did and what the world made of it. Since those days in the late 1960's a spectrum of research and practice has been collected under the term. Journals, magazines, conferences, and workshops have used it in growing numbers. From time to time some have questioned whether or not the second word of the term, "engineering", is properly applied to what it is that "software engineers" do (e.g. [Parnas 1997]). The debate has been sporadic, but it has probably been good for the community. It seems odd, however, that there has been hardly any discussion of the first word of the term, namely "software". When, on infrequent occasion, the meaning of this term has been questioned, mostly in informal conversation, the question has been met with visible discomfort, and some attempt to dismiss it. The purpose of this paper is to try to address the question head-on.

What is software? If our community feels comfortable in believing that it is engaged in the practice of engineering "software", it seems that the community should show some curiosity about what it is that is the subject of its ministrations. But, when asked to ponder what "software" is, computer software engineers seem to assume that the only kind of software is computer software. They provide answers that roughly equate software with code to be executed on a computer. When prodded, most will readily agree that the software they produce consists of more than just the code, but also somehow incorporates specifications of various kinds, designs, and perhaps testing regimes and results as well. But when it is suggested that there might be types of software other than computer software, some computer software engineers have questioned the value of considering the possibility. Here we suggest that considering this possibility might lead to an understanding of what these various kinds of software have in common, and thus what the nature of "software" is. Some have suggested that the quintessential nature of "software" may be imponderable and unknowable. This may indeed be the case, but it seems worth noting that humans have in the past asked many "unanswerable" questions, about the nature of such things as love, God, truth, and reality. While the answers often have not been very satisfying, the pondering and discussion of them has typically been interesting, revealing, and sometimes ennobling. For these reasons, and others, it does not seem inappropriate to offer this short essay, hoping that it may help to start a debate that turns out to be, at least, interesting.

1.1 Why ask the Question?

In addition to the sheer intellectual joy of pursuing a hard, fundamental, and potentially unanswerable question, there are additional more pragmatic reasons for thinking about the essential nature of software. One such reason is that if there are others who work with software then it might be possible that their experiences in doing so might be of value to those of us who work with computer software. Other software practitioners might have encountered problems and issues that are analogous to those that concern us. In doing so they may have found some effective approaches to some problems that frustrate us. At the least, their struggles with analogous problems might at least underscore the universality and importance of the problems. Indeed idiosyncrasies of the problems posed in these analogous domains might well provide new perspectives on the problems that might be useful to us in our own work.

1.2 The Importance of Measurement

As noted above, and following Lord Kelvin, it seems promising to suggest that a path to understanding of the nature of software might be through grappling with questions about how to measure it. The Empirical Methods community has been a key focal point of ongoing efforts to measure software. A central challenge the community has faced is the continuing effort to measure the size of a piece of software. Some attempts have focused on how to count the number of "lines" of computer code, others have grappled with trying to measure the size of non-code artifacts, and the complexity of any and all of these artifacts. Other attempts have instead focused on process issues, suggesting that measuring the time, money, and effort taken to develop a piece of software might also be a good way to measure the size of the software item itself. These ongoing efforts do not yet seem to have led to universal agreement about how to measure the size of software but they have demonstrated correlations between many of the suggested measures. The magnitude of this ongoing challenge suggests the profundity of the question, and also suggests that growing understandings of how to measure size may well be leading to important deep understandings about the nature of software as an entity. We now suggest that these attempts and preliminary successes might be of value and interest to practitioners in other computer-software-like areas. And it indeed raises the question of whether these other practitioners might have had some success in measuring their own artifacts that could be of interest and value to computer software engineers.

2   Other Kinds of Software

It is worth noting that the word "software" is applied to artifacts from domains other than computing. In entertainment, for example, software is sometimes used to describe programmatics, such as videos and television productions. The term seems to be used to contrast this sort of product with "hardware", which refers to physical devices such as VCRs, CD players, and television sets. There are other domains that seem to be very much about "software" but some of these domains may not ever use the word, nor be very conscious of the relevance of what is known about computer software to what they do. Thus, we guide our search for an understanding of what "software" is by searching for other disciplines that seem to deal with "software", even if they may not use that term in describing their work. Thus, for example, it might suffice to simply identify points of similarity between what computer software engineers do and what is done by practitioners of these other disciplines.

2.1   Processes are (like?) software

In a previous paper [Osterweil 1987] it was suggested that "Software Processes are Software Too", intending to suggest that those who focus on the engineering of computer software might perhaps widen the scope of their attention to address processes for developing computer software as well. The point here was that processes seem as though they might be items of software that execute on virtual machines that consists of more kinds of devices than only computers. Subsequent work has tended to confirm the plausibility of that suggestion [Osterweil 1997, Clarke 2008, Simidchieva 2008].

   Process research has suggested that process software has strong similarities to computer software. In particular, experience has shown that many processes are highly concurrent, and that software concepts such as locking and synchronization can help the understanding and control of such processes. It has also been observed that exceptions are common in processes, and that exception management approaches that are analogous to those taken by modern programming languages also facilitate the understanding and control of processes. As with computer software, process software needs to address requirements that should be carefully thought out, should have an architecture, and should be designed prior to implementation. In addition, process software is subject to continuous need for change and evolution, which is highly problematic. Attempts to define real world processes have typically resulted in surprisingly large, repetitive, and ungainly process definitions. Experience has shown, however, that judicious use of formal declarations can help avoid dangerous confusions. Moreover, notions of abstraction, modularity, and hierarchy can lead to process definitions that are clearer, more concise, and demonstrate better reuse than those that do not attempt to exploit abstraction.

Thus, it seems that there is growing evidence that those who deal with the development and use of process definitions face and deal with many of the problems encountered by those who develop computer software. This seems to suggest that there could be value in considering processes to indeed be a type of software. On the other hand experience has also shown that real world processes often raise other issues less commonly dealt with by computer software developers. Processes, for example, make use of resources in ways that are often quite complicated. The prevalence and centrality of this complex usage of very diverse resources in many processes seems to be less analogous to what is typically found in contemporary computer software. This suggests that computer software engineers might consider the relevance of resource specification and utilization to their own work.

2.1.1   Measurement of Processes:

It seems that, while there are strong intuitions about the size of processes, there has been relatively little effort to specify rigorously-defined measures of process size. It is certainly not uncommon to see some processes referred to as "large" or "comprehensive", and even as "ungainly" or "clumsy", suggesting that people have strong intuitions about the size and suitability of processes. But there seem to have been few attempts to try to back up these intuitions with definitions and rigor.

Instead, efforts to be quantitative about processes have focused on measuring the execution characteristics of processes. Thus, for example, as noted above, Empirical Methods researchers have suggested that measures of the amount of time and resources required to develop a computer software product seem to provide some useful sense of the size of the product. And so, analogously, there has been a considerable amount of effort devoted to measuring execution parameters of software development processes. Similarly, practitioners in other areas such as healthcare and management are typically concerned to measure and improve the running time of their processes. In some cases, this has caused these practitioners to seek to materialize these processes in the form of process models, in the hope that study and analysis of these models might facilitate the improvement of the execution characteristics of their processes. But even in such cases there seems to have been relatively little attention devoted to measuring the size of these processes themselves.

Interestingly, in our own work, where we think of processes as being a kind of software we, accordingly, define processes using a programming-like language.

Thus we "measure" the size of a process by the number of steps (the analog of statements in a programming language), thereby pushing the problem of measuring size back onto the software development community.

Thinking more directly about the meaning of "size" in the process domain, however, has caused us to ponder whether the size of a process might be measured by the inherent ability of the process to change the state of the real-world situations to which they are applied. It seems, perhaps, more promising to consider how to measure the size of the state of the domain in which a process operates, and to then use this size as the basis for measuring the magnitude of the change(s) the process might effect, and thus the size of the process itself.

2.2   Legislation is (like?) software development:

We also suggest that laws are a form of software, and that legislation is a form of software development. Laws provide rules that govern the execution of governmental and societal activities. Many laws are proscriptive and in this way and seem not unlike the rules that could be written using a rule based language (e.g. see [Breaux 2008, Sergot et.al. 1986]). Other laws are more prescriptive, some even describing the ways in which various institutions are to be established, organized, and operated. Such laws sometimes prescribe the ways in which such institutions and their activities are to be coordinated with each other. Thus laws seem to define processes in many cases, and in these ways they resemble process definition vehicles. The languages used to define laws may seem to be informal, and may seem to be written in natural language. But this is apparently something of an illusion. Most legislative bodies mandate that their laws incorporate reserved words and phrases that have meanings that are often much more precisely defined than words used in natural language. Thus the text of a law is typically peppered with words that are relatively precisely defined, interspersed with words that are used colloquially. It typically impossible for a novice to tell which words are of which type.

It is interesting to note, moreover, that laws and legal documents (e.g. leases) often begin with a prefixed section in which additional terms may be defined, and in which the bindings of values may be made. Thus, for example, a lease typically begins with a paragraph containing words that bind names (i.e. instances of types) to the terms "lessor" and "lessee" (which are essentially types). The similarity to the declaration sections that precede bodies of computer code seems noteworthy.

Additional parallels can be found in, for example, the organizational structure of the government of countries such as the United States. This structure mandates three principal branches; the legislative, which creates software (i.e. laws), the executive, which executes the software (e.g. by creating bureaucratic machinery), and the judiciary, which analyzes bodies of software (e.g. an entire corpus of laws) to determine the extent to which it is, or is not, consistent. Thus these three branches correspond to computer software development notions of development, execution, and analysis.

We note moreover that laws, like computer software, typically need to be evolved as the needs and perceptions of their users change. As with the case of computer software, laws change the way in which the world works (not uncommonly in unexpected ways), thereby changing the context in which the laws work, thus changing the underlying requirements for the laws and creating the need for evolution. Thus, legal software, like computer software, seems to operate in a closed loop with the real world, each both inducing and reacting to change in the other. As a consequence, laws are typically amended, and at times entire bodies of law (e.g. tax codes) are completely discarded and replaced. All of this should be quite familiar to computer software engineers.

Further parallels between laws and computer software are not hard to identify. We thus suggest that laws are also a form of software and that legislation is a form of software development. We note in passing that this observation might cause computer software engineers to have a bit more sympathy for legislators. More to the point, however, it suggests that software engineers might learn something from studying legislation as an activity, and conversely that legislators might perform better if they were to study computer software engineering.

2.2.1   Measurement of Laws

As noted above people often have strong intuitions about the "size" of a law. Some laws are characterized as being "omnibus", suggesting that they are very broad in scope, others are sometimes characterized as being "landmark", suggesting that they have been placed in a new or different societal domain or interest area. Most typically, however, the size of a law is described in terms of the number of pages of documentation it takes to describe the law and its workings. As in the case of using lines of code to describe the size of an item of software, this measure seems facile and unsatisfying. Counting the articles, clauses, etc. is, perhaps something of an improvement, but not a particularly satisfying one, as these lexical measures do nothing to account for the complexity, substance, or reach of the law.

Here too it seems interesting to note that a more satisfying measure might be based more upon some quantification of the capacity for the operation of the law to change the state of affairs in the world. Some laws are capable of moving large amounts of money from one place (e.g. the taxpayer) to another (e.g. the government). Some laws are capable of incarcerating large numbers of people for long periods of time. Some laws cause large corporations to make major changes in their processes. Here too measuring the magnitude of the changes in state that can be effected by this type of software would seem relatively more measurable, and perhaps a better basis for measuring the "size" of a law.

2.3   Recipes are software

Cooking recipes seem to be a form of software as well. Recipes typically begin with a specification block that usually identifies the ingredients that are needed, a form of input parameter specification, and the equipment that is to be used, a sort of abstract machine specification. The steps in a recipe are often the names of procedures (e.g. "fold in" an ingredient, "bring [something] to a 'rolling boil' ", and so forth) that are defined elsewhere. Sometimes these steps are defined in the cookbook that contains the recipe, but often it is assumed that the execution agent (i.e. the cook) will access them from some sort of cooking process asset library (e.g. a cookbook intended for beginners).

Most recipes have rather straightforward sequential control flow between their steps, but it is not uncommon for complicated recipes to specify threads of control that are to be executed in parallel, often with synchronization conditions. In addition, many such steps also incorporate exception management. In the preparation of some sauces that use eggs, for example, an exception arises when the eggs start to curdle. There are clearly specified predicates used to identify such exceptions (i.e. what the appearance of the sauce is), and clearly stated exception handling procedures for dealing with them (e.g. remove from heat, rapidly stir in some other ingredient). Experienced cooks will recognize that the concurrent execution of several recipes (e.g. in preparing a complicated dinner party) can create severe resource contention problems (e.g. not enough ovens or burners), and that a more rigorous and thorough approach to resource specification and scheduling could help avoid serious difficulties such as deadlocks, races, and starvation (of both cooking processes and diners).

Note that while many recipes lack explicit requirements, some do indeed specify requirements such as, "this recipe is a good way to deal with leftover chicken". In addition, note that recipes are a particularly good example of time-critical real-time software. Timing specifications such as "boil for 5 minutes", and "cook in a 450 degree oven for 30 minutes" are common, and quite analogous to specifications found in real-time computer software. More interesting, perhaps, is the instruction, "stir occasionally for the next hour", which does not seem to be something that is easily specified using commonly available computer software language primitives.

2.3.1   Measurement of Recipes

In the domain of recipes there also seems to be a great deal of intuition about size. Thus, for example, some recipes are regarded as being "difficult", "complex", etc. Often this refers to the presence in the recipe of techniques that seem to require a lot of experience or practice (e.g. the making of certain sauces). But notions of size and complexity can also arise from recipe features that are quantifiable and quantified. Thus, many recipes incorporate specifications of the amount of time required for completion. Virtually all recipes incorporate ingredients lists with precise quantities specified. In that sense, a dimension of the size of the recipe is implied by the size of the ingredients (both quantity and diversity), and the size of the finished product. Many such recipes also features concurrency and the need for careful synchronization of parallel threads. In such cases, the number of parallel threads is easily quantifiable, and the tolerances required in synchronizing these threads are often specified as well. It is interesting that the quantification of recipe software seems to be better developed than the quantification of most other kinds of software.

2.4 Other Types of Software

Kit-building, assembly instructions, and driving directions seem to be other examples of software in different domains. Considering the ways in which these endeavors have features that are analogous to computer software development is an exercise that is left to the reader. In addition, the reader is strongly encouraged to think about other domains and endeavors that also seem analogous to computer software and its development. The prevalence of these domains in modern society is striking, suggesting that computer software engineering has much to study, and perhaps much to contribute, in these domains. *In most of these domains measurement and quantification seems relatively poorly developed, suggesting the need for progress in all, and the possibility that progress in any (e.g. computer software engineering) could be of significant value to many.*

Rather than dwelling upon the specifics of these diverse types of software, it seems more useful to examine the ways in which they address their fundamental problems to see what this might teach us about the nature of "software".

3   What makes these different types of software like each other?

The foregoing sections suggest that there are many features that these different types of entities have in common. As an aid and a prelude to suggesting what the nature of software might be, this section enumerates some of these features.

3.1 They are non-tangible, and non-physical, but often intended to manage tangibles

Perhaps what is most immediately noticeable is that all of these types of entities are non-tangible and non-physical, but often are intended to support the handling of entities that are tangible and physical. Thus, for example, recipes are intended to specify the preparation and management of food items, but the recipes themselves are intangible. Similarly, laws are intended to provide guidance, structure, and control of such tangibles as citizens and property, but the laws themselves are intangible.

3.2 Hierarchical Structure is a common feature.

Hierarchy seems to be a common vehicle for addressing the complexity that is inherent in all of these products. Laws are usually structures of larger sections (articles, chapters, etc.), and lower levels (e.g. clauses), aimed at providing needed elaborative details. Recipes may also be divided into section or phases, each aimed at the production of a different component. Processes are usually divided into phases as well.

3.3   They consist of components having different purposes

In legislation, cooking, and process, as with software development, there seems to be a primary focus on the executable component of the end-product. But the end-product also incorporates other types of components that are often at least as important. Thus, the actual law that results from legislation typically receives much attention. But the law itself typically is drafted only after hearings and conferences aimed at identifying precise requirements, and agreeing upon the design and architecture of the institutions and processes that are to be implemented by laws. Indeed many laws begin with a preamble of some sort that is intended to state the requirements for the law. Thus, for example, the Constitution of the United States of America begins with a preamble, "...in order to form a more perfect union, ... promote the general welfare, ... secure the blessings of liberty ... " that is clearly an, admittedly very high level, requirements specification.

Good cooking recipes also are more than just sequences of instructions for the cook. As noted above, the recipe often begins with a specification of what the recipe is good for, and what needs it is intended to address. In addition the cooking instructions are typically supplemented by explanations of why the cook is being asked to perform certain steps. Thus, for example, a recipe for risotto instructs the cook to coat rice grains with oil in a particular way. But a superior recipe also explains that this is done to foster the slow incorporation of liquid into the rice to impart a particular desirable texture. Note that good recipes also incorporate incremental evaluation steps. Cooks are instructed to test ingredients (usually by tasting them) as the production of the end-product proceeds. Typically this is intended to improve the quality of the final result by supporting the early identification of errors, leading to more prompt and effective correction of the errors.

3.4   All are expected to require modification/evolution

Modification and evolution are expected for all of these types of entities. Thus, for example, laws are typically amended and replaced as internal defects are discovered, and as judicial processes demonstrate their incompatibility, either internally, or with respect to other laws. Evolution also takes place as there are changes in the problems that a law is intended to address. Recipes are updated from time to time to accommodate the availability of new kitchen devices, and changes in the availability of certain ingredients. Processes also need to be changed as defects are discovered, efficiency improvements are identified, and as there are changes in the problem that a process is intended to address.

Because all of these types of software are non-physical and intangible, there seems to be a shared belief that needed evolution and change are relatively easy. In all of these cases, this belief is largely illusory. The reasons have much to do with another feature shared by these different types of software, namely their interconnectness.

3.5 Interconnections are key

While the interconnections among the various components of physical and tangible products may be more visible, the quantity and variety of interconnections among the various components of software seem to be no less either in number or in importance. It is relatively easy to see the way in which columns hold up floors and roofs in buildings, and the way the cables hold up the roadway of a suspension bridge. The way in which the structure of clauses and chapters of a law address the need for equity and justice, however, is no less real and important, although it may be far less clear. Similarly, the process of qualifying a voter directly supports the need for an election to assure the "one vote per voter" fairness requirement, although here too the way in which this is done may not be immediately clear.

As noted above, these different forms of software all consist of components of different types (e.g. requirements, architecture) in addition to the actual executable component of the software. But in all of these cases, these different types of components must satisfy very specific relationships with each other. The need to maintain these relationships complicates the modification and evolution of these components. Thus, a change to a specific clause in a law, much like a change to a computer software module, must be done in consideration of how that change will affect all of the other software components to which the changed component relates. A changed law must not cause inconsistency with other related laws, and must continue to be responsive to all of the requirements for the law.

The invisibility and intangibility of these constraints seems to be at least largely responsible for perpetuating the illusion of easy modifiability of all of these types of software. But the actuality of these constraints defies the illusion.

3.6 Analysis and verification are universal underlying needs

The existence of the relations just described is, in all cases, useful as the basis upon which various approaches to analysis and verification rests. As noted above, the judicial system exists to carry out analyses aimed at determining the consistency of various laws with each other, and with stated requirements to which specific laws must adhere. Thus, for example, American courts often decide the "constitutionality" of laws, namely the extent to which the laws may or may not be in violation of the constraint that they conform to the Constitution of the United States (n.b. including the statement of requirements embodied in its Preamble).

Cooking recipes are typically also analyzed, for example, in trial kitchens where their performability is studied. This is in addition to the more usual verification done by tasters who determine whether execution of the recipe does indeed result in the creation of a product that meets requirements for tastiness, colorfulness, and servability.

Processes are also typically verified by executing their executable component(s) and then determining the extent to which they meet requirements for speed, efficiency, and the production of desired results. Processes are sometimes used as the basis for simulations aimed at the same kinds of determinations, but using simulated, rather than actual, situations. Recent work has shown that static analyses are also useful in verifying the effectiveness of processes [Clarke 2008].

4   Characterizing software

The preceding set of characteristics that seem to be shared by a few notable software domains suggests that these characteristics might be taken as an, at least initial, set of properties of a type of entity that we might refer to as "software". Instances of this entity seem to be characterized by being non-physical and intangible, and yet structured by potentially large and complex sets of constraints that complicate what seems to be a frequent need for modification and evolution. While software is itself non-physical and intangible, a principal goal for instances of the type software is for them to contain one or more components whose execution effects the management and control of tangible entities. Computer software is characterized by the fact that it is intended to execute on a computer. Other types of software execute on different physical manifestations. Thus, for example, laws are executed by government bureaucracies, and recipes are executed on cooking paraphernalia such as ovens, bowls, measuring devices, and mixers.

As a structured entity, software is characterized at least in part as being a collection of constraints and relations that define what it means for it to be well-formed. These constraints are then available for use in determining whether and how the entity may be inconsistent and thus in need of correction. In the case of computer software, there has been considerable effort directed towards creating formal notations for defining these relations, and thus supporting rigorous analyses. Other software domains seem to rely more heavily upon less formal approaches.

The evolutionary forces that act upon all forms of software are also most strikingly universal. Software's role in managing physical and tangible entities that are part of the real world thereby connects software to the vagaries of change that are constant in the real world. The needs and requirements that have been shown to be part of all types of software are rooted in the real world. Thus the constraints between the executing component of software and its requirements component thereby induce the need for change in all components of a software entity as responses to changes in the real world. The need for all of these changes to be consistent with respect to the substantial number of constraints that characterize all types of software are what make software change difficult. In software domains (e.g. legislation) where the constraints are not particularly rigorously defined or explicitly stated change is correspondingly problematic.

This informal description of some key characteristics of software is but an early suggestion of the nature of this entity. More formal and rigorous definitions would be far more satisfying. One approach might be to use Object Oriented technologies to try to specify the class "software", perhaps starting by defining its attributes and methods. An Entity-Relation approach might be used to place more emphasis on the relations that structure and constrain a software entity. The use of a type hierarchy might help to distinguish among the various kinds of software (e.g. legal, computer, cooking, etc.). Another approach might be to consider a software entity to be representable by a hyper-multigraph, with the different relations constraining the software entity being represented by different edges and hyper-edges between nodes that have different "colors" corresponding to the different types of the components that they represent.

A key reason for studying the applicability of these formalisms might be as a way to evaluate them as vehicles for measuring and quantifying items of software. Software size might be parameterized, for example, by the number and diversity of constraints used to define its well-formedness, or by the number of software product entities that are actually constrained by these constraints. We note that constraints often have the effect of broadcasting or propagating changes, both to different software product elements and to the tangible real-world entities that they affect.

Accordingly, our suggestion that software size might be measured by the potential of a software product to cause change in the state of its domain could be a definable function of the number and diversity of these constraints. The Empirical Methods community would seem to be in an excellent position to explore such possibilities for establishing cogent and useful measures of these sorts.

5   What can computer software engineering contribute to other forms of software engineering?

The foregoing suggests that computer software engineering may have technologies and approaches that could be of considerable value to those who engineer other types of software. As noted above, a key characteristic of software seems to be that it is highly structured, with its structure being defined by a potentially large and diverse collection of relations and constraints. The utility and evolvability of software entities seems to rest importantly upon how effectively these constraints can be evaluated and brought into consistency with each other. As just noted, computer software engineering has evolved a formal discipline aimed at supporting this need, but other software engineering disciplines such as law may not have been as successful in doing so. *As noted, this discipline might be a useful basis for establishing useful and intuitive measures and quantifications of computer software.* There have indeed been some attempts to apply computer software engineering formalisms and approaches to laws. *Perhaps work on measuring computer software size could lead to better measures of the size of laws.* More such work seems clearly indicated. There is also a great deal of interest in applying computer software engineering approaches to the engineering of processes. Workflow languages and systems are examples of this (e.g. see [Georgakopoulous et.al. 1995]). They support facilitating the creation of processes for coordinating the efforts of humans in areas such as clerical paperwork processing. Other more ambitious efforts have aimed at developing process definition languages and applying analysis approaches borrowed directly from the domain of computer software engineering [Clarke et.al. 2008, Osterweil 1987]. *Useful measures of the size of processes would come directly from success in defining useful measures of the size of application computer software.*

Computer software engineering approaches could presumably add value to such other software domains as cooking and kit-building instruction development. As scheduling is a serious problem in the parallel execution of large numbers of complex recipes (e.g. in the kitchen of a large restaurant), recipe analysis could be applied to study superior utilization of such resources as ovens and burners. This might reduce the size and cost of kitchen facilities and lead to faster delivery of meals. Kit-building and driving instructions could also be improved by the application of such computer software engineering technologies as exception management. Most kit-building, assembly, and driving instructions ignore the possibility of errors in their execution, even though such errors are not uncommon, and can lead to serious problems. Computer software engineers are evolving approaches to assuring robustness that are based upon identifying the symptoms of incorrect execution, and the fashioning of handlers to deal with the consequences. Applying such disciplines to driving instructions would help drivers to recognize when they have gone astray and would guide them back on course. Clearly, early detection of such errors is, as in the case of computer software development, most desirable.

The application of automation is another particularly promising contribution that computer software engineering might make to the engineering of other kinds of software. Computer software engineers have over the past decades shown that computers can themselves be invaluable aids in developing computer software that is of higher quality, and yet has been built more rapidly and more inexpensively. Computer automation can facilitate the analysis of software, as well as its testing, documentation, distribution, installation, and evolution. It seems natural to consider how these benefits of automation could be applied to other forms of software as well. Indeed, one notes that computer automation is beginning to be applied to the storage and retrieval of legal and cooking software, and automated analysis and testing is beginning to be applied to process software. Automated creation of driving instructions from requirement specifications, and constrained by the architecture of road networks is now also beginning to gain prevalence and acceptance. All of this suggests that a systematic investigation of automation needs in non-computer software domains could lead to important applications of automation in those domains, perhaps mirroring the use of automation in computer software engineering.

6 What can computer software engineers learn from the study of other forms of software?

It is clearly gratifying to contemplate how the technologies that have been developed by our computer software engineering community may have the potential to improve the workings of other important communities. But it is potentially even more important for our community to see what we can learn from doing so. Some examples of potentially valuable learning are suggested here.

6.1 Resources

The large and complex systems that are being built today are increasingly attempting to support and coordinate the activities of various kinds of agents, using various kinds of resources. Yet the languages and notations that computer software engineers use to model, design, and implement such systems seem to pay scant attention to how resources are required and utilized in such systems. In the domain of process software, for example, resources often play an important role. In designing and specifying systems for such domains as hospital care, many key issues revolve around the utilization of such resources as doctors, beds, MRI devices, and surgery suites. Modeling of the way such resources participate in hospital processes is complicated, for example, by the existence of various substitution rules. For example, a nurse may not provide certain services such as prescribing medications, and a doctor will prefer not to provide other services, such as drawing blood for testing. But under certain circumstance, these rules and preferences are overridden. Specification of the circumstances can be difficult, and challenging. Resources are modeled in other domains such as management and networking. But the formalisms used in those domains do not seem to provide the semantic power needed to specify all of the complex substitution rules relating to very diverse types of resources that are required in order to model hospital resources in a way that supports the definition of medical processes sufficiently precisely.

In short, the way in which the real world uses resources poses challenges that seem to stress existing approaches to resource specification and management. Applying computer software engineering technologies to the process software domain underscores these challenges and suggests the need to address them with new research.

6.2   Timing

As noted above, attempts to specify processes and recipes (for example) emphasize the need to improve capabilities for dealing with time. All processes impose timing constraints, and thus process languages require facilities for specifying them. Existing languages and real-time systems offer some capabilities that are undeniably useful. But, as noted above, specification of some processes seems to require more. Thus, for example, cooking recipes specify that sauces need to be stirred "occasionally" for some period of time. Medical processes specify that nurses should monitor a transfusion patient "from time to time" for adverse reactions. These concepts are well-understood in the real world, but not well modeled in languages that computer software engineers would offer for use by process software engineers and recipe software developers.

6.3   Verification and analysis of legislation

While we may like to believe that legislative software engineers have much to learn from computer software engineers, it may well be the case that the reverse is true as well. As noted above the judicial system seems to have as its focus the verification and analysis of legal software (laws). It is interesting to note that laws, like computer software, are typically put into use before their consistency with other laws has been definitively and exhaustively determined. Certainly the details of a new law are debated and studied, but at some point the law is enacted without the completion of the analysis. In some sense, the experiences of those subjected to the enacted law pick up at that point, and serve as testcases for an ongoing regime of testing. When the dictates of a new law seem to a legal subject to be inconsistent with another law, a trial may be used to resolve the consistency question.

Computer software engineers seem to have adopted a roughly analogous approach. New computer software is analyzed statically, and with a certain amount of dynamic testing. The computer software is then installed and delivered, at which time users continue the testing process. Thus, legal systems seem to have arrived at a sense of how much analysis is needed before testing begins. As legal software engineers have been doing this for at least hundreds of years longer than computer software engineers, it is quite possible that they have learned something about this that could be of value and use to computer software engineers.

Moreover, legal software engineers have also evolved the notion of "case law" whereby a persuasive body of legal precedents and interpretations eventually assumes the power of law, even though no legislation governing these cases has ever been passed. In some sense it seems that a sizeable body of testcases can eventually comprise an item of software, or at least a component of an item of software. Computer software engineers do not currently seem to have an analogous practice, although recent work aimed at determining invariants by studying execution traces through computer software may perhaps indicate the beginnings of development of such an analog.

7 Conclusion

It is interesting to contemplate the premise that computer software engineers may not be the only people who engineer software. There seems to be considerable evidence that the hard problems that computer software engineers address with their work may have strong analogs to other problem domains, and indeed to the practices of these other domains. This paper suggests that careful examination of these other domains seems warranted, as the approaches of one could be of interest and value to others. In particular computer software engineering may be of considerable value in improving the state of the practice in such areas as law and process. Moreover, application of automation approaches taken in computer software engineering may have deliver particularly good benefits to these other software engineering domains. Conversely, however, some of these other domains are much older and have longstanding approaches and traditions that could be of value and interest as possible areas of study and beneficial application to computer software engineering.

This paper has also suggested that cogent, useful measures of software of all kinds seem to be lacking. Following Lord Kelvin, it seems that deeper and firmer knowledge of the nature of all of these different sorts of software would follow from the ability to measure and quantify such software. And, indeed, one is struck by the observation that virtually all of these sorts of software suffer from analogous inabilities to do such measurement. This paper has taken as an example of this, the lack of cogent measures of software size. A possibility that has been advanced here is that software size might be measured by the potential for an item of software to change the state in the domain in which the software operates. The Empirical Methods community seems to be in an excellent position to address the evaluation of this specific proposal, and the evaluation in general of different ideas for quantification and measurement of software. This would seem to offer considerable prospects for good progress in the development of the many disciplines that are appropriately viewed as software disciplines.

Ultimately, careful examination of these various software engineering domains, *aided by effective approaches for measuring in these domains,* may lead us to a clear understanding of the elusive nature of the entity that we call "software".

References

[Breaux and Anton 2008] T. D. Breaux and A.I. Anton, "Analyzing Regulatory Rules for Privacy and Security Requirements," *IEEE Trans. on Software Engineering*, v. 34, #1, 2008, pp. 5-20.
[Chen et.al 2008] B. Chen, L.A. Clarke, G.S. Avrunin, L.J. Osterweil, E.A. Henneman, and P.L. Henneman, "Analyzing Medical Processes", ACM SIGSOFT/IEEE 30th International Conference on Software Engineering (ICSE'08), Leipzig, Germany, May 2008, pp. 623-632.

[Clarke et.al 2008] L.A. Clarke, G.S. Avrunin, and L.J. Osterweil, "Using Software Engineering Technology to Improve the Quality of Medical Processes", ACM SIGSOFT/IEEE 30th International Conference on Software Engineering (ICSE'08), Leipzig, Germany, May 2008, pp. 889-898

[Georgakopoulos et.al. 1995] D. Georgakopoulos, M. F. Hornick, and A. P. Sheth, "An overview of workflow management: From process modeling to workflow automation infrastructure", *Distributed and Parallel Databases*, v.3, # 2, 1995, pp. 119-153.

[Naur and Randell 1968] P. Naur and B. Randell, eds., *Software Engineering, Report on a conference sponsored by the NATO SCIENCE COMMITTEE*, Garmisch, Germany, 7-11 October 1968. Scientific Affairs Division NATO, Brussels, Belgium. Also available at http://homepages.cs.ncl.ac.uk/brian.randell/NATO/nato1968.PDF.

[Osterweil 1987] Leon J. Osterweil, "Software Processes are Software Too", ACM SIG-SOFT/IEEE 9th International Conference on Software Engineering (ICSE 1987), Monterey, CA, March 1987, pp. 2-13.

[Osterweil 1997] Leon J. Osterweil, "Software Processes Are Software Too, Revisited", ACM SIGSOFT/IEEE 19th International Conference on Software Engineering (ICSE 1997), Boston, MA, May 1997, pp. 540-548.

[Osterweil 2008] Leon J. Osterweil, "What is Software?". Automated Software Engineering 15 (3-4), pp. 261-273 (2008).

[Parnas 1997] D.L. Parnas, "Software Engineering: An Unconsummated Marriage", *Communication of the ACM*, v.40, #9, 1997, p. 128.

[Sergot et.al. 1986] Sergot, M., Sadri, F., Kowalski, R., Kriwaczek, F., Hammond, P., and Cory, T., "The British Nationality Act as a Logic Program", in *Communications of the ACM*, v. 29, #5, 1986, pp. 370-386.

[Simidchieva et.al. 2008] B.L. Simidchieva, M.S. Marzilli, L.A. Clarke, and L.J. Osterweil, "Specifying and Verifying Requirements for Election Processes", in dg.o 2008: Proceedings of the 9th Annual International Conference on Digital Government Research (2008), S. A. Chun, M. Janssen, and J. R. Gil-Garcia, (eds.), Digital Government Society of North America, pp. 63-72.

Only the Architecture You Need

Richard N. Taylor

1 Introduction

Software architecture has been around for a long time. Even prior to the identification of software engineering as a discipline in 1968, there was an explicit focus on techniques for software design. The 1970s saw many publications detailing various design techniques and strategies. In 1976 Peter Freeman stated, "Design is relevant to all software engineering activities and is the central integrating activity that ties the others together" [1]. More design techniques and strategies emerged in the 1980s, many of them addressing larger-scale systems. "Software architecture" as the label for this type of work took off in the 1990s, notably with the appearance of Perry and Wolf's landmark paper [2]. Subsequent development of the field focused on various types of architectural models, description languages, analysis techniques, development environments, canonical solutions, and design processes. Example architectures abounded, conferences and workshops held, and many books emerged.

Yet despite all this progress, all too often architecture is ignored in application development. Consider the following dialog from an imagined movie, "The Treasure of the Silicon Valley,"[1] starring a venture capital investor performing due diligence for a potential acquisition, conversing with a start-up's lead software developer:

> If you're the chief software engineer on the project, show me your architecture.

> Architecture? Architecture?! We don't need no stinkin' architecture!

---

[1]With acknowledged inspiration from, and apologies to, "The Treasure of the Sierra Madre," a 1948 film by John Huston.

R. N. Taylor (✉)
Institute for Software Research, University of California, Irvine, Irvine, CA, USA
e-mail: taylor@ics.uci.edu

© The Author(s) 2018
V. Gruhn, R. Striemer (eds.), *The Essence of Software Engineering*,
https://doi.org/10.1007/978-3-319-73897-0_5

This dialog is all too understandable. The VC wants to know what he's buying into and wants to perform his own analysis of the properties of the start-up's system. And most assuredly, he does not want to have to read a million lines of undocumented Python and JavaScript to get that insight. The developer, on the other hand, has been immersed in the details of the application since day one. He knows what he has, believes in what he has, and sees any call for an explicit architecture as a nonproductive demand on his nonexistent free time.

Very different dialogs appear in other "movie scripts." Developers in regulated industries, or those working under government contract, are well acquainted with the use of architectural models to facilitate communication and to demonstrate achievement of some mandated properties. What is appropriate and what is necessary can vary widely, just as projects and usage contexts vary widely.

The remainder of this chapter, then, considers several different development contexts, ranging from "personal software engineering" to large-scale organizational development of high-consequence software. For each we consider what kinds of architectural discipline are needed and what purposes such architectural information serve. Our perspective is one of cost-benefit analysis. Investment in architectural modeling and analysis should not exceed the benefits reaped by performing such tasks.

2 Software Architecture: Essence, Benefits, and Costs

Before considering the various development contexts and how they differ in terms of their need for architectural discipline, we provide a little background on software architecture and introduce some key terminology. This is not a full presentation of the key elements of software architecture, but rather a quick highlight of a few concepts that will appear throughout the remainder of this chapter. Software architecture is a well-developed field with numerous techniques and strategies developed to aid the architect. Many of these, along with careful definitions of the rich vocabulary, are fully presented in [3].

To begin, software architecture, as a term, derives from analogy to the architecture of buildings. The analogy, while imperfect, is strong and provides several key insights:

- Architecture exists independently from the building/source code.
- The properties of structures (whether buildings or code) are induced by their architectures, for example, how accommodating of change they can be.
- The necessary skills of an architect are different from the skills of a building contractor/programmer.
- The *process* of design and construction is not as important as the architecture (i.e., the *product* is ultimately what matters at the end of the day, rather than how you got there).

- Architecture is a body of knowledge that can be studied, taught, and improved.
- Every building/application has an architecture, whether implicit or explicit, whether good, bad, ugly, or elegant.

The best definition of software architecture is that articulated by Eric Dashofy and put forth in [3].

Definition A software system's *architecture* is the set of principal design decisions made about the system.

This definition places the notion of *design decision* upfront. Design decisions encompass every aspect of the system under development, including structure, functional behavior, nonfunctional properties, user interaction, and decisions related to the system's implementation and deployment. Every application embodies at least one design decision, and hence all systems have architectures.

Not all design decisions carry equal weight, however. *Principal* is a key modifier of "design decisions." It is a matter of degree and pertinence that grants a design decision "architectural status," that is, that makes it an *architectural design decision*. This also implies that not all design decisions are architectural. Indeed, many of the design decisions made in the process of system building (such as the programming details of the selected algorithms) will not impact a system's architecture.

Determining which decisions are principal is a function of context. It is the system's stakeholders (including, but not restricted to, the architect) who rightfully decide which design decisions are important enough to include in the architecture.

Given that stakeholders may come with very different priorities from a software architect, even nontechnical considerations may end up driving determination of the architecture. Moreover, different sets of stakeholders may designate different sets of design decisions as principal. Thus this definition of software architecture is neither simplistic nor simple. Architecture concerns the core decisions, and in a significant system those decisions do not come automatically or without dispute.

Architectural models are means of capturing architectures in a tangible form. Once again from [3], we have these definitions.

Definitions An architectural *model* is an artifact that captures some or all of the design decisions that comprise a system's architecture. Architectural *modeling* is the reification and documentation of those decisions. An *architecture description language* (ADL) is a notation for capturing architectural decisions as a model.

Lastly, we consider architectural styles, whose role will figure prominently in the subsequent discussion.

Definition An *architectural style* is a named collection of architectural design decisions that (1) are applicable in a given development context, (2) constrain architectural design decisions that are specific to a particular system within that context, and (3) elicit beneficial qualities in each resulting system.

Many architectural styles are widely known, such as client-server, event-based, REST (REpresentational State Transfer) [4], and SCADA. Styles are essential tools in a software designer's toolbox. Styles capture the hard-won lessons of past experience, enabling a designer to reap known benefits in specified contexts in a new design.

2.1 Benefits

The benefits sought through a focus on software architecture include:

- Effective communication
- Conceptual integrity: intellectual control and management of complexity
- Adequate basis for supporting knowledge reuse
- Support for cost-effective product lines, including management of related variants

The most widely acknowledged benefit of a focus on software architecture is improved communication. That communication may be among developers or between developers and various stakeholders. Seemingly ubiquitous PowerPoint presentations of system designs, with circles, boxes, arrows, and colors, are attempts to communicate some of the key design decisions of a system. (Whether those attempts are effective or accurate is an entirely different subject.) Whatever the means of modeling, the objective is to communicate the essential decisions to others so that, for example, developers can proceed with their tasks knowing the context into which their work fits, or so that other designers can offer their opinions about the suitability of the design, based on their analysis of the represented decisions.

Maintaining conceptual integrity of a system as it evolves over time is perhaps the greatest challenge to a project manager. As systems evolve, responding to pressures for additional or changed features, new platforms, or simply to fix bugs, it is easy for their architectures to drift from their original key decisions. Knowing whether a new decision is consistent with key decisions made previously is of fundamental importance. Determining such consistency demands that there be a record of what those decisions are, and that is the function of explicit models of the architecture. With a model there is at least the hope of assessing the impact of a newly proposed change; without a model the project manager is left with only his memory.

Knowledge reuse is essential to the economic success of an enterprise; rediscovering insights and reinventing solutions is a recipe for failure. Knowledge reuse on a small scale became well known and popularized in the 1990s through use of design patterns: solutions to small-scale problems that are nonetheless common in programming [5] and which have been subsequently captured for reuse by others. Stepping up in scale to subsystems of modules and to whole applications, architectural styles enable developers to similarly reuse solutions captured through prior experience, thereby achieving the benefits yielded by adherence to those styles.

On a still larger scale, companies often flourish when their products dominate a market segment. Dominating a segment often results from acquiring deep knowledge of the domain and having experience developing multiple solutions to problems in the domain. New products in a domain are often incremental variants of prior products that leverage that knowledge. A domain-specific reference architecture can capture these insights in ways similar to design patterns and architectural styles and can provide guidance for the design and management of software product lines.

2.2   Techniques . . . and Costs

The literature of software architecture is full of techniques, strategies, languages, and tools intended to help the architect from initial conception of a system through its full product lifetime. Virtually all of the techniques center on, or require, some form of architectural model. Models form the basis for communication, analysis, and, if they are good models, implementation and evolution.

Modeling languages run the gamut from informal and shallow (most PowerPoint architectures) to technically rich and deep, upon which formal and automated analyses can be performed, and in some cases from which implementations can be automatically generated, or at least started.

Doing a good job of modeling—in which the key decisions are all identified and captured—is not an easy or quick task. Modeling languages are not all easy to use. Indeed, generally speaking, the easier a modeling language is to use, the less information it captures and the less useful it will be as a project proceeds; conversely, the most powerful languages have narrow ranges of applicability and can require costly and rare expertise to effectively employ.

The key issue in the application of any software architecture technology is the cost-benefit ratio.

Capturing knowledge, of the kind that enables new products in a domain to be built efficiently, is also costly. It requires, as new products are built and experience gained, that an investment be made in reflecting on that experience and refining domain models and architectures for potential future use. The potentiality is a risk; if the captured knowledge is not reused later in new products, then that effort was wasted.

Risks exist too, based on the current state of software architecture tools and techniques. Some modeling languages, for example, may provide significant benefit to architects during initial design stages, through facilitating communication and providing the basis for analysis. But when it comes time to push the design into implementation, the modeling language may provide little help. Indeed, with many languages, the task of showing conformance between the architecture of the code (the realized architecture) and the architectural model (the intended architecture) may be quite difficult. Moreover, when problems arise during implementation and a need for change to the intended architecture is identified, many design tools provide no help in "mapping back" to enable a disciplined approach to the redesign.

2.3   Summary and Roadmap

The benefits that have the potential to be realized through a disciplined application of software architecture are many and substantial. But the costs can be significant. The key, then, is to understand the demands of a development context, and for that context identify just the architecture techniques that are cost-effective. The following sections of the chapter will attempt to briefly do just that, examining three notional development settings: personal software engineering (working by yourself, for yourself), working in a team in a small corporate setting, and working in a large company on high-consequence software.

3   Personal Software Architecture

The imaginary screenplay between the venture capitalist and the start-up entrepreneur found in the Introduction section could very plausibly arise from a common scenario. An individual, the entrepreneur, learns programming in college and then decides to use his new skills by writing an app for his iPhone—writing it both for the pleasure and interest of doing so, and also because he has a particular way he likes to plan and record his vacations. His app, "MyTravel," allows him to record an itinerary, include photos and commentary, and export to his personal blog. Naturally by doing good development work, his friends are impressed, want their own copy, and later ask him to add additional features. By word of mouth the popularity of the app increases until the group of friends decides to form a small company to further enhance and market the product. Sometime later as success grows, the need for venture capital appears and the "no stinkin' architecture" dialog ensues.

But why would the inventor be so resistant to talking about architecture? Simply because of how his company evolved. At the outset of his efforts, he was just "messing around" and the project just accreted features in a haphazard fashion after that. He was just working for himself, with no intention of ever forming a company. He never took the time to focus on "architecture."

There is a deep falsehood in this narrative, however. Unless the developer was truly ignorant, he will have used Apple's app developer tools, such as Cocoa, the XCode software development kit, the Quartz framework, and user interface guidelines. And prominent in those materials is this statement: "MVC is central to a good design for a Cocoa application[2]." That is, Apple is directing developers' attention to a particular architectural style, MVC (Model-View-Controller), and saying that it is of critical importance in the design of new iPhone applications. The Apple website goes on to say, "The benefits of adopting this pattern are

---

[2]https://developer.apple.com/library/content/documentation/General/Conceptual/DevPedia-CocoaCore/MVC.html, Accessed July 2017.

numerous. Many objects in these applications tend to be more reusable, and their interfaces tend to be better defined. Applications having an MVC design are also more easily extensible than other applications. Moreover, many Cocoa technologies and architectures are based on MVC and require that your custom objects play one of the MVC roles." Thus the individual developer is compelled from the outset to be knowledgeable about and to utilize an important concept from software architecture.

The need for personal architectural knowledge goes beyond MVC, however. iPhone applications, and indeed virtually every user interface-intensive application, rely heavily on event-based architectural concepts. From handling interrupts through publish-subscribe architectural styles, to highly decoupled applications, event-based styles are powerful and common. Their power arises from supporting strong decoupling (which indeed may cross host and address space boundaries) and unpredictable sequences of events, leading to high extensibility. They are seductive and dangerous, however, because while an individual developer may initially only use events to coordinate two or three actors in an application, mentally keeping track of how the events are handled, the situation can quickly become confusing. Indeed, unwelcome surprises may appear as the developer slowly starts to recognize all the possible event interactions that may occur.

Cocoa and Quartz introduce even more architectural concepts into the solo entrepreneur's world. Cocoa's AppKit is a framework used to implement the user interface of an application. Quartz is a framework used to manipulate images. A framework is a programmatic bridge between concepts (such as "window" or "image") and lower-level implementation technologies. Frameworks can be very architectural in orientation, wherein they cleanly map architectural styles to code; unfortunately, they may also be rather random collections of nonetheless useful code.

So, indeed, our intrepid entrepreneur was using multiple explicitly architectural concepts from the outset, though he may have not known them under that label.

As time progresses, a key question for the entrepreneur is whether his memory is sufficient to remember all the design choices he has made, and to make future changes to his application in a manner that is consistent with the previously made decisions—or at least to be able to recognize when a prior decision is being changed, and then to understand all the downstream consequences of that change. To what extent has he bothered to record his design decisions in some accessible medium?

The cost-benefit analysis for a developer working on his own, for himself as a client, is pretty simple, though the analysis itself is "risky." He must know the concepts of software architecture, for they will surely figure into his development. But to what extent does he need to invest in capturing his decisions in a model of some sort? If his memory is good, or if the application has a very limited time horizon, then little or no such investment is warranted. But if there is a chance that the usage and development will progress to a context beyond that of personal development, then the investment might be very well worth it. It is that context that we examine next.

4 Team Software Architecture

The role of software architecture grows in importance dramatically as development shifts from an individual working for himself to a team developing a product for use within a company or for external sale. The consequences of poor decisions or poor engineering are much more severe, the need for communication within the team and across the company is critical, and the complexity of the product and project is much greater.

Though the sources of increased complexity are perhaps obvious, as an example consider some of the possible ways the "MyTravel" app could grow. The app could support ingestion of travel itinerary information from a wide range of external travel vendors by importing the information from confirmation emails. The app could enable export of selected information to Facebook. A dramatically larger user base could drive the back end of the app to the cloud, improving access and providing scalability. With wide usage and broad third-party integration, the need for security and authentication arises, very possibly supported by services available in the cloud.

4.1 Communication

Perhaps the single greatest need for architecture in this context arises in support of communication. Not only must all developers be on the same page, but also the development team must meet its accountability obligations, both to management within the company and potentially to external clients. If the architecture is not captured in any tangible form, then communication is limited very unsatisfactorily to mental recollections and verbal communication. If, rather, explicit models are used, both during design and during subsequent system evolution, then they may serve as the anchor for all types of communication. But what kinds of models? The options range from informal text and diagrams ("PowerPoint architectures") to semiformal UML, to precise architectural specifications in a formal architecture description language. The choice turns on what benefits are needed from the models, both immediately and also over the project's lifetime. The typical tragedy, unfortunately, is that this key decision is often made thinking only of immediate communication needs, such as to satisfy some corporate review board, and not, for example, with an eye to how a different downstream development group is going to attempt to decide through reviewing past documents whether a particular program reorganization will break security properties of the system. Making the choice of what to model and how to model, then, requires professional maturity and engineering discipline, qualities that are often in short supply.

Furthermore, the larger the team and the more diverse the set of project stakeholders, the greater the need for specialized visualizations, or projections, of a chosen architectural model. When talking to a customer, for instance, a less detailed view of the architecture is probably desirable. When internally reviewing the architecture for performance properties, a more detailed view is likely essential. Support for multiple views of a single model is unfortunately uncommon among modeling techniques.

4.2   Complexity

The complexity of a project is often the initial reason for creating a team to develop it. And often as a project evolves, its complexity only increases, as additional interconnections with external systems increase, additional features are added, and new usage modes considered. While the development team may initially select a satisfactory, coherent architecture, how is intellectual control over that architecture maintained over time? As features accrete, how does the team prevent the once-clean architecture from slowly devolving into a "big ball of mud?" Certainly explicit models and team discipline are part of the answer, but additional success can be found in judicious choice of architectural style; some styles are far more accommodating of change than others. Indeed, some styles, such as event/message based, are explicitly designed to foster and accommodate change.

Accommodating the need to *scale* to new dimensions of users, or data, or platforms is a particularly common and particularly difficult type of change to satisfy unless good architectural engineering is applied. Coping with issues of scale requires understanding the source of scaling pressures and then choosing or combining techniques suited to meet those challenges. The techniques available include, obviously, choice of architectural style and, especially, choice of appropriate connector technology. Further, with suitable modeling some types of scalability analysis can be undertaken prior to any system implementation.

A compelling illustration of this approach is the World Wide Web. The well-known REST architectural style mentioned earlier [4] arose from a careful consideration of the demands on an open, network-based, hypertext-oriented information integration system. REST was developed as a judicious combination of multiple simpler and well-known styles, such as replicated data, client-server, layered, and virtual machine, plus some additional constraints.

Through a team's shared understanding of a style—why it was chosen, what its constraints are, what benefits it elicits—and maintaining adherence to that style, a system's conceptual integrity can be preserved.

Essential to understanding and applying advanced architectural styles is understanding the rich range of connector technologies available. Perhaps the most common weakness in the educational background of new developers is lack of understanding of such connectors, and how different types of connectors can contribute to keeping system complexity under control while achieving scale and extensibility goals. Many new developers come armed only with method calls, the simplest and perhaps most limiting of all connector types. More capable connectors often come hidden inside various middleware packages. "Enterprise software buses," for example, can provide a much richer and dynamic connection style, and the many network protocols offer still other connection means. For a full treatment of connectors, see [6] or [3].

5 Summary

In a team setting the costs of development are higher than in the individual setting and the consequences of poor engineering are similarly higher. What was sufficient practice in the individual developer context is no longer adequate. There is a greater need for planning, and much greater need for support of communication between developers, customers, and management. Failure to adequately prepare for future years of product development and modification can lead to numerous downstream costs and problems, from scalability issues to costly errors and data breaches. How much architecture do you need? Again, the balance is between the costs of applying it and the benefits so realized. The essentials, for most projects and teams, are:

- Explicit modeling using some form of architectural description technology to support communication and analysis
- Broad knowledge of and ability to select and apply a range of architectural styles
- Similar depth in understanding and applying connector technologies

What happens when the organizational setting is even more consequential? For example, when the product competes in a governmentally regulated industry, or when the organization develops not just one product in a market space, but a large family of related products? We consider this context next.

6 High-Consequence Software

"High-consequence software" may mean software whose usage occurs in contexts where errors or failures can result in death or large-scale economic loss. The phrase may equally be used to describe software whose economic importance is so great that the fortunes of a company, or even an ecosystem of companies, may rise or fall depending on issues with the software. In either situation, the implication is that the context in which the software is designed, built, and used is larger still from what we have considered so far. Diverse (and distant) user communities may be involved, regulatory oversight may exist within multiple jurisdictions, and the development "organization" may no longer be a single company, but involve a cooperating set of agents. The "software" too may no longer represent a single application, but a family of related products, with variants for differing usage contexts. In many dimensions, then, the context is more complex and the stakes are higher.

The large consequences of key decisions and the large risks that may be entailed imply that professionalism is not an option, it is essential. But given the wide diversity of high-consequence software, what aspects of software architecture technology are essential?

First, in any high-consequence situation, is an even greater need for attention to techniques previously mentioned. Increased investment in modeling is warranted in support of communication, addressing the larger and more diverse community of stakeholders. Because of increased size and system complexity, specialized projections of the model likely will be needed. Independent regulatory oversight may demand specific, particular projections of a system in order to demonstrate compliance properties.

Similarly needed is a clear focus on and identification of key styles. As an illustration, consider the importance of precisely identifying the plug-in architecture for supporting third-party extensions to Adobe's Photoshop product, Apple's identification of the role of the MVC style, or the Web's identification of the REST style. In these cases, and many similar ones, explicit styles are key to enabling an ecosystem of independent development organizations to cooperate and mutually thrive.

Beyond such increased attention to the previously discussed techniques, two additional emphases deserve brief discussion. The first is domain-specific software architectures and its closely related cousin, architecture-based product families.

DSSAs and product families spring from slightly different origins but end up in a similar place. The key notion of a DSSA is capture and reuse of deep domain knowledge and experience with developing solutions within that domain. The key notion of a product family is management of related product variants. Seen together the notion is exploitation of deep experience (domain and solution) through management of a family of related products—in short, a technically based product line[3]. The technical bases for such product lines are configuration management, domain knowledge capture, and reference architectures. These concepts merge with architectural styles and explicit modeling to yield careful management, product generation, and highly efficient platform and market specialization.

Configuration management is a well-understood, universally practiced discipline, at least in its simplest form: version control. The focus in the high-consequence context is sensibly managing the relationships between features, deployment platforms, and architectural entities.

Domain knowledge capture is the discipline of effectively recording the fundamental characteristics of an application domain in such a way that new products in the domain can be described using terminology that enables unambiguous description of novel requirements as well as clear mapping of continuing requirements to concepts and entities in prior products. Domain knowledge may well be half of a development organization's competitive advantage; the other half is based in its experience with prior solutions in that domain.

---

[3]We explicitly distinguish this concept from "product lines" that are nothing more than applying a uniform marketing badge on products having no common technical foundation.

When an organization reflects on its product experiences and captures effective solution strategies (i.e., architectural decisions) in a form that supports reuse, those strategies are termed a reference architecture. A good reference architecture is a company's "secret sauce"; it is the knowledge that enables it to produce new solutions within a domain faster and cheaper than its competitors. It is an architectural style on a very large, grand scale. The fundamental question, though, is, how is that knowledge, that reference architecture, captured? Often it is merely in the heads of the company's lead engineers. What happens if those engineers resign? The cost-benefit analysis must consider how difficult and expensive it will be to invest in reifying that knowledge, versus the potential downsides should the key engineers depart to work for competitors.

The second additional emphasis is security engineering. Data breaches and security violations seem only exceeded in news articles by hyperventilation over AI and big data. The ubiquity of the problem, and the inability of repeated patches to do anything more than slightly delay the next problem, indicates that security is not an add-on feature. Security properties must be considered from the outset of a system's design. Indeed, it must be a key element in designing a system's architecture. Explicit architectural models are a starting point for security analysis and design. Consider the alternative—if the key design decisions are not recorded and made analyzable, then how can an engineer determine whether there are system vulnerabilities? Given the enormous range of system designs, there is little in general that can be said about designing for security properties, but an emerging view is that no perimeter defense will ever be sufficiently protective for decentralized systems [7, 8]. Rather, security must be considered at all levels of design, from the most abstract architecture to specific coding choices. In any event, explicit consideration is necessary.

7   Conclusion: Excuses Are Not Strategies

"We don't need no stinkin' architecture!" Really? Young companies always seem to have time to address today's emergency, but never the time to engineer at the right time to prevent future emergencies. That is an excuse, not a strategy.

Excuses are not strategies, but neither is untempered exhortation to use every type of software architecture technology. In the end, it is a cost-benefit analysis that must be applied, but it must be an analysis that looks beyond the next quarter's earnings report. Indeed, it must look to a significant product horizon. Only mature organizations can afford to do that, but only mature organizations survive.

Acknowledgments My understanding of software architecture has been enriched immensely through my long-standing collaborations with Professor Nenad Medvidovic of the University of Southern California and Dr. Eric Dashofy of The Aerospace Corporation.

References

1. Freeman, P.: The central role of design in software engineering. In: Freeman, P., Wasserman, A. (eds.) Software Engineering Education, pp. 116–119. Springer, New York (1976)
2. Perry, D.E., Wolf, A.L.: Foundations for the study of software architecture. ACM SIGSOFT Software Engineering Notes **17**(4), 40–52 (1992)
3. Taylor, R.N., Medvidovic, N., Dashofy, E.M.: Software Architecture: Foundations, Theory, and Practice, 736 pgs. Wiley, Hoboken, NJ (2010)
4. Fielding, R.T., Taylor, R.N.: Principled design of the modern web architecture. ACM Trans. Internet Technol. **2**(2), 115–150 (2002)
5. Gamma, E., Helm, R., Johnson, R., Vlissides, J.: Design Patterns: Elements of Reusable Object-Oriented Software. Addison-Wesley Professional Computing Series. Addison-Wesley Professional, Reading, MA (1995)
6. Mehta, N.R., Medvidovic, N., Phadke, S.: Towards a taxonomy of software connectors. In: Proceedings of the 2000 International Conference on Software Engineering, pp. 178–187. ACM Press. Limerick, Ireland, 4–11 June, 2000. http://sunset.usc.edu/classes/cs599_2000/Conn-ICSE2000.pdf
7. Gorlick, M.M., Strasser, K., Taylor, R.N.: COAST: an architectural style for decentralized on-demand tailored services. In: Proceedings of the 2012 Joint IEEE/IFIP Working Conference on Software Architecture (WICSA) & 6th European Conference on Software Architecture, pp. 71–80, IEEE. Helsinki, Finland, August 20–24, 2012. doi:10.1109/WICSA-ECSA.212.15
8. Gorlick, M.M.: Computational state transfer: an architectural style for decentralized systems. Ph.D. Dissertation. Department of Informatics, University of California, Irvine (2016). http://isr.uci.edu/sites/isr.uci.edu/files/techreports/UCI-ISR-16-3.pdf

Variability in Standard Software Products

Introducing Software Product Line Engineering to the Insurance Industry

Alfred Bröckers

1 Introduction

The development of industrial goods and consumer products has become remarkably mature over the past century. The availability of large numbers of different products has driven their widespread use. The large number of variants was not achieved by developing each of them individually. Moreover, many goods were and are developed in a way that allows for easily adapting them for different purposes. For example, in the automotive industry, different kinds of trucks are developed serving multiple purposes. There are trucks for long-distance transportation, others deliver ready-mixed concrete to construction sites, etc. Despite these different purposes, the commonalities in their design outweigh by far. Therefore, the different variants are developed based on a common platform and can even be produced on the same production line.

Over the last two decades, software product line engineering (SPLE) emerged as an area of software engineering that follows the same pattern that traditional industries adopted so successfully. However, until now, this promising approach has not spread across all industries that are dominated by—or at least driven by—the use of software systems. This applies especially to the insurance industry: Over the last decades, developing individual software systems or tailoring existing software solutions was the only option for insurance companies. However, competition in the insurance industry and tight IT budgets as a consequence have raised the demand for standard software products over the past few years. To cope with a significant diversity of insurance companies, variability is required from such software products. SPLE promises to provide this variability.

A. Bröckers (✉)
adesso insurance solutions GmbH, Dortmund, Germany
e-mail: broeckers@adesso.de

© The Author(s) 2018
V. Gruhn, R. Striemer (eds.), *The Essence of Software Engineering*,
https://doi.org/10.1007/978-3-319-73897-0_6

The fact that in the insurance sector the knowledge required to define a platform for a product line is distributed across insurance companies and software vendors, the size of the investment, and the speed of innovation makes it difficult for a vendor to introduce product lines following conventional transition strategies. This chapter proposes a transition strategy that fits to the specific situation in the insurance industry. It might be transferred to other industry sectors which exhibit similar conditions. This strategy enables small- to medium-sized software vendor organizations to base their business on software product line engineering.

The next section introduces software product line engineering as far as needed for this chapter. The following section explains why software product lines are a promising approach to establishing software products for the key processes of the insurance industry and why in this domain traditional introduction strategies most likely will not suit the current practice of software development. Subsequently, the chapter introduces the extended pilot project strategy that overcomes the shortcomings and discusses the pros and cons of the approach.

2   Software Product Line Engineering

Software product line engineering [1] is an area of software engineering. It follows the pattern that traditional industries adopted to provide consumers from a single domain with a large variety of products. According to this approach, development for a software product is based on a software platform that is common to a whole software product line. Deriving a software product from such a platform consists of customizing and extending the platform to the specific needs of the target group (individual customer or group of customers that share the same requirements). Up to this point, this sounds familiar from traditional approaches to adopt existing software solutions and customize them. Characteristic to software product line approach is that the platform is built for this purpose specifically: The platform already defines the possible range of variability of the product line. It accounts for the aspects that can vary across the products which can be derived. The set of variable aspects must be considered very carefully. Missing variability may limit the product range and exclude relevant products from the product line. On the other hand, accounting for variability that does not really vary across the product line raises development and maintenance cost for the platform and the derived products alike.

In software product line engineering, the overall development process consists of *domain engineering* for developing and maintaining the platform for a product line and *application engineering* that deals with deriving specific software products from a platform [1].

Domain Engineering The result of domain engineering is a software platform that is used by application engineering for building software products. The platform contains all the artifacts that are known from traditional development approaches, such as requirements and design documents, code, as well as test artifacts. In traditional "build-and-customize" approaches, differences first come into play when building the final application. In software product line engineering, the commonalities and (known or expected) differences across the product line are accounted for completely when building the reusable base unit, the platform. Domain engineering defines the complete variability of the range of software products that can be derived.

The variability of a product line is defined in terms of the so-called *variation points* [1]. A variation point defines an aspect that can vary across the different members of the product line, that is, the software products that can be derived from the platform. The different specific forms for such an aspect are called *variants*. Domain engineering is not limited to identifying the variation point. If the set of variants (or a subset thereof) for a variation point is well known, they can be developed during domain engineering. Different solution patterns can be used for implementing variation points. Examples are:

- Configuration parameters, for example, read from flat files, XML structures, or databases for simple situations
- (Model-based) code generators
- Design patterns for framework development [2]

Application Engineering An application engineering project develops a specific software product required by a single customer or customer group. Each project must decide if the product line fits the problem at hand. This is the case if the commonalities that the platform of the product line implements apply. Furthermore, the project has to find out if the required system can be derived from the platform: For each of the variation points, a suitable variant is selected. The variant might already exist as part of the platform or can be developed as part of the application engineering project.

In traditional software customizing approaches, application projects must deal with the complete complexity of the whole reuse basis. In SPLE, developing a software product or application is reduced to selecting or developing variants for a known set of variation points. That reduces the development and maintenance cost significantly.

The goal of software product line engineering is to provide customers with different software products at significantly reduced cost compared to individually build products. The cost of a software product, derived from a platform, is the sum of the cost of the application engineering project and a portion of the cost of domain engineering for the product line. This portion is roughly the nth part of the overall domain engineering cost, where n is the number of members of the product line. According to [3], the break-even compared to single systems development is reached between three to four systems.

Software product line engineering has not yet spread across all the software-driven industries. From the 15 product line examples given in [1], only two can be identified to be not from the command and control software or embedded software domains. Only one of them is from the financial industry domain.

3 SPLE in the Insurance Industry

In the public perception, the internet of things (IoT) and the ever-increasing penetration of software into traditional consumer products are the main innovation drivers. Software-related innovations in the service sectors are often not recognized. It is just those sectors in which the importance of software to business success is expected to increase significantly. The internet is only one driver of this development. Thus, the demand for software and standard software products in these sectors and especially in the insurance industry is expected to increase accordingly.

For software vendors, the diversity of products, processes, and IT landscapes in the insurance industry is an obstacle to successfully introducing standard software products. Software product lines promise to provide the variability required to solve this problem. Still, the specific situation of software development within the insurance business makes it difficult to introduce software product line engineering. This section gives a short introduction to the state of the practice of software development for the insurance industry and then describes the obstacles to introducing product lines.

3.1 Current Situation

Providing insurance services to consumers and companies alike has always been a business that is intangible and primarily based on administering data on insurance contracts and claims. With the emergence of computer technology, software automated this business without any need for sensors and actuators beyond classical input/output devices such as computer terminals and printers. Therefore, software has always been a vital part of day-to-day business for many decades in insurance companies.

Today, software systems largely pervade any business process within the industry. For business processes that are not specific to the insurance industry, standard COTS software has become a common practice. Examples are standard systems for accounting, collections/disbursements, or output management. For business processes that are specific and characteristic for the insurance industry (core insurance processes), most companies use software systems that are specifically built for these purposes. Among these, there are systems for contract management, claims processing systems, and sales management systems.

Until only a few years ago the pervasive pattern for an insurance company was to develop these core insurance systems individually for its own purposes. Large numbers of software and business consultants were required for these in-house developments. Typically, after the initial development, these systems went into maintenance for a period of 15–30 years before reaching the end of their life cycle. Over this long timespan, they accumulated more and more functionality. Thus, when replacing such a system, the business functions that have been paid for more than a decade must be provided in a much shorter timeframe to maintain the functional status quo. Furthermore, replacing a software system almost always involves technology that is new to the old maintenance team. Therefore, for most small- to medium-sized insurance companies, replacing an insurance core system with an in-house development is an investment that can hardly be justified.

As a result, the trend goes to buying complete software systems even for the core insurance processes. However, there are many differences between the individual insurance companies. Among these, there are the size of each company, its culture, the target customer group, the channel of distribution, and the products sold. In addition, each system to be replaced is embedded into a larger IT architecture with numerous other systems. Examples are other core insurance systems or support systems such as database management systems. To account for these differences, a software system needs to be customized significantly before it can be introduced.

Having customized and introduced an existing software system, an insurance company has to decide on the maintenance strategy. Establishing an in-house project for maintenance and further development is one option, although the cost advantage compared to in-house development is limited to the introduction time: Even if several companies individually customize the same system, maintenance of the customized systems equals pure in-house developments. Even worse, for a single insurance company, maintaining the customized system might be burdened with the complexity of redundant functionality that is needed elsewhere.

Another option is to outsource further development and maintenance to the vendor or to some IT service provider. The insurance company will expect synergy from further development of the initial product. However, depending on the extent of the customization, additional costs arise: Each new release of the initial system carries the risk that the changes interfere heavily with the individual modifications and extensions made when introducing the system.

3.2 Transition Strategies

Software product line engineering is one way out of the dilemma between the demand for standard software products and the variability inherent to the insurance industry. adesso insurance solutions GmbH is a software vendor that applies this approach to software development and maintenance of its in|sure software suite. The in|sure suite contains software for the core business processes of insurance companies. The way the in|sure suite is divided into software systems follows a pattern that can be found in many insurance companies around the world: For the health insurance segment, it contains systems for managing contracts and a claims management system. Likewise, for the property/casualty insurance segment, there is a contract management and a claims management system. For the life insurance segment, there is a combined system for contract and claims management.

Within the in|sure suite, each of these systems constitutes a product line. There is a defined set of variation points for each system. When introducing an in|sure system to an insurance company, those variation points are used to derive a customer-specific variant. Most of the variation points address the following aspects:

- Insurance products that the company offers to its customers
- Processes that are specific to the insurance company
- Selection of systems that the in|sure system must communicate with

The means that are used to implement variation points (for an in|sure system) include modelling and code generation techniques (e.g., EMF-based insurance product modelling), typical pattern techniques for framework development [2], customer-specific include statements, and simple configuration files.

The goal of applying SPLE to the in|sure software suite is to account for the variability during the initial development and the maintenance phase. That means the variants that a customer has selected or implemented survive a release upgrade of the platform.

The current practice of software development for the insurance industry results in some major obstacles for introducing SPLE as a strategy for developing standard software systems for the core processes of insurance companies. Basically, there are four transition strategies for organizations [4]. Only two of them apply: the big bang strategy and the pilot project strategy.

Big Bang Strategy Specific to this strategy is a domain engineering phase that is carried out prior to the first application project. That means platform development (except for maintenance and further development) is completed before the first software product is derived. Although the availability of a completed, stable platform even for the first application engineering project is highly desirable, it is hard to achieve: For the big bang strategy, the commonalities and the required variability have to be well known and well defined in advance. Even future trends of the industry must be known as well. Furthermore, domain engineering for a complete platform is a large capital investment and—sometimes even worse—an investment in time. For example, for standard software products such as the in|sure systems, time to market is vital for business success. When following the big bang strategy, there is no proof nor evidence of the feasibility of the platform for a very long time.

Pilot Project Strategy In this strategy, the domain engineering is carried out as part of a pilot project. The pilot project can be regarded as the first application engineering project. It develops the platform, defines the variation points, and develops the variants needed for the first software product. A platform for a product line can only emerge from a pilot project, if profound and settled domain knowledge is accounted for when defining the variation points. This knowledge is hardly achievable for a project that focuses on a single product mainly. In addition, there will always be a tendency to sacrifice the domain engineering character of the project to budget and schedule pressures inherent to software development. Following the pilot project strategy, there is no natural counterpart to this effect.

Although both transformation strategies have already proven successful in many organizations, there are three main reasons why applying them will not lead to the intended results.

Availability of Domain Knowledge The quality of the platform, especially the reuse benefits, highly depends on the availability of profound domain knowledge that is available to domain engineering. In domains where software development consists of in-house development mainly, the knowledge is widespread. In the insurance industry, the domain knowledge required to develop a platform for a software product line is spread over many insurance companies and almost as many small- to medium-sized software development consultant companies.

Domain Knowledge of Insurance Companies Within each insurance company, there is a high-level understanding concerning the insurance domain and the commonalities and differences between companies. Otherwise, competition would put them out of business easily. However, the detailed knowledge on the specifics of business processes and insurance products is widespread across the company workforce, including IT departments. Although some of the employees within a company may have cross-company knowledge, for example, from changing their job, it will be outdated most likely and limited to two or three companies.

There are initiatives, driven by own interest or by sector associations, to define common strategies for new challenges, for example, new legal regulations. These initiatives are limited to single challenges. Neither do they cover established business practices nor the future trends that could be part of competitive advantages.

Domain Knowledge of the Software Industry Most insurance companies have developed the software systems for their core business processes in in-house projects. Typically, a considerable number of external consultants are hired for those projects. Often the consultants or their employer consultant companies are specializing in software development for insurance companies. Therefore, a consulting company could be regarded as a valuable source of cross-company knowledge. Although individual consultants may stick to an insurance company, consulting companies usually have several customers (even at the same time). The recent project history dominates the domain knowledge. It consists of the experience accumulated in the heads of the employees mainly; after all, in most cases, the customer owns the intellectual property right in the project results. The consequence of relying on the domain knowledge of a consulting company is most likely an incomplete, distorted picture of the requirements of the whole industry. Often a high staff turnover makes this situation even worse.

Speed of Innovation Some of the current software systems that are used as a basis for traditional buy-and-customize approaches provide a wealth of functionality that has been gathered over many years. Introducing these systems is accompanied with large individual maintenance cost and technological backlog. However, the functionality is the predominant factor when selecting new software systems. To be able to compete with the traditional approaches, a new software product—regardless if developed from scratch or derived from a platform—must contain the complete functionality needed of the targeted insurance company. This challenge is exacerbated by new must-have features, required either from market pressure or by law: Digitalization of business process has been driving the demand for software over the last year and is far from being completed. Completely new kinds of products emerge, often enabled by the possibilities of the internet. Regulatory requirements (e.g., data privacy, EU directives) have been rising over the past few years and are expected to increase.

In summary, the demand for functionality is increasing dramatically. Unlike other domains, which are used as successful examples for software product line engineering, in the insurance industry there is no hardware development (such as for sensors, actuators, machines that must be controlled) that slows down the speed of innovation. Given this situation, it is virtually impossible to complete a full domain engineering phase and a consecutive application engineering project, keeping the pace of new emerging requirements. To a software vendor, the upfront investment is a high risk: The first software product with business functions that are partially even enforced by law might be completed too late.

Innovator's Dilemma Most of the companies that specialize in software development for the insurance industry follow a traditional business model: They charge their customers according to the consulting or development work performed. To this business model, software product line engineering is a disruptive technology. If a company invests significantly in a disruptive technology, it will inevitably face the *Innovator's Dilemma* [5]. In the battle for limited monetary and personnel resources, the established model almost always wins. For the big bang approach, the large upfront investment with an uncertain business success exacerbates this effect.

Software product line engineering is a promising approach to software development for the insurance industry. It allows for introducing standard software products for the core processes of the insurance industry that account for the variability of insurance companies. Unfortunately, known transition strategies that have proven to be successful in other domains do not fit well.

4 The Extended Pilot Project

Over many years, insurance companies have extended their in-house developed software systems with a plethora of business functions. When replacing these systems, most of those companies will not be able to maintain their status quo in time and reasonable budget following the in-house project pattern. As stated before, standard software products are a solution to this problem. Those systems must account for the variability that insurance companies need to compete in their market. Software product line engineering promises to provide this variability. The preceding section showed that the known strategies for introducing product lines do not fit the situation.

As an alternative to these strategies, this section proposes the *extended pilot project* as an approach that is a compromise between a big bang approach, based on the domain knowledge of several insurance companies, and a pilot project for a single company. The approach involves several insurance companies as charter clients. It overcomes the obstacles to introducing software product lines shown in the preceding section, without compromising on the general validity of the product lines to their respective target group.

This first section introduces the basic setup of the extended pilot project and then defines some criteria that should be considered when selecting insurance charter clients. It defines the roles of the software vendor and the charter clients in the extended pilot project approach. Finally, the pros and cons of the approach are discussed.

4.1 The Setup

The fundamental idea of the extended pilot project approach is to develop the platform as part of a first application engineering project. Unlike with the simple pilot project approach, the resulting platform is aimed at more than a single product right from the start. Involving several insurance companies ensures the functional breadth and the variability that is needed for an entire product line (or at least the first release thereof). Figure 1 gives an overview. The setup is as follows:

- For each of the typical systems that support the core business processes of an insurance company, a specific product line is defined. The product line for managing health insurance policies is an example.
- Several insurance companies are involved in developing the platform for the product line. Their involvement is not distributed evenly. First, there is the pilot charter client, or pilot client for short. The platform for the product line and the product are developed as part of a single project: Domain engineering and application engineering are carried out in parallel. In addition to the pilot client, other insurance companies are involved. Each of these charter clients intends to start an application engineering project that derives its own specific software product in a succeeding application engineering project.
- During the pilot project, the additional charter clients monitor to which extent the software product fulfills their own requirements. The aspects in the functional specification of the system, where the requirements for pilot charter client and additional charter clients differ, act as candidates for introducing variability to the platform. Only the variants for the pilot client are developed as part of the pilot project. Other variants are left either to maintenance and further development of the platform or to following application engineering projects.
- As soon as the pilot platform reaches a state that is sufficiently stable, the additional charter clients can start their own application engineering project. They benefit largely from matching the platform against their own demands throughout the pilot project.

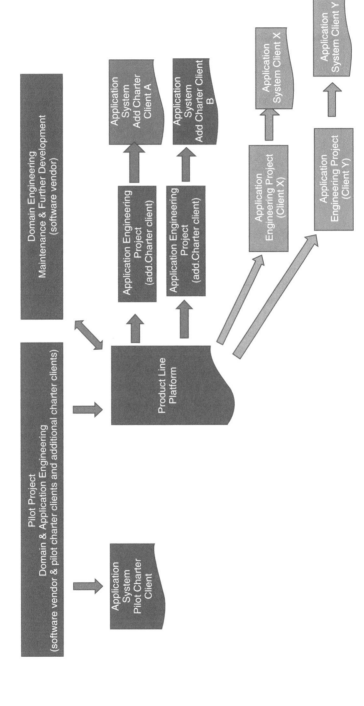

Fig. 1 Overview of the extended pilot project strategy

- After the pilot project has been completed, the platform for the product line enters maintenance state. New customers can derive their own insurance software systems from the platform. Furthermore, from that point on, all application engineering projects including those of the charter clients are equal with respect to maintenance. Maintaining the platform is a pure domain engineering effort carried out by the vendor.

4.2 Selecting Charter Clients

To a software vendor, charter clients shall be considered customers. That means, in the global market of today, the choice is up to the customer and not vice versa. Still, introducing software product lines as part of the business model is a critical endeavor. Therefore, it is important for the vendor to select the charter clients very carefully. The most important selection criteria are a strong motivation, the number of charter clients to include in the extended pilot project, and the contribution of each charter client to the domain coverage of the project.

Motivation The pilot project is of crucial importance for the vendor and for all charter clients. Software development projects almost always face the danger of termination before completion. The reasons are manifold, ranging from internal reasons such as weak project performance to external reasons such as priority changes within the company. While in a traditional project, a termination has only consequences for a single company, in our setup a considerable impact on the entire platform and therefore on all companies involved is inevitable. Thus, each of the charter clients should have a strong motivation to take part in the endeavor. This is especially true for the pilot charter client. Losing a pilot charter client halfway down the road will set the whole endeavor at risk. The pilot client benefits from a much more direct involvement compared to additional charter clients:

- The pilot client has more impact on the definition of the platform, although from a platform point of view this effect is detrimental.
- When defining the platform and the individual variants, the pilot client gets an unbiased alternative view on his business practices.
- The pilot client benefits from the fact that he gets a new system prior to any other client. That might be a competitive advantage.

For an additional charter client, the investment is much smaller than for a pilot charter client. Although the consequences of losing an additional client are much smaller, the impact cannot be ignored. The additional charter client benefits from its involvement:

- While reviewing the platform specifications, he influences the scope and content of the platform. Furthermore, in cooperation with the other charter clients, he defines explicitly the variability that is built into the platform. The impact even goes beyond his own variants.

- In a subsequent application engineering project, an additional client obtains a software system that is customized to his own requirements—a software system that he otherwise would have to acquire at much higher risk and cost.

Number of Charter Clients The number of charter clients has to be balanced carefully. If too few clients are selected, the whole transition strategy degenerates to the pilot project approach with the known effects described before. On the other hand, if too many charter clients are involved, organizational overhead, politics, and discussions on minor details will choke off the progress of platform and product development.

Common sense in the software engineering community is that reuse (and product line engineering is a sophisticated approach to reuse) pays off when a software item is reused three times at least. For software product lines, the break-even is reached at about three derived software products. For this reason, to reduce the economic risk to a manageable size, a software vendor will select a pilot charter client and two charter clients at least. To account for the risk that a charter client cancels its involvement, even more charter clients are desirable.

However, if the number of charter clients exceeds a certain number, some problems outweigh the advantages of adding clients: Quickly obtaining content-related decisions on platform features and on variation points becomes much more difficult. Competition between charter clients and politics step into the decision-making process. Even organizing frequent steering committee meetings becomes virtually impossible. In the insurance industry example, a practical maximum number of charter clients is about five.

Domain Coverage When selecting charter clients, the domain coverage is an important criterion. With respect to software product line engineering, domain coverage can be divided into functional coverage of the platform, variability coverage, and variant coverage. At best, the pilot charter client is a typical representative covering a larger portion of the domain.

Functional coverage is the extent to which the selected charter clients represent the target group of the product line. As an example, Fig. 2 shows how the functional demand can be distributed across the target group and three charter clients.[1] If the functional coverage is too low, the functional scope of the platform may be too narrow to attract further customers.

Variability coverage is the extent to which the selected clients vary. If they do not vary sufficiently, variation points important to the target group will be overlooked. In this case, major rework on the platform will be necessary.

The quality of the platform benefits, if for each variation point the platform development accounts for a representative breadth of variation. Therefore, the charter clients should differ within the boundaries of the target group, requiring substantially different variants. Otherwise, the variation point implementation may

---

[1]Figure 2 intentionally exaggerates the differences in functional demand. In reality, the differences can be much smaller.

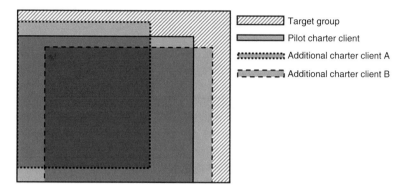

Fig. 2 Distribution of functional demand across the target group and charter clients

be inappropriate for future clients. However, *variant coverage* is hard to recognize in advance.

4.3   Cooperation of Software Vendor and Charter Clients

In our setup, there are several players involved in the pilot engineering project. There are the software vendor, the pilot charter client, and additional charter clients. This paragraph discusses how these players cooperate to provide a platform for a product line and to develop a software product for the pilot charter client. To achieve this, the first application engineering project is set up much like a development project for an individual software system, solely to be used by the pilot chart client: The typical roles of a project such as project manager, requirements engineers, designers, programmers, testers, etc. are staffed using employees of the software vendor and the pilot charter client. The software vendor and the pilot charter client account for the additional cost of domain engineering by providing additional personnel.

Each of the additional charter clients provides two to three proven domain experts taken from its own organization. These experts take part in the functional specification as their main task. This enables them to monitor the specification for completeness and to identify the need for variation with respect to their own organizations. Furthermore, the experts discuss each variation point of the platform and the possible variants with other experts within their own organizations.

Even though the common platform is the result of the pilot project as the first application engineering project, the individual primary interests of the players diverge considerably. Sooner or later the divergence might result in conflicts that set the success at risk. To manage the emergence of these conflicts, a steering committee should be established. This committee consists of top-level decision makers from the software vendor and from the charter clients. It meets on a regular basis and provides for a balance between the interests.

4.4   Pros and Cons

This section discusses the advantages and disadvantages of the introduction strategy described in this chapter: In the insurance industry case, the traditional pilot project strategy would involve a single insurance company. In contrast, the extended pilot project strategy involves several companies. This ensures a functional scope that is much more relevant to the target group and a much higher level of variability.

The big bang introduction entails the risk of supposed demand for variability. Under the pressure to identify sufficient variability, the domain engineering will tend to define more variation points than required. There is no counterpart.

In the extended pilot project strategy, the fact that the platform specification and the variability built into it are validated against the demand of several clients minimizes the risk of supposed variation points: When discussing variation points, the charter clients separate the variability that is really needed from the variability one might think about. The charter clients can even turn supposed variability into common features of the platform. Minimizing the variation leads to an increase in reuse, which in turn reduces the cost of the individual software products.

However, the focus on the demand of the pilot charter client can contain some risks: The extended pilot project provides the pilot charter client with a software system for his organization. Although there is a motivation to develop a platform that a whole product line is based on, the ubiquitous time and budget pressures lead to a tendency to omit aspects that have no relevance to himself. It is the task of the vendor and the additional charter clients to counteract. If conflicts arise, they must be resolved by the steering committee. If this is not possible, the minimum solution is to account for extending the platform later, for example, in the second or third application engineering project or as part of platform maintenance.

5   Summary

Software product line engineering is a promising approach that does not only apply to domains where software products are a well-established concept. Furthermore, it can be applied to domains where—due to a demand for variability—the traditional in-house development project still dominates the development of software. For example, adesso insurance solutions has adopted software product lines to provide software products for the core business processes of insurance companies.

However, software product line engineering is a disruptive technology. To a software vendor, introducing this technology is a long-term investment and a business risk. The current structure of the software development practice, the spread of domain knowledge, the speed of innovation, and the general risks, associated with adopting disruptive technologies, are the major obstacles. Known transition strategies for introducing software product line engineering do not fit this situation well.

The extended pilot project strategy is an approach that accounts for these obstacles explicitly. When following this approach, a pilot project develops the platform for a software product line and derives the first software product. In contrast to other transition strategies, it involves several insurance companies to achieve the functional breadth and the variability needed for the product line.

There are some criteria that the insurance companies taking part in the endeavor have to meet: Each of them must have a strong interest in the product line, given as an explicit plan to derive its own software product. Their individual demand for functionality and variability must contribute to the intended domain coverage of the product line. Finally, the minimum number of companies to be included in the pilot project should account for the risk of a company dropping out. At the same time, the number must be limited to minimize political and competitive effects and to keep organizing feasible.

References

1. Pohl, K., Boeckle, G., van der Linden, G.: Software Product Line Engineering- Foundations, Principles and Techniques. Springer, Berlin (2005)
2. Gamma, E., Helm, R., Johnson, R., Vlissides, J.: Design Patterns – Elements of Reusable Object-Oriented Software. Addison-Wesley, Boston, MA (1994)
3. Weiss, D.M., Lai, C.T.R.: Software Product-Line Engineering – A Family-Based Software Development Process. Addison Wesley, Reading, MA (1999)
4. Boeckle, G., Bermejo, J., Knauber, P., Krueger, C., Leite, J., van der Linden, F., Northrop, L., Stark, M., Weiss, D.: Adopting and instititionalizing a product line culture. In: Proceedings of the 2nd Conference on Product Lines, San Diego, LNCS 2379, pp. 48–59. Springer, Berlin (2002)
5. Christensen, C.M.: The Innovator's Dilemma: When New Technologies Cause Great Firms to Fail. Harward Business School Press, Boston, MA (1997)

Using Design Thinking for Requirements Engineering in the Context of Digitalization and Digital Transformation: A Motivation and an Experience Report

Angela Carell, Kim Lauenroth, and Dirk Platz

1 Introduction and Motivation

Digitalization and digital transformation are omnipresent terms inside and outside the software engineering community. Many governments consider digitalization of industry and society as the primary challenge of this decade (cf. [1]). However, people inside the software engineering community often consider both terms as buzzwords that do not provide meaning. They often argue that everything in software engineering is about digitalization and that digitalization and digital transformation are nothing novel for them. Unfortunately, this narrow perspective prevents the community from recognizing that the world outside the software community has a different understanding. This understanding reveals a significant change of the software business that has a tremendous impact on the way a software is developed.

This chapter, which draws upon practical experience, first shows in Sect. 2 how digitization, digitalization, and digital transformation have affected or are currently impacting the discipline of requirements engineering. In particular, the digital transformation that has begun is leading to disruptive changes here, as is also the case with many other areas of software engineering. A key finding is that requirements engineers have to adopt the mindset of designers to cope with the challenges that emerge from projects in the context of digital transformation.

In Sect. 3, we explain the methodology of design thinking as a current framework that has proven itself in practice to live up to the new required mindset. Then, we will present two concrete adesso AG project examples of how design thinking came to be employed at the company and the results it achieved in specific project

A. Carell (✉) · K. Lauenroth · D. Platz
adesso AG, Dortmund, Germany
e-mail: angela.carell@adesso.de; kim.lauenroth@adesso.de; platz@adesso.de

© The Author(s) 2018
V. Gruhn, R. Striemer (eds.), *The Essence of Software Engineering*,
https://doi.org/10.1007/978-3-319-73897-0_7

situations. These results were quite surprising from the point of view of a "classical" requirements engineer. Section 4 contains the summary and the conclusions.

2 From Digitization to Digital Transformation

The way software and digital technology impacts business and society can be separated by three different terms: digitization, digitalization, and digital transformation. Inspired by the work from [2], we use these three terms to form three levels of impact of digital technology. These three levels can be considered at the same time as a kind of historical development. However, these three levels are a mental model that is used to characterize and explain phenomena that the authors have observed. They should not be understood as a strict framework that allows for a precise classification. Instead, these levels should be considered as a way of looking at the impact of digital technology that helps to understand the changes that the authors recognized in their professional life.

2.1 Level 1: Digitization

Digitization literately means the conversion of analogue information into a digital (binary) representation [3]. This conversion is a prerequisite for making information processable for digital technology. Processing large amounts of information was one of the primary reasons for developing computers [4]. The impact on business and society on this level is limited; the digital technology is mainly used inside organizations without much visual surface to end customers and society.

Examples of digitization are:

– Banking: Bills are no longer paid with cash, but with credit cards or electronic cash cards.
– Business Administration Systems: Several industries use computers to manage their business, for example, insurance companies manage contracts and claims with software.
– Office software: Letters and documents are written by using a dedicated office software and are no longer written on paper or with a typewriter.
– Records to compact discs (CD): Music is no longer stored in an analogue way on records. The music industry now sells compact discs with digital music.
– Analogue to digital photography: Digital cameras provide a new way of taking pictures.

The essential characteristic of digitization is that there is an analogue model of the process or artifacts that is digitized. The user of this new digitized product or service typically recognizes only a minor change. For example, the early digital cameras had the same format as the analogue cameras. Applications for insurances or insurance claims were made with paper-based forms that were digitized later in the insurance company by an insurance clerk.

From a software engineering perspective, the challenge was to *understand the analogue product or service on a detailed level to create the digital equivalent.* The challenge has led to the development of the software engineering discipline requirements engineering (RE). The focus of RE is the proper understanding of stakeholder (i.e., customers, users, etc.) requirements and the documentation of these requirements to make them available for a structured software engineering process [5].

2.2   Level 2: Digitalization

With the increasing power of computer hardware and the advent of broadband Internet connection at the end of the 1990s, a new level in the use of software and digital technology can be recognized. The term digitalization is often used to describe this phenomenon (cf. [6]). Instead of focusing on the transformation of information into a digital format, whole processes and businesses start to move from the analogue world to the digital world. The impact on business and society can be considered medium, underlying business models and the society remains unchanged, the main goal is to improve the existing products and services. The result of this development is that people were increasingly exposed to digital technology in several places of their daily and professional lives in the late 1990s. Examples of digitalization are:

– Online shopping: customers buy various products over the Internet.
– Online banking: customers start doing their bank business over the Internet.
– Online music: customers buy music over the Internet and listen to music with a digital device (e.g., MP3 player).

This transition from digitization to digitalization appears to be minor from a technical perspective, since the devices remain unchanged. They became more powerful in terms of processing power, memory, storage, and network capabilities. From a software engineering perspective, the challenge of understanding the business remains, but two new challenges emerged in this phase.

Firstly, the software in the context of digitalization is mainly used by people that were unexperienced and often novices in terms of computer and software. Therefore, the software had to be designed in a way that enables intuitive usage and supports the user as much as possible. This challenge eventually led to the establishment of usability engineering in software development [7].

Secondly, potential products and services that were suitable for digitalization must be identified prior to the development. This task constituted a significant challenge because *knowledge about the business must be combined with a proper understanding of the potential benefits of digital technology.* History showed that this task was very difficult and that the potential of digital technology was overestimated by orders of magnitude in the late 1990s. The peak of this negative development was the so-called dot-com bubble [8].

2.3   Level 3: Digital Transformation

The growing dissemination of digital technology (e.g., smartphones, mobile Internet, portable computers) in the late 2000s and the successful digitalization finally led to a phenomenon called digital transformation. Digital transformation is characterized by significant changes in business models and in society enabled by digital technology (cf. [9]). Examples of digital transformation are:

– Crowdfunding: A project, product, or venture is funded by many people. Software platforms (e.g., Kickstarter or Indiegogo) made this concept popular and provide a service for presenting ideas to people and allowing them to support the idea with a certain amount of money. Crowdfunding provides a real alternative business model for project funding compared to credit-based funding from a bank (cf. [10]).
– Music streaming flat rate: The customer pays a fee (typically monthly) to a platform provider (e.g., Spotify) that allows the customer to listen to all the music provided by the platform. The central changes in the business model are that the customer no longer buys a certain song but pays a fixed fee and that artist receives payment based on the number of listened songs.

From a technical point of view, the difference between digitization and digitalization again is minor since the devices remain more or less unchanged besides further increases in power (e.g., for streaming large amounts of music data).

On the level of digitalization, existing business models or products were improved, that is, it was clear that the underlying business is sustainable (e.g., selling books). The major challenge was to identify a proper way for the digitalization of the business. On the level of digital transformation, this underlying assumption is no longer valid and an additional challenge emerges: *changes in business models and society are only successful if people (customers/users) see value in a new digital product or service* (e.g., paying money every month for listening to music). The real user needs play an essential role. Users had to adopt their way of working to the systems capabilities (good requirements engineering was useful to bring the system as close as possible to the user's requirement). Nowadays, fundamental user needs (that are not addressable by asking) must be identified to be successful.

2.4   Conclusion: The Growing Need for a Holistic Design Competence in Software Engineering

From a technical perspective, the three levels of digitization, digitalization, and digital transformation are equal or at least very similar. Devices such as computers, smartphones, or tablets are used to power software that has been developed to perform one or more tasks in a certain context. The technical development of software (i.e., the act of coding and selecting technical realization alternatives) remains more or less unchanged since the medium software itself does not change. From a historical perspective, the major change is the growing power of the devices, the increased mobility and connectivity of new devices, and the development of new programming languages (e.g., Java in the late 1990s) (cf., e.g., [4]).

From the outside perspective, the three levels show a significant difference in their impact on the context in which the software is developed:

– Digitization means that an analogue information medium changes to a digital medium within an otherwise stable context (e.g., maintaining insurance policy in a software database instead of a paper folder).
– Digitalization means that analogue processes are replaced or extended with digital processes within an otherwise stable context (e.g., doing bank business via the Internet instead of going to a bank's office).
– Digital transformation means that the whole context is changed by digital technology (e.g., funding a project via Kickstarter instead of applying for a credit).

The main conclusion from this list is that each level increases the scope of what is covered by the development of the software. In digitization, the software development can fully rely on the context and can focus on the proper software representation of the analogue model. In digitalization, software development must come up with a proper idea of the digital process for an existing analogue process. Here, software development has to become creative together with the business to develop an optimal solution. Typically, there is an analogue model of the process, but a simple transfer of the analogue process is typically not feasible, since digital technology offers different possibilities (e.g., buying books over the Internet is a different experience compared to a physical bookstore). Finally, digital transformation has the largest scope since the business model and the digital product/service determine each other and are created in parallel. In this situation, there is no analogue model that can be used as a reference point for the development activities. Instead, the business model and the software must be developed in parallel since both influence each other.

Development paradigms that fully rely on business stakeholders (or product owners) to provide the requirements for the software under development are not appropriate for digitalization and digital transformation since stakeholders typically do not have a profound understanding of the technical capabilities of software. On the other hand, trained software developers typically do not have a proper understanding of the business context to come up with optimal ideas. Hence, these development paradigms suffer from a competence gap since business people typically only focus on the business side and software people typically only focus on the technical side of the software.

This chapter argues that software development must drop the assumption that there is somebody out there that has a proper understanding of what shall be developed. Instead, software development should start to guide the process of designing a software in the sense of industrial or product designers. Industrial designers have a holistic view on a product and feel responsible for the overall shape of a product (appearance, functionality, and quality aspects). They interact with stakeholders and create ideas for the product instead of purely collecting requirements from the stakeholders (cf. [11]).

This paradigm shift has a significant impact on software engineering and especially on the disciplines of requirements engineering and usability engineering, since these disciplines are the interfaces to the stakeholders and the front-end of the software development process. The central change is the way requirements and usability engineers have to work and interact with their stakeholders. Instead of focusing on the collection, documentation, and validation of requirements, both disciplines have to participate actively in the creation process of the software.

3 Design Thinking as a Method to Think About Software

Implementing the paradigm shift is by no means an easy task. It requires people that use designer's ways of working (cf. [12] for a comparison of designer's working style with other disciplines) and substantial methodical support. Design thinking is a framework that has the potential to provide this support in terms of principles, process models, and techniques. The following subsections will provide a brief overview of design thinking and present two case studies for the successful application of design thinking in two development projects of the adesso AG.

Besides design thinking, there are other methods with similar goals, for example, contextual design [13], design sprint [14], or liberating structures [15]. A comparison of such methods is not the objective of this chapter. An overview of creativity/design techniques in requirements engineering can be found, for example, in [16].

3.1 A Brief Overview of Design Thinking

Design thinking can be defined as a methodological approach (a framework). Above all, though, it is an attitude amenable to consistently developing innovation potential and new solutions from the users' perspective.

> Design thinking is a human-centered approach to innovation that draws from the designer's toolkit to integrate the needs of people, the possibilities of technology, and the requirements for business success. (Tim Brown, president and CEO of IDEO) [17]

This approach has been in development since around 1996 and emerged from the collaboration of Terry Winograd and Larry Leifer with David Kelley (Stanford

University) and the design company IDEO. In 2005, d.school was founded at Stanford University, which helped to spread the idea of design thinking.

Design thinking is based on specific principles that differentiate the process from other creative processes and make it particularly useful for an IT context. These are described below.

Principle 1: Users' Needs Take Center Stage

Design thinking involves a human-centered design approach. This means that the needs of the users are placed at the center of attention and the design is consistently viewed from the perspective of future users. This approach is particularly relevant for projects in the context of digital transformation, since the success of such projects is decisively dependent on the acceptance of the end user.

Empathetically "stepping into users' shoes" and understanding their needs and wishes are essential aspects of this approach. However, design thinking goes far beyond classic human-centered design approaches: It delves much deeper into the needs of the users and attempts to uncover their latent needs, that is, those that cannot be articulated. The findings thus obtained provide important information that can be used to develop creative solutions and discover innovative potential.

> Deep empathy for people makes our observations powerful sources of inspiration. We aim to understand why people do what they currently do, with the goal of understanding what they might do in the future. [18]

Unlike participatory design [19], in which the users actively participate in the development of the solution, the actual generation of ideas takes place without direct user involvement. Representatives of design thinking assume that users themselves often have no access to their real needs. Asking them directly about ideas will hardly yield any revolutionary, new solutions. For example, the following quote has been ascribed to Henry Ford: "If I had asked people what they wanted, they would have said faster horses." At the same time, though, design thinking does not mean that the user is kept out of ideas development. Instead, the developed solutions are evaluated step-by-step with users and thus systematically refined and further improved upon. Users are not asked directly for solutions, though.

Principle 2: Deep Understanding Rather Than Large Numbers of Cases

In contrast to other methods, design thinking does not rely on large-scale qualitative user surveys or questioning focus groups. These have little use in design thinking, as this approach is not about identifying aspects that are equally common to *most users*. Instead, design thinking aims to discover interesting, surprising, astonishing, or even irritating things and to take these as starting points for developing innovative ideas. The process is similar to a gold digger digging for small gold lumps (nuggets); design thinking involves searching for nuggets that can act as starting points for creative solutions. This is why the term "nuggeting" is used in this context.

In order to find these "innovation nuggets," persons from extreme groups are often surveyed or observed. Extreme groups consist of persons who either do something extremely often or intensively or take a position of extreme denial. The idea behind observing these groups rests on the assumption that these persons

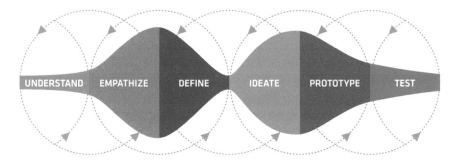

Fig. 1 The design thinking process

exhibit behavior and reveal needs that are also present in other user groups, but in a much weaker form, and are therefore very difficult to access.

Principle 3: Interdisciplinary Team

The team represents a central element of a successful design thinking project. It should consist of members who are open to new things and dare to try something new. They must be able to look beyond their own ranks, to appreciate the opinions and perspectives of others, and thus to constructively deal with them. Ideally, teams are recruited from different areas to create a diversity of perspectives—this is the only possible way to tackle problem-solving in a manner that is "different from the norm."

Principle 4: Follow a Clear Process

Design thinking follows a process [20] that consists of both divergent and convergent phases (Fig. 1). Divergence is based on diversity and illuminating a problem from different perspectives. Convergence leads to a consolidation and merging of ideas all the way up to the solution. The process is not to be understood as a rigid linear sequence; it may include feedback loops and iterations.

Phase 1: Understand

In this phase, the main focus is on understanding the problem that is posed (this is also called a challenge) and its essential elements. In design thinking, it is assumed that the problem formulation at the beginning of the design thinking process can only provide a rough description of the problem area. It can only be refined and fleshed out in the course of the process on the basis of the insights gained. In this phase, however, an initial understanding of the problem context is wholly sufficient. In terms of the methodology, the idea is to mainly research data and facts, identify relevant actors and situations, and explore the possible scope of design.

Phase 2: Empathize

This phase is essentially about building up empathy with users in order to understand their views of the world or the problem. This phase expands the focus (divergence) set by the challenge and provides deep insights into what users think and feel and, above all, where their real needs lie. Tim Brown describes this very aptly: "We need to return human beings to the center of the story. We need to learn to put people first" [21]. This involves techniques that are particularly suited to building empathy, such as the empathy-oriented interview, observation, and active entry into a situation to experience it through the user's eyes [22].

Phase 3: Define

At this point in the design thinking process, all the information and insights gathered so far are examined in detail, patterns are identified, and, above all, unexpected and surprising aspects are worked out (nuggeting). In contrast to a cross-sectional analysis of interviews, during this phase, all team members share all their impressions and information with each other. The collected impressions and experiences are used to reformulate and specify the initial problem (convergence). This refocusing may even be quite radical, namely, when the presumed cause of a problem proves to be incorrect.

> 'If a problem is not worth solving, it's not worth solving well.' Focusing our energy on the right question can make the difference between incremental improvement and breakthrough innovation. [18]

Phase 4: Ideate

The idea-finding phase begins with the reformulated challenge (point of view). First of all, personae (prototypical users) are developed in order to be able to grasp the target group for the future solution in as concrete of terms as possible. Personae are used to repeatedly compare the solutions to be developed against users' needs. In the next step, as many different ideas as possible (divergence) are developed, based on the focused challenge and the defined persona(e). For example, creative techniques can be used, ranging from purely intuitive (e.g., brainstorming, analogy, bisociation) and discursive techniques (e.g., Osborne checklist, Ishikawa) to combinations of both (e.g., Walt Disney method, Triz) [23]. The objective of using these methods is to resolve so-called priming effects—priming refers to the unconscious activation of certain associations while generating ideas due to previous experience or other impulses. After a large number of ideas have been collected in this way, the solutions are evaluated, and the promising ones are selected.

Phase 5: Prototyping

Once ideas are identified that are to be pursued further, the process moves on to implementing concept prototypes. Unlike in software development, this is generally not a viable piece of software or any other concrete modeling of an IT system (e.g., mock-up). It is rather an initial design thinking prototype that serves to visualize an idea quickly and concisely, in such a way that it can also be rejected quickly. A prototype can therefore be made from a variety of materials (e.g., paper and cardboard or Legos). It can also be a role play, a storyboard, and so on. It is essential that these concept prototypes offer the user possibilities for interaction.

Phase 6: Test (Trial)

Advanced prototypes are tested in a real context during the test phase. Unlike prototyping, it is crucial here to test the prototype in the context in which it is to be actually used later on. The context or the testing in the real situation once again creates empathy for the target group and their needs and provides insight into the context-related factors to be considered for the final solution.

In the following section, two example projects will show how design thinking is used in the practice of an IT company.

3.2 Example 1: Online Jewelry Shopping

The Challenge

A jewelry chain (the customer) has been selling its goods (watches, jewelry) through its conventional chain store. For some time now, it has also been selling them via an online marketplace as well as a mobile channel. The sales figures for the mobile channel in particular have lagged behind the customer's expectations. To address this issue, initial approaches and ideas for optimizing the online business were to be worked out within the framework of a design thinking project. The challenge was thus as follows: "How can we make more people buy jewelry through the mobile channel?"

Design Thinking Setting

The design thinking project was tailored to fit into 5 workshop days. The design thinking team consisted of 12 people from various different professions (three customer representatives from the area of customer IT, two Web designers, two app developers, two concept developers, one secretary, and two moderators).

The Design Thinking Process

After a concise customer briefing, the team worked on the topic of "jewelry retail" and became familiar with products, services, target groups, and competing portals ("understand" phase). For the observation phase ("empathize" phase), it was decided to first determine customers' needs related to the jewelry purchase independently of the actual sales channel, as well as to gather information about what people associated with jewelry—including what positive and negative experiences they had with jewelry and jewelry purchases. The way in which the interviewees purchased jewelry was irrelevant for this approach at that point, and so the interviews were conducted on a Saturday morning on a shopping street of a major German city. Passers-by were interviewed at random. Back at the workshop, the collected findings from the stories interviewees told were shared within the team and parsed for contradictions, surprising insights, and amazing (nuggeting) factors ("define" phase). Surprisingly, many people wanted to express their particular appreciation for the person to be presented with the jewelry through their choice and purchase of a piece of jewelry. The original challenge was revised on the basis of this insight. It was no longer generally a matter of getting more people to buy via the mobile channel. Instead, it was much more precisely about the question of how to create value for the recipient through the purchase of a piece of jewelry. This new challenge prompted the team to think about online portals that are designed more like treasure or memorabilia boxes, or where jewelry can be linked with individually stored images of other memorabilia.

Conclusion

The design thinking project yielded more than 250 ideas for a future mobile shop for the customer. Not a single line of code was written, nor were wireframe or mock-up models created. The IT experts involved had to fully accept this process that had nothing to do with IT. However, their IT know-how was still very valuable to the process, and they themselves learned a lot about the potential customers of the future IT solution—more than they would have ever learned in any other project. They continued to maintain this customer-centric perspective during the subsequent software development process.

3.3   Example 2: Developing Innovative Software for Dentists

The Challenge

For this design thinking project, the focus was on developing a new and, above all, innovative software for dentists. The existing IT solution was already highly outdated, its user interface was very inconvenient, and, above all, the software failed to sufficiently meet the legal requirements for documentation and quality assurance. Within the framework of the design thinking process, a viable innovative idea was to be developed within 3 months from scratch, then tested on initial IT prototypes, and worked out in the form of a rough specification. The challenge was as follows: "How can we create an IT system for dentists that significantly reduces the cost of documentation for them?"

Design Thinking Setting

For this project, the actual design thinking team consisted of IT experts, educators, dentists, and social scientists. The customers to be surveyed were specifically selected by the client. The prerequisite was that both dentists themselves as well as nonmedical specialists (users of the future solution) were to be surveyed. In addition, both groups were to be as heterogeneous as possible in terms of age, gender, and size of practice, with attitudes ranging from "highly professional" to "pragmatically relaxed." Three-day workshops were held independently with each group.

The Design Thinking Process

First, persons affected by (stakeholders) and users of a new dentistry system were identified in working with both groups ("understand" phase). The design team was surprised to learn that apart from the obvious groups (such as dentists and dental assistants), cleaning specialists had been named as well. After all, the cleaning process and the cleaning agent used must also be documented via the software, according to the reasoning. In the next step, personae were developed for the main stakeholders. These were to be designed in such a way that they would differ significantly in their professional attitudes, views, and working methods ("empathize" phase). The workshop participants were able to draw on the abundance of their daily experiences and worked very intensively on creating the most detailed and accurate characterizations possible. Subsequently, the participants developed a key set for each persona, which summarized the general requirements for the software from the perspective of said persona (point of view: How can we make it happen that persona X . . .). These statements were elaborated amidst intensive discussions, which generated many insights for the design thinking team ("empathize" phase). Finally, a series of ideas were generated for each persona during the ideation phase. Prototypes of these ideas were implemented selectively with paper and cardboard ("prototyping" phase). The group discussed the solutions with verve and commitment. The design thinking team questioned the solutions over and over again and wanted to know, above all, *why* a solution was supposedly suitable for a certain persona. At some point in the process, one participant erupted in frustration:

> He [dentist persona] only wants to work with his patients—he doesn't want to document anything at all. He became a dentist because he enjoyed working with patients. He doesn't want to be an expert in dentistry IT.

The design thinking team then developed an idea of how the IT system could be used to inform patients about their treatment as best as possible on the basis of pictures and other visualizations. Documentation, then, merely occurred in the background.

Conclusion

In this process, the software developers worked intensively for a very short time (two periods of 3 days each) on the conditions in different dental practices, taking legal requirements and practical concerns of the day-to-day business in these practices into account. The workshops with the dentists and assistants were not seen as a participatory development process, but rather as a source of inspiration for developing a truly innovative solution for the dentistry software of the future. The empathy developed during the design thinking process for the users and their needs was felt all the way through to the creation of the specification document: It was examined over and over again and questioned as to whether it was still on target where needs were concerned.

4   Summary and Conclusions

We have shown that the different levels of digitalization require correspondingly adapted procedures or methodologies for requirements engineering. This requires new frameworks or models for projects in the context of digital transformation. This is particularly due to the fact that these projects call for specifying completely new business models and realizing these by means of IT, which can only succeed if users' actual needs are met and satisfied as best as possible. One of the main challenges is that these needs often cannot be identified by asking questions, but must instead be tracked down.

Design thinking presented in this chapter serves as a suitable framework for this purpose; adesso has successfully used this method in many project situations within the context of digitalization and digital transformation. We have illustrated this by providing examples of two real projects. One of the main advantages of this methodology is that people and their needs are at the center of the design process.

In practice, we have found that it is helpful in such projects if, in addition to the classic management roles (a project manager responsible for budget, quality, and time and an architect responsible for the technical implementation), a third management role is established with responsibility for designing software according to the subsequent user's requirements.

The third management role is key to:

- Ensuring the necessary focus in these projects on the design of the software from the point of view of the user
- Avoiding conflicts of interest as far as possible, because an architect may, in case of doubt, decide against the user of the software and in favor of a simple technical solution

These three management roles should already be filled at the start of the project and cooperate with each other in the course of the project according to their responsibilities.

As with all frameworks and methods, when each new project is initialized, one must examine the extent to which design thinking is adapted to the project context and to what extent project-specific customizing of the methodology is required.

We are doubtless still at the beginning of the digital transformation and thus also at the beginning of the further necessary changes to the mindset of successful requirements engineers. The particular goals are to create new software systems that are very popular among users and, consequently, to successfully establish new business models in the marketplace from the point of view of the respective client.

References

1. Digital Agenda, Federal Ministry for Economic Affairs and Energy. https://www.bmwi.de/Redaktion/EN/Artikel/Digital-World/digital-agenda.html, last accessed 2017/07/19
2. Khan, S.: Leadership in the digital age – A study on the effects of digitalization on top management leadership. Master Thesis, Stockholm Business School (2016)
3. Merriam-Webster Dictionary. https://www.merriam-webster.com/dictionary/digitization, last accessed 2017/07/19
4. History of Computer. http://www.computerhistory.org/timeline/computers/, last accessed 2017/07/19
5. Pohl, K., Chris, R.: Requirements Engineering Fundamentals: A Study Guide for the Certified Professional for Requirements Engineering Exam – Foundation Level – IREB Compliant. Rocky Nook (2015)

6. Vogelsang, M.: Digitalization in Open Economies, Contributions to Economics. Physica-Verlag, Heidelberg (2010)
7. Nielsen, J.: Usability Engineering. Morgan Kaufmann (1993)
8. DotCom Bubble, Wikipedia. https://en.wikipedia.org/wiki/Dot-com_bubble, last accessed 2017/07/19
9. Kane, G., Palmer, D., Phillips, A.N., Kiron, D., Buckley, N.: Strategy, Not Technology, Drives Digital Transformation. MIT Sloan Management Review (2015)
10. Ordanini, A., Miceli, L., Pizzetti, M., Parasuraman, A.: Crowdfunding: transforming customers into investors through innovative service platforms. J. Serv. Manag. **22**(4), (2011)
11. What is ID? Industrial Designers Society of America. http://www.idsa.org/events/what-id, last accessed 2017/07/19
12. Durling, D., Cross, N., Johnson, J.: Personality and learning preferences of students in design and design-related disciplines. IDATER 96 (1996)
13. Beyer, H., Holtzblatt, K.: Contextual Design. Defining Customer-Centered Systems. Morgan Kaufmann (1997)
14. Knapp, J., Zeratsky, J., Kowitz, B.: Sprint: How to Solve Big Problems and Test New Ideas in Just Five Days. Simon & Schuster (2016)
15. Lipmanowicz, H., McCandless, K.: The Surprising Power of Liberating Structures: Simple Rules to Unleash A Culture of Innovation. Liberating Structures Press (2014)
16. Lemos, J., Alves, C., Duboc, L., Rodrigues, G.N.: A systematic mapping study on creativity in requirements engineering. In: Proceedings of the 27th Annual ACM Symposium on Applied Computing, pp. 1083–1088. ACM (2012)
17. Homepage. http://pure.au.dk/portal/files/45289412/Bilag_11_Om_IDEO.docx, last accessed 2017/07/20
18. Kelley, T., Kelley, D.: Creative Confidence. Unleashing the Creative Potential Within Us All. HarperCollinsPublishers, London (2013)
19. Kensing, F., Blomberg, J.: Participatory design: issues and concerns. Comput. Supported Coop. Work. **7**, 167–185 (1998)
20. Kelley, T. (with Jonathan Littman): The Art of Innovation. HarperCollinsBusiness, London (2001)
21. Brown, T.: Change by Design, p. 39. HarperCollinsPublisher, New York (2009)
22. Hasso Plattner Institute of Design at Stanford. https://static1.squarespace.com/static/57c6b79629687fde090a0fdd/t/58890239db29d6cc6c3338f7/1485374014340/METHODCARDS-v3-slim.pdf. last accessed 2017/07/31
23. Kumar, V.: 101 Design Thinking Methods. A Structured Approach for Driving Innovation in Your Organization. Wiley (2012)

Towards Deviceless Edge Computing: Challenges, Design Aspects, and Models for Serverless Paradigm at the Edge

Stefan Nastic and Schahram Dustdar

1 Introduction

Recently, Cloud Computing, Edge Computing, and the Internet of Things (IoT) have been converging ever stronger, sparking creation of very large-scale, geographically distributed systems [1, 2]. Such systems intensively exploit Cloud Computing models and technologies, predominantly by utilizing large and remote data centers, but also nearby Cloudlets [3, 4] to enhance resource-constrained Edge devices (e.g., in terms of computation offloading [5–7] and data staging [8]) or to provide an execution environment for cloud-centric IoT/Edge applications [9, 10].

Serverless computing is an emerging paradigm, typically referring to a software architecture where application is decomposed into "triggers" and "actions" (or functions), and there is a platform that provides seamless hosting and execution of developer-defined functions (FaaS), making it easy to develop, manage, scale, and operate them. This complexity mitigation is mainly achieved by incorporating sophisticated runtime mechanisms into serverless or FaaS platforms. Hence, such platforms are usually characterized by fully automating many of the management and operations processes. Therefore, serverless computing can be considered as the next step in the evolution of Cloud platforms, such as PaaS, or more generally of the utility computing.

While originally designed for centralized cloud deployments, the benefits of serverless paradigm become especially evident in the context of Edge Computing [11]. This is mainly because in such systems, traditional infrastructure and application management solutions are tedious, ineffective, error-prone, and ultimately very costly. Luckily, some of the existing serverless techniques, such

S. Nastic (✉) · S. Dustdar
Distributed Systems Group, TU Wien, Vienna, Austria
e-mail: nastic@dsg.tuwien.ac.at; dustdar@dsg.tuwien.ac.at

© The Author(s) 2018
V. Gruhn, R. Striemer (eds.), *The Essence of Software Engineering*,
https://doi.org/10.1007/978-3-319-73897-0_8

as sandboxed execution of polyglot tenant-provided code, can be applied on Edge without substantial modifications. The most common approach to runtime execution environments is to utilize Linux containers (such as Docker). Unfortunately, due to inherently different nature of Edge infrastructure, for example, in terms of available resources, network, geographical hyper-distribution, very large scale, etc., fundamental architecture and design assumptions behind cloud-based serverless computing need to be reexamined and specifically tailored for the Edge infrastructure in order to realize *Deviceless Edge Computing*. Some of the main research challenges of the emerging Deviceless Computing include:

- *Resource pooling and rapid elasticity.* Traditional serverless platforms utilize commodity infrastructure, small footprint, and short execution duration, combined with statistical multiplexing of a large number of heterogeneous workloads over time [12]. Elasticity at the Edge implies challenges not present in the Cloud, mostly due to different nature of the infrastructure, the topology of network connectivity, and locality-awareness.
- *Security.* Unlike serverless platforms which often operate in secured environments, the Edge is exposed to various attacks, requiring much better protection and isolation for the individual hosts, tenants, and applications.
- *Automated provisioning and management at scale.* Due to dynamicity, heterogeneity, geographical distribution, and the sheer scale of the Edge infrastructure, traditional management and provisioning approaches are hardly feasible in practice. Thus, novel techniques, which will provide a uniform view and interaction with both Cloud and Edge, are needed [13].
- *Scheduling on loosely coupled and scarce Edge resources.* Scheduler is one of the core components in cloud-based serverless computing. However, at the Edge, application scheduling, orchestration, and configuration management cannot be done in an easy and predictable manner (e.g., by Deviceless platform runtime mechanisms) due to the limited nature of Edge resources and their inherent volatility.
- *Deviceless application development.* In Deviceless paradigm we trade explicit device management for slightly complex application business logic. This means that the development context of such applications needs to grow beyond writing custom business logic to also consider the involved Edge resources and their capabilities, but on a higher level of abstraction, for example, in code.
- *Edge-centric governance.* Due to inherently different nature of Edge-based systems, traditional governance approaches need to be reevaluated and particularly designed to be suitable in the new Edge context. In particular, governance objectives (law, compliance, etc.) are not easily mapped to concrete operations processes (e.g., querying sensory data streams or adding/removing devices). Additionally, making the governance approaches feasible in deviceless paradigm requires full automation of such operational governance processes.

In this chapter, we continue our line of research towards realizing the novel paradigm of Deviceless Edge Computing, by extending the previously defined concepts [11] and by building on our existing work in the area of Edge Computing and

IoT, which serve as the main enablers of Deviceless Computing. In particular, we propose a reference architecture for the Deviceless Edge Computing. Furthermore, we analyze the main aspects of realizing the Deviceless Computing paradigm from two main points of view: (1) required support for application development, in terms of programming models (Sect. 4), and (2) required runtime support for deviceless applications, in terms of main deviceless platform mechanisms (Sect. 5).

The remainder of the chapter is organized as follows: Sect. 2 presents the state of the art. Section 3 introduces a reference architecture of a Deviceless Edge Platform. In Sect. 4 we present our programming model for developing deviceless functions. Section 5 introduces the provisioning model and a middleware for provisioning Deviceless Edge applications. Finally, Sect. 6 concludes the chapter and gives an outlook of future research.

2 Related Work

Recently, the serverless computing paradigm has been rapidly emerging in the IT industry, since its appearance in AWS Lambda[1] in 2014. Major public Cloud providers have introduced comparable FaaS offerings—Azure Functions,[2] Google Cloud Functions.[3] In addition to commercial offerings, several open-source initiatives have emerged, including Apache OpenWhisk[4] (originally developed by IBM, now under incubation at ASF jointly with Adobe and additional companies), as well as several projects developed in the open by various vendors such as Iron Functions,[5] Fission,[6] and Kubeless.[7]

In spite originating as a special case of Cloud computing, the FaaS/serverless paradigm has since evolved to also become applicable beyond the traditional Cloud data centers. For example, the PubNub BLOCKS[8] offering enhances their real-time data stream capabilities running on a network of Edge data centers (e.g., used in IoT applications to stream events and logs between the Edge and the Cloud), with the ability to invoke custom handlers (provided by the application developer) on the data path. Similarly, Amazon Lambda@Edge[9] allows to run custom Javascript handlers on web traffic going through their CloudFront (CDN) facilities. Moreover, there are recent attempts to expand applicability of "serverless" even further, to

---

[1] http://aws.amazon.com/lambda/.

[2] http://azure.microsoft.com/en-us/services/functions/.

[3] http://cloud.google.com/functions/.

[4] http://openwhisk.org/.

[5] http://open.iron.io/.

[6] http://fission.io/.

[7] http://github.com/bitnami/kubeless.

[8] http://goo.gl/IIjkZi.

[9] http://docs.aws.amazon.com/lambda/latest/dg/lambda-edge.html.

IoT gateways and devices—both commercial (e.g., Amazon Greengrass[10]) and exploratory (e.g., OpenWhisk). However, most of these attempts are at early stages, and architectural and design assumptions behind such approaches need to be reevaluated, for example, to address the challenges described in Sect. 1, in order for the serverless paradigm to be fully adopted in Edge computing environments, as opposed to being an extension of Cloud (e.g., in CDN).

The core principle of the serverless paradigm includes fully automated orchestration, lifecycle management, and scheduling of both user-defined functions and underlying resource pools. Recently, different approaches have emerged that focus on utilizing principles of Service-Oriented Architecture (SOA), dynamic service orchestration, and Cloud computing techniques, in order to facilitate execution of data processing applications (e.g., with cloud offloading), but also provisioning and management of vast Edge infrastructure. For example, in [14] the authors introduce sensor-cloud infrastructure that virtualizes physical sensors as services and provides management and monitoring mechanisms for the virtual sensors. However, their support for provisioning and orchestration of virtual sensors is based on static templates, which are not intended for dynamic reconfigurations and optimizations required in Deviceless platform. OpenIoT framework [15] utilizes semantic Web technologies and CoAP to enable web of things and linked sensory data. They mostly focus on discovering, linking, and orchestrating Internet-connected objects. Further, the authors focus on developing a virtualization infrastructure to enable sensing and actuating as a service on the Cloud. They propose a software stack which includes support for management of device identification, selection, and aggregation. In [16] the authors develop an infrastructure virtualization framework for wireless sensor networks. It is based on a content-based pub/sub model for asynchronous event exchange and utilizes a custom event matching algorithm to enable delivery of sensory events to subscribed cloud users and a range of mechanisms to support SaaS applications. These approaches provide valuable insights, advances, and a solid baseline to underpin the Deviceless Edge Computing paradigm.

3 Deviceless Edge Platform

3.1 Approach

The main objective of our approach is to provide a full stack platform for supporting executing and automatically operating Deviceless applications across Cloud and Edge in a unified manner. The key role of the distributed *Deviceless Edge Platform* is to facilitate automated management of the underlying resource pool and optimal placement of applications/functions in order to support the envisioned deviceless

---

[10]http://aws.amazon.com/greengrass/.

execution model. This approach allows for combining the benefits of the Edge (lower response time, ability to manage heterogeneous data) with the computational and storage capabilities of the Cloud. For example, time-sensitive data, such as life-critical vital signs, can be analyzed at the Edge close to where they are generated instead of being transported to the Cloud for processing. Alternatively, selected data can be forwarded to the Cloud for a further, more powerful analysis and long-term storage.

3.2 Platform Usage and Architecture Overview

Figure 1 shows a high-level view of the platform and main *top-down control process* (left) and *application execution and results delivery process* (right). The proposed deviceless paradigm is particularly suitable for managing different granularity of user-defined business logic functions *bottom-up*. This means that the Edge focuses on local views (e.g., per Edge gateway) while the Cloud supports global

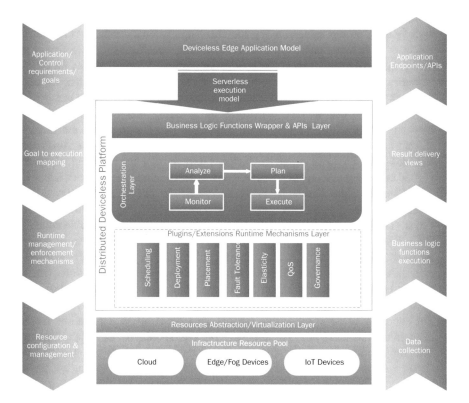

Fig. 1 Deviceless platform architecture

views, for example, combining and analyzing data from different Edge devices, regions, or even domains. For example, in the case of data analytics applications, data is collected from the underlying devices and delivered to the applications via consumption APIs. More importantly, the application business logic such as data analytics can be performed on Edge nodes, Cloud nodes, or both, and the results can be delivered from any of the nodes directly, based on the desired view. Moreover, the *top-down control process* allows decoupling of application requirements (*What*) from concrete realization of those requirements (*How*). This allows developers to simply define the application behavior and business logic and application goals (e.g., regarding provisioning) instead of dealing with the complexity of different management, orchestration, and optimization processes. Moreover, Fig. 1 shows the Deviceless platform's core architecture:

- *Business Logic Wrapper and APIs Layer* focuses on executing and managing user-provided functions, for example, delivering required data to the function and creating results endpoints. To this end, it wraps the user-defined functions in executable artifacts such as Linux Containers and relies on the underlying layers to perform concrete runtime actions and execution steps.
- *The Orchestration Layer* is responsible for interpreting and executing user-defined functions, requirements, and configuration models. This layer acts as a "gluing" component bringing together application's configuration model, business logic functions, and platform's runtime mechanisms. Therefore, the Orchestration Layer receives the application configuration directives, in terms of high-level objectives such as to optimize network latency. It interprets and analyzes these goals and decides how to orchestrate the underlying resources, as well as the user-defined functions, by invoking the underlying runtime mechanisms. To this end, this layer contains micro (Edge-based) and macro (Cloud-based) orchestration and control loops. For example, it can utilize the Scheduling and the Placement mechanisms to determine the most suitable node (Cloud or Edge) for executing a function in order to reduce the network latency.
- *The Runtime Mechanisms Layer* is an extensible plug-ins layer, providing mechanisms to support executing the actions initiated by the Orchestration Layer. The Deployment, the Scheduling, the Elasticity, and basic reasonable defaults for the Quality of Service (QoS) are the core runtime mechanisms. More precisely, the platform has to determine the minimally required elastic resources, provision them, deploy, and then schedule and execute analytics functions, which will satisfy the QoS requirements. On the other hand, the Governance, the Placement, the Fault Tolerance, and the extended QoS mechanisms are optional. For example, in some cases, the sensory data, used by an application, could be confidential and some geographical regions should be excluded. Placing the computation (functions) closer to the data and deciding whether to use Cloud or Edge resources could improve the QoS. Additionally, having a k-fault-tolerant platform that can mitigate the risks of failures to acceptable level further improves the QoS.

In the remainder of the chapter, we particularly focus on two key aspects of Deviceless Edge platform: its programming support for deviceless applications and its support for application management and operation.

4 Programming Support for Deviceless Edge Computing

The main purpose of our programming model is to provide a programmatic view on the whole application ecosystem, that is, the full stack from the infrastructure to software components and services. The main principle behind our programming model is *everything as code*. This includes providing support for writing deviceless functions' business logic, as well as representing the underlying infrastructure components (e.g., gateways) at the application level and enabling developers to programmatically determine their deployment and provisioning. Figure 2 shows a component diagram with the logical structure of Deviceless Edge applications. The main components of such application include custom business logic components, that is, user-defined functions; resource provisioning and deployment logic (custom or stock component provisioning); and operational governance logic. In the remainder of this section, we mainly focus on the programming support for deviceless functions. More details on programmatic provisioning and governance can be found in [17].

4.1 Programming Support for Deviceless Edge Functions

In our programming model, we consider a unified notion of deviceless functions. However, we provide versatile abstractions, which enable expressing the functions' business logic depending on the nature of their respective interactions with Edge or Cloud resources. Figure 3 shows a simplified UML diagram of the programming

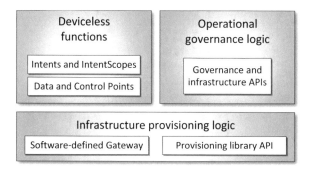

Fig. 2 Overview of deviceless application structure

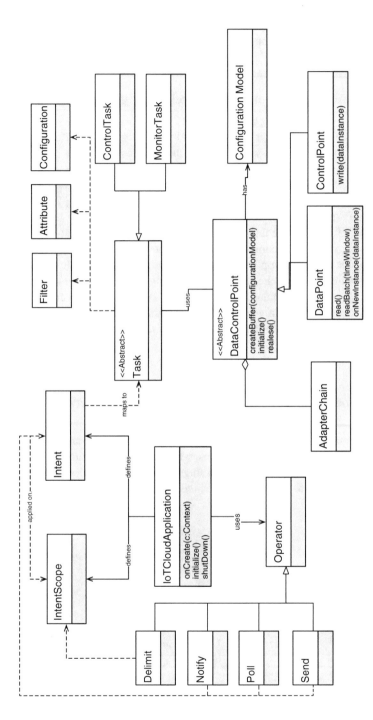

Fig. 3 Simplified UML of programming model for Deviceless edge functions

model. Its key abstractions are *Data and Control Points* and *Intents*. Deviceless functions can be executed in Edge devices to implement control and monitor tasks. For example, a monitoring task includes processing, correlation, and analysis of sensory data streams. Data and Control Points are provided to support such a task development. Deviceless functions executed in the Cloud usually define virtual service topologies by referencing the tasks. At the application level, we provide explicit representation of these tasks via *Intents*, that is, developers write *Intents* to dynamically configure and invoke the tasks. Further, developers use *IntentScopes* to delimit the range of an *Intent*. For example, a developer might want to code the expression: "stop all vehicles on golf course X." In this case, "stop" is the desired *Intent*, which needs to be applied on an *IntentScope* that encompasses all vehicles with the location property "golf course X."

4.2 Intents and IntentScopes

Intent is a data structure describing a specific task which can be performed in a physical environment. In reality, *Intents* are processed and executed on the Deviceless platform, but enable monitoring and controlling of the physical environments by triggering corresponding deviceless functions. Based on the information contained in an *Intent*, a suitable task/function is dynamically selected, instantiated, and executed. Depending on the task's nature, we distinguish between two different types of *Intents*: *ControlIntent* and *MonitorIntent*. *ControlIntents* enable applications to operate and invoke the low-level components, that is, provide a high-level representation of their functionality. *MonitorIntents* are used by applications to subscribe for events from the sensors and to obtain devices' context.

Figure 4 shows the *Intent* structure and its most relevant parts. Each *Intent* contains an ID, used to correlate invocation response with it or apply additional actions on it. Additionally, it contains a set of headers, which specify meta-information needed to process the *Intent* and bind it with a suitable task during the runtime. Among other things, headers carry *Intent's* name and a reference to an *IntentScope*. Further, an *Intent* can contain a set of attributes, which are used by the runtime to select the best matching task instance in case there are multiple

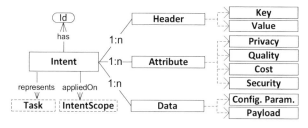

Fig. 4 Intent structure

Intent implementations available. Finally, *Intent* can contain data, which is used to configure the tasks or supply additional payload. Generally, *Intents* allow developers to communicate to the system what needs to be done instead of worrying how the underlying devices will perform the specific task.

Our programming model also allows developers to define *IntentScopes*. IntentScopes need to be defined explicitly and implicitly, that is, developers can explicitly add entities to the scope by specifying their IDs or recursively prune the *GlobalScope*. Formally, we use the well-known set theory to define *IntentScope* as a finite, countable set of entities (set elements). The *GlobalScope* represents the universal set, denoted by S^{max}; therefore, $\forall S(S \subseteq S^{max})$, where S is an *IntentScope*, must hold. Further, for each entity E in the system general membership relation $\forall E(E \in S | S \subseteq S^{max})$ must hold. Therefore, an entity is the unit set, denoted by S_{min}. Empty set $\emptyset$ is not defined; thus, applying an *Intent* on it results with an error. Finally, a necessary condition for an *IntentScope* to be valid is as follows: *IntentScope* is valid iff it is a set S, such that $S \subseteq S^{max} \wedge S \not\equiv \emptyset$ holds. Equation (1) shows operations used to define or refine an *IntentScope*. The most interesting operation is $\subseteq_{cond} S$. It is used to find a subset ($\hat{S}$) of a set S, which satisfies some condition, that is, $E \in \hat{S} \mid E \in S \wedge cond(E) = True$.

$$S = S_{min}|S^{max}| \subseteq_{cond} S \mid S \cup S \mid S \cap S \mid S \setminus S \tag{1}$$

4.3 Data and Control Points

Generally, the main motivation for introducing the Data and Control Points is to enable developing deviceless functions that encapsulate a domain-specific task. Hence, they are used to develop domain libraries of deviceless functions. In this context, a domain library contains a set of reusable functions that are responsible to encapsulate domain-specific knowledge, most notably domain model and common behaviors, in a reusable manner. For example, a building automation expert developer could develop a domain library to facilitate development of higher-level functionality for building management systems. To this end, Data and Control Points represent and enable management of data and control channels (e.g., device drivers) to the low-level sensors/actuators in an abstract manner. Generally, they mediate the communication with the connected devices (e.g., digital, serial, or IP based), enable application-specific customizations of the channels, and also implement communication protocols for the connected devices, for example, Modbus, CAN, or I^2C.

The *DataControlPoint* (Fig. 3) is an abstract class which provides main operators and lifecycle management hooks for the Data and Control Points. Both DataPoints and ControlPoints inherit from this component and encapsulate the specialized behavior for reading sensory data (DataPoints) and preforming the actuations (ControlPoints). In general, the DataControlPoint allows the developers to perform concurrent reads and writes, regardless of whether the low-level drivers support sequential or concurrent reads and writes. In this way, the applications have an impression of exclusive usage of the available devices. Another important feature of DataControlPoint is that they enable developers to configure custom behavior of underlying devices. For this purpose, each DataControlPoint can have a ConfigurationModel associated with it. For example, an application can configure sensor poll rates, activate a low-pass filter for an analog sensory input, or configure unit and type of data instances in the stream.

The most important concept supporting the DataControlPoint is the Virtual-Buffers, which are provided and managed by the Deviceless Edge Platform. In general, such buffers enable virtualized access to and custom configurations of underlying sensors and actuators. They act as multiplexers of the data and control channels, thus enabling the device applications to have their own view of and define custom configurations for such channels. To this end, the VirtualBuffers wrap the device drivers and share a common behavior with them. For example, they can be initialized, shut down, and released. Both buffers and drivers lifecycle are managed by the platform. Finally, to support application-specific configurations such as sensor poll rates, filters, or scalers, each virtual buffer can have an AdapterChain. Adapter chains reference different Adapters, which are specified and parametrized via DataControlPoint's ConfigurationModel. Any raw sensing value is passed through such adapter chain before being delivered to a DataPoint.

5   Provisioning Support for Deviceless Edge Computing

In this section, we shift focus from deviceless functions and application level support to the core Deviceless Edge Platform components. In particular, we discuss resource provisioning in Deviceless Edge Computing, as it is the cornerstone for resource pooling and rapid elasticity at the Edge. Moreover, provisioning component (middleware) is a crucial enabler for deviceless paradigm, because it decouples the developers and their applications from the underlying devices. In the following, we discuss our deviceless provisioning model and the middleware.

5.1   *Software-Defined Gateways*

Software-defined gateways (SDGs) are the core abstraction in deviceless provisioning model. Their main purpose is to support virtualizing Edge compute resources, for example, IoT devices, in order to provide isolated and managed execution environments for deviceless functions.

To achieve this, SDGs encapsulate functional aspects (e.g., communication capabilities or sensor poll frequencies) and non-functional aspects (e.g., quality attributes, elasticity capabilities, costs, and ownership information) of the Edge resources and expose them to the deviceless platform (provisioning middleware).

The functional, provisioning, and governance capabilities of the units are exposed via *well-defined APIs*, which enable provisioning and controlling the SDGs at runtime, for example, start/stop. Our conceptual model also allows for composing and interconnecting SDGs, in order to dynamically deliver the Edge resources and capabilities to the applications. The runtime provisioning and configuration is performed by specifying late-bound policies and configuration models. Naturally, the SDGs support mechanisms to map the virtual resources with the underlying physical infrastructure. However, this is out of the scope of this chapter. Finally, some of the most important features of SDGs include:

• They provide software-defined API, which can be used to access, configure, and control the units, in a unified manner.
• They support fine-grained internal configurations, for example, adding functional capabilities like different communication protocols, at runtime.
• They can be composed at higher level, via dependency units, creating virtual topologies that can be (re)configured at runtime.
• They enable decoupled and managed configuration (via late-bound policies) to provision the units dynamically and on-demand.
• They have utility cost functions that enable pricing the Edge resources as utilities.

Figure 5 gives the architectural view of SDGs and depicts the most important components of software-defined gateways. In the figure, the double line shows virtual boundaries of the SDG prototypes. Our provisioning model does not require building custom SDGs from scratch. Instead, it provides SDG prototypes and defines mechanisms (implemented by the middleware) to customize them, based on application-specific requirements. At their core, the SDG prototypes define an isolated runtime environment for the SDGs and application-specific components. The main purpose of the SDG prototypes is to provide isolated namespaces, as well as limit and isolate resource usage, such as CPU and memory. Therefore, the SDG

Fig. 5 Software-defined gateway (SDG) architecture

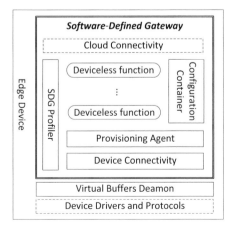

prototypes are used to bootstrap higher-level SDG functionality. It is important to mention that SDG prototypes do not propose a novel virtualization solution. Instead, they rely on proven techniques, namely, kernel-supported virtualization approaches, which offer a number of lightweight execution environments/drivers such as LXCs, libvirt-sandbox, or even chroot. Such environments are generally referred to as containers that can be used to "wrap" the SDGs. Conceptually, virtualization choices do not pose any limitations, because by utilizing well-defined APIs, our SDGs can be dynamically configured, provisioned, interconnected, and deployed, at runtime. The SDG prototypes are hosted in the IoT Cloud and enriched with functional and provisioning capabilities, which are exposed via the well-defined APIs. There are a number of components (cf. Fig. 5) which are preinstalled in each SDG prototype in order to support such APIs.

5.2 Deviceless Provisioning Middleware

Figure 6 gives a high-level architecture overview of our middleware. Generally, the provisioning middleware is designed based on the microservices architecture and it is distributed across the Cloud and Edge devices. The main components

Fig. 6 Architecture overview of the deviceless provisioning middleware

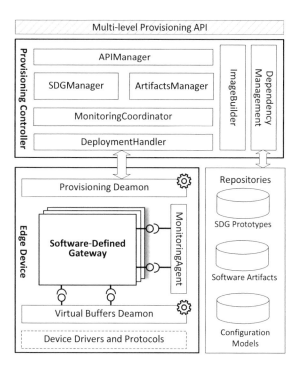

of the provisioning middleware include (1) the *Software-Defined Gateways*, (2) the *Provisioning and Virtual Buffers Daemons* that run in Edge devices, and (3) the *Provisioning Controller* which runs in the Cloud. Previously, we have briefly discussed the SDGs; in the remainder of this section, we mainly focus on describing the Provisioning Controller component and point an interested reader to our earlier publication [13], where we discuss the Provisioning and Virtual Buffers Daemons in great detail.

The Provisioning Controller (Fig. 6, top) provides a mediation layer that enables the Deviceless Edge Platform to interact with the Edge infrastructure in a conceptually centralized fashion, without worrying about geographical distribution and heterogeneity of the underlying Edge devices. Internally, the Provisioning Controller comprises several microservices: *APIManager, MonitoringCoordinator, SDG- and ArtifactsManager, DeploymentHandler, and DependencyManagement service*. These microservices are self-contained units, which communicate over REST APIs and can be individually deployed. This enables our Provisioning Controller to support elastically scalable execution of provisioning workflows, since we can dynamically spin up additional instances of microservices under heavy load and scale out the Provisioning Controller to support a large number of connected Edge devices. Due to space limitations, in continuation, we only describe the most important microservices of the Provisioning Controller.

The main responsibility of the *APIManager* is to manage the *Multilevel Provisioning API*, that is, it encapsulates the middleware provisioning capabilities in well-defined APIs and handles all API calls from user-defined provisioning workflows. Although our middleware provides multilevel provisioning support, this distinction is only relevant to the middleware internal components, since the APIManager hides all such details from the users, who effectively observe only simple API calls and corresponding responses. Therefore, the APIManager is responsible to resolve incoming requests, map them to the respective handlers, that is, *SDGManager* or *ArtifactsManager* (depending on the request type), and deliver results to the calling workflow. Among other things, the actions performed by these managers involve selecting requested SDGs or artifacts by querying the corresponding SDG- and Artifacts-Repository, building the package images, and delivering them to the Edge devices. All device state-snapshots are maintained by the MonitoringCoordinator, which manages static device meta-information and periodically sends monitoring request to the *MonitoringAgent* in order to obtain runtime snapshots of current device state. Finally, since the user-defined functions and SDG images are not readily available in Edge devices, the *DeploymentHandler* is responsible to deliver them to the Edge devices (i.e., *Provisioning Daemons*) or SDGs (i.e., *Provisioning Agents*) at runtime. The DeploymentHandler relies on the *DependencyManagement service* to resolve the required dependencies and *ImageBuilder* to prepare (package and compress) them into deployable images. Resolving the dependencies on the cloud is particularly useful, because it saves a lot of processing and networking, from the perspective of whole infrastructure, since otherwise each Edge device would have to perform the same set of actions, for example, downloads.

6 Conclusion

The chapter introduced a novel vision of the Deviceless Edge Computing paradigm. In order to clarify some of the most important aspects of this emerging paradigm, we have analyzed the key challenges associated with Deviceless Edge Computing and presented a generic reference architecture of a Deviceless Platform. Moreover, we have presented *Intent-based programming model* and an approach for *automated provisioning* of the Edge infrastructure, based on *Software-Defined Gateways*. We discussed how these two approaches facilitate two main challenges: *deviceless application development* and *automated provisioning and management at scale*, respectively.

As we have discussed, the presented approaches significantly reduce the complexity related to development and runtime management (e.g., provisioning, deployment, and configuration management) of deviceless applications. However, there is still a long road ahead to fully realize the vision of the Deviceless Edge Computing. In the future, we plan to continue our line of research, by focusing on addressing the most important research challenges such as (1) enabling resource pooling and rapid elasticity, at the Edge, (2) scheduling deviceless functions execution on loosely coupled and scarce Edge resources, and (3) addressing the key governance and security issues related with deviceless applications. To this end, we plan to focus on "filling the gaps" in the proposed reference architecture, by developing the required models and platform mechanism.

Acknowledgment This work is sponsored by Joint Programming Initiative Urban Europe, ERA-NET, SMART-FI project under project No. 6683255.

References

1. Amazon: Amazon Web Services IoT. https://aws.amazon.com/iot/. Accessed June 2016
2. Sundar Pichai (Google Official Blog): Building the next evolution of Google. https://googleblog.blogspot.co.at/2016/05/io-building-next-evolution-of-google.html. Accessed June 2016
3. Satyanarayanan, M., Bahl, P., Caceres, R., Davies, N.: The case for VM-based cloudlets in mobile computing. Pervasive Comput. **8**(4), 14–23 (2009)
4. Bahl, V.: Cloud 2020: emergence of micro data centers (cloudlets) for latency sensitive computing (keynote). In: Middleware 2015 (2015)
5. Cuervo, E., Balasubramanian, A., Cho, D.-K., Wolman, A., Saroiu, S., Chandra, R., Bahl, P.: Maui: making smartphones last longer with code offload. In: Proceedings of the 8th International Conference on Mobile Systems, Applications, and Services, pp. 49–62. ACM, New York (2010)
6. Chun, B.-G., Ihm, S., Maniatis, P., Naik, M., Patti, A.: Clonecloud: elastic execution between mobile device and cloud. In: Conference on Computer Systems. ACM, New York (2011)
7. Messer, A., Greenberg, I., Bernadat, P., Milojicic, D., Chen, D., Giuli, T.J., Gu, X.: Towards a distributed platform for resource-constrained devices. In: Proceedings 22nd International Conference on Distributed Computing Systems, 2002, pp. 43–51. IEEE, New York (2002)

8. Stuedi, P., Mohomed, I., Terry, D.: Wherestore: location-based data storage for mobile devices interacting with the cloud. In: MCS (2010)
9. Distefano, S., Merlino, G., Puliafito, A.: Sensing and actuation as a service: a new development for clouds. In: NCA, pp. 272–275 (2012)
10. Nastic, S., Sehic, S., Voegler, M., Truong, H.-L., Dustdar, S.: Patricia - a novel programing model for iot applications on cloud platforms. In: SOCA (2013)
11. Glikson, A., Nastic, S., Dustdar, S.: Deviceless edge computing: extending serverless computing to the edge of the network (2017)
12. Breitgand, D., Glikson, A., et al.: Sla-aware resource over-commit in an IaaS cloud. In: CNSM'12
13. Nastic, S., et al.: A middleware infrastructure for utility-based provisioning of IoT cloud systems. In: The First IEEE/ACM Symposium on Edge Computing (2016)
14. Yuriyama, M., Kushida, T.: Sensor-cloud infrastructure-physical sensor management with virtualized sensors on cloud computing. In: NBiS (2010)
15. Soldatos, J., Serrano, M., Hauswirth, M.: Convergence of utility computing with the internet-of-things. In: IMIS, pp. 874–879 (2012)
16. Hassan, M.M., Song, B., Huh, E.-N.: A framework of sensor-cloud integration opportunities and challenges. In: ICUIMC (2009)
17. Nastic, S., Truong, H.-L., Dustdar, S.: SDG-Pro: a programming framework for software-defined IoT cloud gateways. J. Internet Serv. Appl. **6**(1), 1–17 (2015)

Data-Driven Decisions and Actions in Today's Software Development

Harald Gall, Carol Alexandru, Adelina Ciurumelea, Giovanni Grano, Christoph Laaber, Sebastiano Panichella, Sebastian Proksch, Gerald Schermann, Carmine Vassallo, and Jitong Zhao

1 Introduction

When software development is portrayed, it is often shown as a rather uncoordinated activity in which some genius programmers get together to hack a program until it magically starts working. While this picture may have been arguable decades ago, professional software development is a very structured activity. It has evolved into a complex process that is heavily relying on various kinds of data about the software itself, about its execution environment, but also about feedback from its users and the market. All these data are used to fuel the development for optimizing technical aspects and user experience. Today's processes fully integrate all phases of software engineering, from requirements to coding and testing, to integration and deployment, and to operations of the software system. Boundaries of development and operations have been reduced to the extent that both activities have been integrated and optimized leading to better performing software in the field.

Today's software development is very well tracked and recorded in various forms of data: requirements data, code and bug repositories, testing data and code, configurations and continuous integration data, deployment scripts, or data in social coding platforms such as StackOverflow. Additionally, runtime data (e.g., from executions in the cloud) are collected and fed back into the development process.

H. Gall · C. Alexandru · A. Ciurumelea · G. Grano · C. Laaber · S. Panichella · S. Proksch (✉) ·
G. Schermann · C. Vassallo
Department of Informatics, University of Zurich, Zurich, Switzerland
e-mail: gall@ifi.uzh.ch; alexandru@ifi.uzh.ch; ciurumelea@ifi.uzh.ch; grano@ifi.uzh.ch;
laaber@ifi.uzh.ch; panichella@ifi.uzh.ch; proksch@ifi.uzh.ch; schermann@ifi.uzh.ch;
vassallo@ifi.uzh.ch

J. Zhao
Tongji University, Shanghai, China
e-mail: 1410787@tongji.edu.cn

© The Author(s) 2018
V. Gruhn, R. Striemer (eds.), *The Essence of Software Engineering*,
https://doi.org/10.1007/978-3-319-73897-0_9

Software developers have to deal with a lot of infrastructure and data, be it static of dynamic data in various forms. Software experimentation provides further means to optimize feature roll-out for different user bases on a global scale. Consequently, process support has become even more essential given this mass of data and the interleaving processes.

From a business perspective, development workflows have been designed to allow the software creation to be planable by estimating efforts and monitoring progress. From a technical perspective, these workflows represent a safety net for the developers, because they both facilitate quality control and help to structure the work.

Inspired by the typical workflows of agile software development, Fig. 1 illustrates one typical release cycle in a simplified workflow. Each cycle starts from a list of requirements and leads to a shipped product, with several phases in between. We have analyzed these phases and have identified several challenges that developers are facing in these individual phases. In the following, we describe these challenges, the data to be used for decision making, and the actions that can be supported. For that we present opportunities to improve over the current state of the art by adapting results and tools that are proposed by recent research.

In Fig. 1, the first step in a release cycle is the planning phase, in which the scope of the next release is planned (1). This step is typically not a technical problem, but driven by business decisions. It is, therefore, considered separate and out of scope for our discussion.

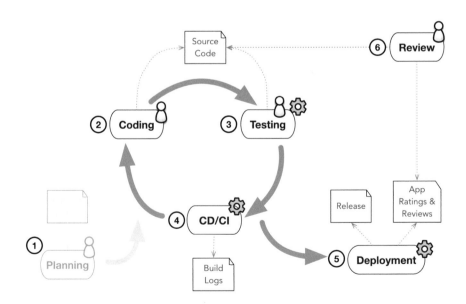

Fig. 1 Release cycle

The core part of the release cycle is the implementation of the product itself (2). Modern software engineering has become less centered around the efficient implementation of algorithms, but more about a smart composition of existing components. Large numbers of frameworks and libraries exist that can be reused to solve a problem at hand. Reuse has several benefits like maintainability and maturity of the code base, but it requires the developer to constantly learn new application programming interfaces (APIs) to use these existing components effectively. Especially inexperienced developers or developers that switch projects are confronted with a huge technology stack that needs to be mastered, before they can contribute to the project. This overwhelming amount of information is not only very frustrating but also hinders productivity.

Heavily interwoven with the actual creation of source code is the creation of test code that double-checks that the implementation of the developer follows the expected behavior (3). Extensive testing is crucial to achieve a high software quality. Traditionally, developer either write small unit tests that test individual classes or resort to manual debugging to assert the expected behavior. Both approaches are suboptimal though, as important test scenarios might be missed. More recently, approaches appeared that can automatically generate test suits. Unfortunately, the quality of the generated tests is low and these suits are hard to maintain. In addition, some components are not easy to test automatically (e.g., user interfaces) and new ways of testing are required.

The most natural artifact that is created in the release cycle is source code. Both the implementation phase (2) and the testing phase (3) create source code as the primary artifact. One of the most important means for quality control in a project is a review of this source code before it can be considered finished. On top of this, source code is a way to communicate with other developers, and developers are required to understand source code on a daily basis. The high amount of source code is a big challenge for developers as it is often hard to find the important bits and pieces.

An important part of a modern release cycle is the existence of a build server that performs all integration tasks on every commit (4). Such a continuous integration/continuous deployment system asserts that the current code base can be used on different systems, for example, it would detect, if the developers forgot to add files to a commit or broke a configuration file. In addition to asserting the deployability of the product, the build server often performs several actions to enforce several quality attributes (e.g., test coverage, code style, code complexity). When build servers fail, they typically maintain a build log that reports about the individual steps of the build. Unfortunately, the cause of the build error is often not obvious. Developers need to understand the errors reported in a build to fix them in source code or through adapting the build configuration. The length of a build log and cryptic error messages take time to process and present a big challenge for developers.

After completing several iterations in this cycle, the updated product will eventually be deployed (5). This can happen in multiple ways; most commonly, a release of the product is created and published as an update to its users. For long-running projects, the number of existing releases is large and projects that exercise continuous delivery principles excessively might create multiple releases per day. Analyzing the historic development of these releases is not only interesting for research but also for project managers that want to study telemetry data of their product. By monitoring trends about, for example, performance metrics, code complexity, or the number of dependencies, it is possible to identify degradations early and to make educated and data-driven decisions about technical details of the product.

A crosscutting concern that is valid across all phases is the review of changes (6). We already motivated the need for summarization techniques to support efficient reviews of source code reviews, but other use cases exist. In case of a deployment to app stores, any release can also be rated by users, which creates a valuable source of feedback for the developers. The vast numbers of ratings and reviews can be leveraged to better understand the requirements and sentiments of the target users. Rating and reviews can be used to decide about the direction of future development. However, to make the amount of data digestible by a human, it is required to summarize it to the most valuable information first.

In the following, we will dedicate one section to each phase of the release cycle. We describe current tools and approaches that add value to the process, describe the data-driven aspects and the current boundaries of feasibility, and sketch the next big idea that is about to impact the corresponding phase. While this chapter has a survey character, we will restrict the referenced works to existing approaches and to promising new results that could be put to action soon. We do, however, omit some visionary solutions for which the adoption cannot be expected in the near future.

2   Recommendation

Programmers extensively leverage application programming interfaces (APIs) to reuse code and unify programming experience when writing code. However, it is still a tough task for programmers to choose and utilize APIs from numerous libraries and frameworks. Even the most experienced programmers may encounter unfamiliar APIs and spend lots of time to learn how to use it. Furthermore, various barriers [68, 106] cause APIs to be hard to learn, such as insufficient examples and ambiguous documentation. As a result, it is a critical job for assisting programmers to learn APIs effectively and efficiently with less effort.

2.1   Code Example Recommendation Systems

To help programmers alleviate burden and better facilitate the usage of APIs, developers can be supported through code example recommendation systems [97]. Over the last decade, several of such systems have been proposed [95, 102, 108].

These systems propose programming information, such as which methods are most likely to call and how to invoke these methods. Traditional code example recommendation systems generally provide suggestions based on API usage data. Existing contributions can be organized in the categories according to the purpose of the detecting techniques.

Code search engines (CSEs) such as Krugle[1] and NerdyData[2] usually leverage text-oriented information-retrieval (IR) techniques to search in a large number of open-source repositories. But they don't provide mechanisms to rank the quality of the found code snippets and usually return too massive results for programmers to choose.

API usage example recommendation systems utilize API examples or API calls to recommend example code. These systems adopt various categories of API usage patterns and various techniques for inferring and clustering API usage algorithms, such as DBSCAN [109], k-nearest neighbor [16], BIDE [128], and RTM [83], or clustering algorithms like Canopy clustering [98]. The quality of the API usage examples found by these tools is derived from the overall quality of the code repositories they utilize and the selected mining algorithms.

Other tools use a semantic analysis approach to explore API usage obstacles through analyzing programmers' questions in Q&A website. Example Overflow [129] uses keyword search based on the Apache Lucene [76] library, which internally uses the term frequency-inverse document frequency (tf-idf) weight [127]. Using Q&A website as code repositories, systems would not be able to critically evaluate various snippets, and bugs may crop up for the examples that are not properly tested.

2.2   Naturalness of Software

The implementation of recommender systems, which aid developers in writing and maintaining code, has often employed machine learning and data mining approaches. The availability of a large and growing body of successful open-source projects and a recent hypothesis, "the naturalness of software", has opened the possibility of applying natural language processing techniques to source code. The hypothesis states that software, as a form of human communication, has statistical properties similar to the ones specific to natural language and that these can be exploited to build and improve software engineering tools [7].

Code suggestion is one of the most popular recommender systems and most used features of any modern IDE; it is typically implemented using manually defined syntactic and semantic completion rules derived from the programming language specification. Hindle et al. [60] observed that code corpora present a high degree

---

[1]http://www.krugle.com/.

[2]https://nerdydata.com/.

of repetitiveness and they were able to exploit this property using a simple n-gram language model to enhance the code suggestion capabilities of Eclipse. Allamanis et al. [4] take advantage of the available open-source code online and learn a language model using a corpus 100 times larger than the previous work and improve their results showing that language models learned over source code, just like natural language, benefit significantly from more data. Tu et al. [120] analyze the limitation of previous models in capturing local regularities that are highly typical for human written programs and build a cache language model that further improves the code suggestion accuracy of previous work.

In [5] the authors tackle an interesting problem using statistical language models of source code: that of learning coding conventions from a code base. Adhering to coding conventions is an important practice of any successful and high-quality software project, as it strongly impacts readability and maintainability and it is often enforced by developers, but it currently lacks support in modern IDEs. Allamanis et al. [5] learn the coding style conventions specific to a software project through simple n-gram-based language models that are subsequently used to detect style violations of identifier naming and formatting and suggest improvements. One of the limits of this approach is that it can only suggest names that appear in the training set of the language models. While this is an adequate solution for local variable names, suggesting method and class names requires a more sophisticated approach. In [6], the authors experiment with a neural log-bilinear language model that is able to recommend neologism, names that do not appear in the training corpus, with promising results.

Natural language processing techniques applied to source code are extremely versatile: researchers have exploited them to evaluate code contributions to open-source projects and analyze whether they are likely to be accepted or not [59], improve reporting of compiler error messages [19], help developers find buggy code that is flagged as unnatural by language models [105], etc. Nevertheless, these techniques come with their own set of challenges. Natural language and source code have different characteristics which have to be taken into account when reusing approaches built and evaluated primarily for spoken and written language. A second problem is that a basic principle of software engineering, reusability, creates a data sparsity problem: it is rare to find multiple implementations of the same task in code, while it is quite common to find many news articles written about the same topic. While programming, developers often define new terms and compose them in novel ways; current NLP methods for natural language texts have been developed expecting that this is unlikely to occur. Another important issue is the evaluation of models trained on source code; there is a need of metrics adapted to source code and of existing benchmarks for researchers to compare their results. In spite of the existing limitations, there is a wide potential to apply natural language processing methods in a wide range of areas in software engineering and support developers in writing and maintaining code.

2.3 *Evaluation*

Independently of the technology that is used to build a recommendation system, be it a traditional recommender learned from examples or a recommender that is built on top of a language model, it will always remain a great challenge to evaluate the value of such a system. Traditionally, researchers have built benchmarks from the vast amounts of source code found in public repositories like GitHub. They would use the source code to learn models and validate the models on other examples. This approach has one significant drawback though: these benchmarks need to be considered as artificial. Previous work has shown that the history recorded in a repository is not representative for actual development [87], because it is incomplete. They find that a representative picture requires more fine-grained evolution data.

To close this mismatch, researchers have started to collect interaction data of developers directly in the IDE. The tools DFlow [79], FeedBaG [8, 101], or Epicea [39] are three examples of such systems that track developers during their day-to-day activities. The resulting datasets [100] present a unique opportunity to learn about patterns in developer behavior and to identify chances to improve their productivity in reoccurring tasks.

Examples of how to use such information are presented in several studies on the typical time budget of developers [9], frequently used commands in the IDE [85], or to find smells in interaction sequences [32]. As some of these trackers also capture source code changes, it is possible to use the interaction data as a ground truth for the evaluation of recommendation systems in software engineering. Prior work has shown that these realistic evaluations report different quality metrics for recommenders, when the evolving nature of source code is not reflected in the evaluation setup [99].

3 Testing

It is widely recognized that software testing is a crucial task in any successful software development process. Indeed, the overall testing cost has been estimated at being about half of the total development cost [12]. The definition of software testing involves several different kinds of activities and processes. In fact, various types of testing need to be performed in order to achieve different objectives and assess the qualities and the reliability of a software system. There are two main categories in software testing. On one side, *functional testing* assesses whether software behaves as intended. This category contains unit, integration, and user acceptance testing. On the other side, *nonfunctional testing* is concerned with program attributes like performance, security, or reliability.

Software testing is extensively handled in research; hence, we focus on two specific topics from both abovementioned categories. We start off by introducing concepts from automated unit test generation. Afterwards, performance testing in the form of software microbenchmarking is discussed.

3.1 Automated Unit Test Case Generation

Unit test is intended as a piece of code that automatically invokes a *unit* of work in a given system, checking assumptions about its behavior. To do that, inputs that exercise such units need to be defined. However, finding those inputs and writing test cases for a large system are extremely costly, difficult, and laborious tasks. An obvious response to this problem is to automate such a process as much as possible. Since the test case generation problem can be easily expressed as an optimization one [3], a tremendous amount of research has been conducted in applying metaheuristic algorithms (especially Genetics Algorithms (GA) [51]) to solve such a problem. The Search-Based Software Testing (SBST), an entirely new line of research, is the result of such a growing interest in the area [77].

The design of a search algorithm tailored to solve any optimization problem usually starts from the definition of the solution representation and the fitness function. In this context, a solution is represented by a set of test inputs. The fitness function is used to represent how *good* is a given solution for a coverage criterion. The most common one is the branch coverage criterion. A fitness function is composed mainly by two metrics: the *approach level* and the *branch distance*. The former expresses how far is the actual execution path from covering the target; the latter represents how far is the input data to change the Boolean value in the closer condition node to the target. Depending on how the targets are handled by the evolutionary algorithm, we can distinguish between single-target and multi-target approaches.

3.1.1 Single-Target Approaches

This class of algorithms has been the first one proposed in the literature as a search-based approach for test case generation [21, 42, 49]. A single-target strategy works as follows: (1) all the targets to hit are listed, (2) a single-objective search algorithm is used to find a solution to each target until all the search budget is consumed or all the targets are covered, and (3) a test suite is built combining together all the generated test cases. Therefore, in such techniques, every individual is a test case that evolves to cover a target.

From the ones presented in the literature, we believe that several tools are mature enough to be used in industrial applications, especially for programs written in C language. For instance, Lakhotia et al. implemented AUSTIN, an open-source tool based on the Alternative Variable Method able to deal with pointers [72]. Scalabrino et al. presented OCELOT, a tool that implements a technique based on the concept of linearly independent path to smartly select the targets and therefore save search budget [110]. Moreover, such a tool is able to automatically generate test cases for the Check[3] framework. More recently, Kim et al. introduced CAVM, an extension of a commercial tool able also to handle dynamic data structures [67]. Despite working pretty well for procedural languages, single-target techniques might suffer of some limitations [45]. For instance, in a program under test, some branches might be more difficult to cover or even infeasible. Thus, in this case, a single-target approach would waste a significant amount of budget. Multi-target approaches, discussed in the upcoming paragraph, have been proposed in last years to overcome such limitations.

3.1.2 Multi-Target Approaches

The first example of multi-target technique has been presented by Fraser and Arcuri [45]. They proposed a *whole-suite* approach where the search algorithm evolves the entire suite with the aim to cover all the branches at the same time. In order to achieve such a result, they define a new fitness function that sums the branch distance of all the targets into a cumulative function that express the *goodness* of the entire suite. Such an approach has been implemented in EVOSUITE,[4] an open-source tool generating JUnit test cases for Java code. Following a similar idea, Panichella et al. proposed MOSA (Many-Objective Sorting Algorithm) [91]. Instead of aggregating multiple objectives into a single value, MOSA reformulates the branch coverage as a many-objective optimization problem. Indeed, in this formulation, a fitness score is a vector of m values, instead of a single aggregate score. In addition, MOSA uses an *archive* to keep track of the best test cases between the many detected by the algorithm. Evaluated on 64 Java classes of large projects, MOSA was able to generate unit test with an average coverage about 84%. Moreover, also such an algorithm is built on top of EVOSUITE. Being available as Maven plugin, such a tool represents an out-of-the-box solution for practitioners that want to automate the process of test case generation.

3.1.3 Limitations and Outlook

The aforementioned approaches only automate the process of generating data able to exercise a part of a system. However, given such input data, a proper test case should be able to check whether the software is behaving as intended, preventing it from potentially incorrect behavior. Such a problem is called the *test oracle problem* [11]. Despite the huge amount of research in testing automation, such a problem

---

[3]https://github.com/libcheck/check.

[4]http://www.evosuite.org.

still remains less solved. Therefore, without test oracle automation, human effort is needed to determine the correct behavior and inhibits better overall test automation. Moreover, such tools often generate test cases that are hard to understand and difficult to maintain [107]. Despite different approaches that tried to address such a problem, there is still room for improvement.

3.2 Performance Testing

Performance testing is a form of nonfunctional testing that deals with the assessment of particular performance counters of a system. A system can range from a piece of software to a deployed application potentially running on multiple computers. Hence, we differentiate between two major types of performance tests: (1) load tests and (2) software microbenchmarks. During load testing, a production-like system is deployed to a dedicated environment, and defined load patterns are executed against that system for a period of time (usually multiple hours). Load testing can be seen as the system/integration testing equivalent for performance. Conversely, microbenchmarking focuses on small fractions of a program (e.g., a function) and evaluates over many executions how performance counters behave for that particular fraction. It is the unit test equivalent for performance. Typical performance counters evaluated are related to time and required resources. Examples are average execution time, throughput, and CPU utilization; and memory consumption, number of allocations, and I/O operations.

In the following, we focus on software microbenchmarking for software-component execution times.

3.2.1 Problems

Recent studies on OOS show that microbenchmarking is not as common and popular as unit testing [73, 119]. The decreased popularity is potentially due to multiple factors described in the following. In order to write good performance tests, an in-depth knowledge about compiler/runtime internals and statistics is required [50]. Moreover, execution should be done on an environment dedicated and set up for reliable performance measurements, and tests need to be executed many times (system warmup, >20 measurements) to reduce nondeterministic influences. This results in two constraints: many developers do not have such a dedicated environment but rather use their own machines or unreliable cloud resources, and test-suite execution times rise up to multiple hours or even days [64]. Further, in most programming languages, there is no established standard for writing microbenchmarks, and current tools that support agile process models (i.e., CI servers) do not provide means for continuous performance assessment [73].

3.2.2 Current Solutions

In recent years, software microbenchmarking has gained interest in both academia and industry. To lower the required knowledge for writing microbenchmarks, tool vendors introduced dedicated frameworks that assist in writing good performance tests. OpenJDK introduced from version 7 on the Java Microbenchmarking Harness (JMH).[5] Newer languages such as Go,[6] Rust,[7] and Swift[8] provide microbenchmarking framework as part of their standard library. On the academic side, Bulej et al. [17] introduce the Stochastic Performance Logic (SPL) that removes the required statistical knowledge from developers for performance test result evaluation. SPL is a declarative way of specifying assertions about a software components performance. One example could be as follows: algorithm A must be faster than algorithm B by a factor of 2. These assertions are transformed into performance tests, and their results are validated with common statistical tests (i.e., hypothesis tests).

Others explored the identification of performance introducing code changes and the reduction of performance test execution time. Jin et al. [64] first study the characteristics of performance bugs and consequently take the insights to compute efficiency rules for performance bug detection. Auxiliary to that, Heger et al. [58] introduce PRCA, an approach that utilizes unit tests and the revision history of a project to find the root cause of a performance problem. Their work bisects the git revision history to find the commit and involved methods that introduced the degradation. Both previously discussed works do not continuously check, but rather check for performance problems ad hoc. Conversely, Huang et al. [61], Alcocer et al. [1], and de Oliveira et al. [35] propose approaches that continuously check for software performance. Huang et al. and Alcocer et al. introduce static approaches to detect potentially performance-risky commits, and based on their assessment flag a commit for benchmark execution or not. Conversely, de Oliveira et al. are the first to introduce a methodology that executes a subset of a performance test suite on every commit. They employ a combination of static analysis, to predict whether a benchmark is potentially able to detect a regression, and historical dynamic benchmark execution data, to predict whether the performance of a benchmark is affected by a commit. Compared to the other approaches, this reduces the benchmark suite to a subset that is of interest and executes a subset on each commit.

3.2.3 Outlook

An unsolved issue so far is the utilization of unstable environments for performance test execution. The premier example of such environments is cloud resources,

---

[5]http://openjdk.java.net/projects/code-tools/jmh/.

[6]https://golang.org/pkg/testing/.

[7]https://doc.rust-lang.org/1.7.0/book/benchmark-tests.html.

[8]https://github.com/apple/swift/tree/master/benchmark.

mostly caused by virtualization and multi-tenancy. Further work in the area of continuously assessing software performance as part of CI needs to be done. We envision a future where performance testing is as common place as unit testing is today, where each build is automatically tested for its performance characteristics, and developers receive quick feedback about these nonfunctional attributes of their software.

4 Continuous Delivery

Continuous Delivery (CD) is an agile software development practice where code changes are released to production in short cycles (i.e., daily or even hourly). A basic CD pipeline is composed by build, deploy, and test stages [123]. This practice is one of the pillars of the agile movement and is widely adopted in both open-source and industry projects by now. The regular invocations of the build-related tools (e.g., static analysis tools) and the corresponding artifacts generated in this process (e.g., build logs) open up new opportunities to better understand the development process and to build tools that support the developers early on.

4.1 Build Breakage

In the CD pipeline, a build is typically triggered during the build stage (i.e., Continuous Integration), whenever a code change is pushed in a version control system (e.g., Git). It is being checked out, compiled, tested, and analyzed for code quality measures. The build can potentially fail in any of these phases due to several reasons, for example, syntax errors, failing tests, or violations of coding conventions. Such a failing build delays the release of a new software version. Indeed, developers have to analyze and resolve the problems causing the build failure before being able to perform a new build. In such a scenario, release engineers spend at least 1 h per day to fix broken builds [66] and an organization loses a lot of man-hours because of many build failures occurring during a working day.

Thus, it's crucial to support developers in (1) identifying faster and better the problem causing a build failure and (2) fixing easily those problems.

The first step to meet those two challenges has been a deep understanding of the types of build failures. We performed a large study [124] of 34,182 build failures occurred in OSS and in a large financial organization, namely, ING Nederland. The purpose of this study was to compute a taxonomy of build failures and compare the frequencies of each category in a closed-source (i.e., ING) and an open-source (i.e., Travis CI[9]) environment.

Through the analysis of the build failures in 349 Java Maven projects from Travis CI and 418 (mostly Java) Maven projects from ING, we derived a Build Failures Catalog including 20 categories. We briefly describe the most important types.

Compilation is the category including builds failed during the compilation of production and test code. A compilation of a code change might not succeed because of language constructs unsupported by the build environment or due to annotations unsupported by the installed Java VM.

Dependencies are another substantial source of build failures. Typical errors in this category are invalid resource configurations or failed downloads due to unavailable artifacts.

Testing failures also break the build. This category is divided in other sub-categories based on the testing activity involved in the failure (e.g., unit testing, integration testing, nonfunctional testing).

Code Analysis enforces code changes to follow predefined code quality criteria. Thus, a build might fail because of non-passed quality gates.

Deployment of artifacts resulting from an introduced code change causes other types of build failures. The deployment environment might be set up incorrectly or the new application version simply doesn't harmonize.

Given this catalog of build failures, we compute and compare the percentages of build failures of different types for both industrial (i.e., ING) and OSS projects. Then we analyzed differences and commonalities. Except for dependencies, we observed a quite different distribution of build failure types in the two domains under analysis.

Specifically, integration testing failures are more frequent in industry than in OSS. Instead, OSS projects exhibit more unit testing failures. Those results suggest that industrial developers are more keen on performing unit tests also before the build (see "Testing" in Fig. 1) and rely on the build server to catch mostly integration issues. In OSS, developers tend to delegate all testing activities to the build stage.

For business-critical projects like the one used by financial organizations, proper nonfunctional testing is crucial. Thus, a separate node is usually used to perform time-consuming testing activities, for example, stress testing and penetration testing. Nevertheless, exclusively industrial developers (at least in ING) started to rely on the build process to spot, whenever possible, nonfunctional issues and specifically load testing failures. It allows them to make the identification of such nonfunctional problems faster and reduce the time and the cost for fixing them.

There are more build failures due to static analysis in industry compared to OSS. Performing a qualitative analysis of both industrial and OSS build failure logs, we observed that most of the OSS projects run static analysis tools directly on the build server, while industry tends to perform static analysis on a different server using

---

[9]https://travis-ci.org.

tool as SonarQube.[10] This choice implies (1) data easy to monitor and query and (2) less overloading of the build server machine.

Finally, we observed a quite low percentage of compilation failures in both domains. This result shows how it's important to compile a code change before building it. This best practice of compiling code before building it makes the identification of the error behind a compilation failure faster and easier (i.e., it's more difficult to spot a compilation error when a code change is already integrated with other changes).

The results of our study suggest the need for supporting developers in maintaining their CD pipeline to make it more efficient, for example, by deciding what to do in private builds on the developer's local machine and what to delegate to build servers, or how to improve the overall detection of the issues by anticipating the execution of nonfunctional tests. We plan to use the taxonomy we built to make the overall process of build failure understanding faster and conceive approaches able to automate the build failure resolution.

4.2   Release Confidence and Velocity

The trend towards highly automated build, test, and deployment processes enables companies delivering their software quickly and efficiently. However, the faster a company moves, the less time is available to perform precautions to minimize the risk of releasing defective changes. Consequently, there exists an inherent trade-off between the risk of lower release quality and time to market. We investigated this trade-off and derived a model [111] based on *release confidence* and the *velocity* of releases during the course of two larger empirical studies [25, 113].

Release Confidence is the amount of confidence gained on the quality gates within a company's development and release process. Those quality gates involve automated (e.g., unit, integration, performance tests) and manual tests (e.g., user acceptance tests) and code reviews.

Release Velocity is the time it takes to assess each single quality gate starting with the developer's commit of a change until the change reaches the production environment, including the time it takes to deploy the newest version.

4.2.1   Model of Release Confidence and Velocity

Our model consists of four categories (*cautious*, *balanced*, *problematic*, *madness*), arranged on a grid from both low to high velocity and confidence. The underlying idea and vision of this model are to serve as a vehicle for self-assessment (i.e., what

---

[10]https://www.sonarqube.org.

is my company's category) and provide guidelines on how a company can transition to other categories (e.g., increase velocity while keeping confidence high).

Cautious is the category characterized by high release confidence and low velocity. Companies put a high emphasis on testing, including both a well-maintained set of automated tests to reduce the risk of human-caused errors during manual testing and supplemental manual tests to cover areas hard to test. Code reviews are a common practice complementing the testing phases. Manual approval processes (e.g., domain-specific requirements, company policies) decrease velocity and hence reduce the number of releases.

Problematic is characterized by low confidence in a company's quality gates and low velocity. Typically, this is not a category a company is placed in by choice. Insufficiently maintained test suites (automated and manual), or test suites not covering all aspects of an application, shortages in testing personnel, the absence of code reviews, and unclear roles regarding the quality assurance are characteristics for this category. Velocity is often low as a direct consequence of this, but also due to lack of automation and architectural issues.

Madness is associated with high velocity and low confidence. Release cycles are short; companies make use of early customer feedback and reduced time to market. However, quality assurance plays a minor role, but often by choice, as companies within this category decide that the benefits of sophisticated quality assurance processes are not worth the investments. Consequently, issues might be fixed fast, but the lack of quality gates leads to risky and stressful releases. This category is often appealing for companies with smaller code bases (e.g., startups) as it enables pushing new functionality fast.

Balanced is characterized by high velocity and how confidence and portrays the vision of continuous delivery and deployment [22, 62]. Companies in this category strive for a balance of having sophisticated and highly automated quality assurance processes and code reviews (for specific critical code sections) to maintain confidence on a high level and tool support that allows releasing by the push of a button. Moreover, this category provides a proper basis for post-deployment quality assurance techniques (i.e., continuous experimentation), testing new functionality on a small fraction of the user base first [113].

4.2.2 Transitioning Between Categories

The derived model serves as a starting point discussing the consequences of the categories and allows investigating research gaps not only on how we can better support companies but rather on how to guide (i.e., transition) them to other categories.

Increasing Velocity One topic of raising popularity is containerization, and especially Docker. Docker allows packaging an application with its dependencies into a standardized, self-contained unit that can be used throughout development and to run on any system, being it the development machine, but also the production server.

Its concept of lightweight virtualization speeds up the process of bringing a change into the production system without having to deal with different hardware and software platforms and their dependencies. In a recent study [26] we investigated the Docker ecosystem on GitHub to understand its evolution and identify quality issues. One of the findings is that there is space for improvement when it comes to the size of Docker images. Many projects rely on rather heavyweight OS images as their base image, which somehow defeats the original purpose of lightweight containerization. Therefore, research should aim for providing guidelines and tool support allowing projects to reduce their image sizes and consequently reduce memory consumption when deployed at scale.

Increasing Confidence Recently, the field of continuous experimentation has received increased attention by both academic research and industry (e.g., Fabijan et al. [41], Kohavi et al. [70]). The ability of experimenting with new functionality on a small fraction of the user base enables companies getting early feedback from real-world users while at the same time keeping the risk manageable in case that something goes wrong. Tooling to support experimentation includes our own tool called Bifrost [112], Vamp,[11] and Spinnaker.[12] Bifrost and Vamp support the automated, data-driven execution of experiments defined in a domain-specific language. Spinnaker serves as an extension to a CI system allowing to define additional steps for experimentation.

5   Deployment

After completing several iterations of the development cycle introduced in the beginning of this chapter, the updated product will eventually be deployed to its users. While professional software developers are mostly concerned with the quality and state of the current and upcoming releases, it is often desirable to reflect on the long-term evolution of a software project. Managers and project coordinators may be interested in learning how different parts of a project evolve, for example, to reallocate resources and estimate future effort [31, 69, 78, 121]. Modern version control systems present a rich opportunity for understanding the history of a project, but the wealth of information contained within them needs to be managed appropriately.

Two of the main challenges in analyzing the history of a project are the computational time and resource requirements. Running a static analysis tool, for example, to detect bugs or compute various software metrics, can easily take several minutes for a single release. Repeating the analysis for hundreds or even thousands

---

[11]https://vamp.io/.

[12]https://www.spinnaker.io/.

of past releases quickly becomes infeasible. Research has yielded two main avenues of solving this problem: (1) scaling analyses via additional resources, such as clustered computations, and (2) increasing the efficiency of analyses by reducing redundant computation.

A prime example of the former is BOA [40], a server framework that allows analysts to formulate and execute analyses which are executed on a Hadoop cluster. BOA supports analyzing metadata of historical commits (e.g., to learn more about how developers have authored code in the past). It also supports the analysis of Java ASTs to do perform static analyses. For industrial companies, a setup such as this can be useful if there is a large volume of historical code to be analyzed on a regular basis—otherwise, the resources may lay idle.

An alternative to adding more resources is to reduce redundancies during the analyses of past revisions as much as possible. This is done, for example, by LISA, a stand-alone library for running arbitrary analyses on multi-revision graphs [2]. Changes between two subsequent revisions of a software project typically concern only a fraction of the source code, while most of the source code remains identical. LISA exploits this fact by loading source code ASTs and other graphs in such a manner that each node (which might, e.g., represent a Java class) is stored only once for any range of revisions where there have been no changes. While analyzing the graphs, for example, to compute code metrics, computations need only be run once for these entire ranges. This reduces the average time per revision by multiple orders of magnitude compared to the naive approach of analyzing revisions individually. This approach is advantageous when resources cannot be permanently assigned for the analysis of historical data.

No matter which way historical data is computed, the goal is to obtain actionable knowledge on the health of a project. An example for how this can be achieved is Evolizer [48], a library that draws data from both version control systems as well as bug trackers and enables the joined analysis of both resources. Evolizer has, for example, been used to link commits with bug tracking data to automatically determine which parts of the source code are more bug prone, since commits to the same file referencing bugs more frequently are likely to be more fragile. Evolizer has also been used to discover which parts of the source code coevolve and are thus logically coupled.

Current research is addressing the challenges in obtaining linked, historical data efficiently, and it has shown that using this data can provide valuable and useful indicators that can allow software developers to manage the complexity inherent in modern software systems. Exploiting historical data like this allows them to make decisions more confidently and increase the effectiveness of allocated resources, improving the quality and reliability of software in the long term.

6 Summarization Techniques for Code, Change, Testing, Software Reuse, and User Feedback

In the current software industry, developers are involved in a fierce competition to acquire and retain users. Thus, in this competitive market, understanding the factors affecting users' experience and satisfaction and how these factors are related to software quality represents a valuable benefit for developers interested to evolve their software applications [52]. Moreover, with the introduction of Continuous Development and Continuous Integration software practices, it is becoming important for software developers to speed up development activities without hindering the reliability and quality of the produced software [23]. Thus, for "modern software companies it is nowadays, crucial to enact a software development process able (i) to dynamically react to market requirements (i.e., users requests), (ii) delivering at same time high quality and reliable software". To achieve this high-level goal, developers have to efficiently deal with the huge amount of heterogeneous data [86, 96] they have at their disposal, for example, bug reports [89, 103], source code [14, 56, 75, 81, 115, 116], test cases [44, 94, 123], mailing lists [36, 89], question and answer site (Q&A) discussions [122, 126], user feedback [37, 38, 92], and other kinds of development artifacts [86, 96].

According to its original definition or concept, a *Summarization approach* has the general capability of automatically **extracting** or **abstracting** key content from one or more sources of information [55], thus determining the relevant information in the source being summarized and reducing its content (see Fig. 2). Specifically, the *extraction* capability consists of "selecting original pieces from the source document and concatenating them to yield a shorter text" while the abstraction capability is different as it "paraphrases in more general terms what the text is about" [55]. Both the two categories of summaries can be either *indicative*, *informative*, or *critical*:

- *Indicative summary*: it provides a direct link to the required content or relevant sources to users, so that they can read the provided information more depth.
- *Informative summary*: it has the goal to substitute the original source of information, by mainly assembling the relevant content, presenting it in a new, more concise, and structured form.
- *Critical summary (or review)*: it reports or selects the main opinions or statements related to a specific discussed topic; thus, it brings the most relevant feedback, both positives and negatives, about a given subject discussed in the source document.

Given the great potential of such approaches, in recent years, *Summarization techniques* [55, 86] have been explored by SE researchers to conceive approaches and tools that support developers to deal with the management of such a huge amount of heterogeneous data, coming from different sources of information [80, 86, 94, 96].

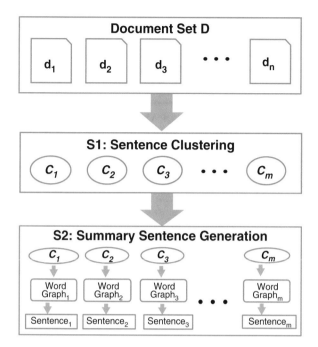

Fig. 2 High-level view of summarization approaches

In this section, we provide an overview of the summarization techniques explored in the literature for supporting developers during program comprehension, development, maintenance, and testing tasks, by leveraging the abovementioned heterogeneous data. A more detailed and exhaustive literature review on summarization techniques proposed in SE research is reported in recent work [80, 86].

6.1 Source Code Summarization

First attempts on the adoption of summarization techniques to SE problems were of Murphy [84] and Sridhara [115].

The work by Murphy [84] was the first that proposed to generate summaries of source code by analyzing its structural information. In particular, he proposed to use summarization techniques of such techniques for generating abstractive descriptions of its behavior, to automatically document or re-document source code with the generated summaries. Sridhara [115] extended such previous work by Murphy, suggesting the use of predefined *natural language templates*, filled with the main linguistic elements (e.g., verbs, nouns, etc.) [33, 34] composing the signature of methods, to generate the summaries.

On top of such previous work, other researchers used a similar strategy to summarize other kinds of software artifacts at different levels of abstraction: parameters [118], groups of statements [117], Java methods [56, 75, 116], Java classes [81], and services of Java packages [57].

The main limit of such work is that they generate source code descriptions or summaries by only analyzing the static information available in the source code itself. Thus, they are not able to describe the high-level behavior and meaning of the described software artifact, something that developers often report in various communication means, such as mailing list [10, 90], issue trackers [89, 90, 104], IRC chat log [90], and other developers communication means. For this reason, recent work proposed to generate source code documentation by mining text data from other sources of information, alternative to source code: question and answer site (Q&A) discussions [122, 126], bug reports [89, 104], e-mails [89], and forum posts.

6.2 Task-Driven Software Summarization

A limit of approaches proposed for *Code Summarization* regards the way in which SE researchers evaluated their usefulness. Indeed, Binkley et al. [14] and Jones et al. [114] highlighted that the evaluation of summarization techniques for SE should not be done by using simple metrics, answering the general question "is this a good summary?". Thus, they proposed the concept of *Task-Driven Software Summarization* where summarization techniques for SE should be evaluated "through the lens of a particular task" (e.g., during bug fixing or testing tasks). Stemming from the observations made by Binkley et al. [14] and Jones et al. [114], recent work proposed approaches for automating particular software maintenance and testing tasks [80, 86], evaluating their practical usefulness in their specific utilization context.

6.2.1 Code Change Summarization

Code change summarization approaches have the goal of augmenting the context provided by differencing tools, generating natural language descriptions of changes occurred at different types of software artifacts [80, 86].

An example of such differencing tools is the *Semantic Diff* tool introduced by Jackson and Ladd [71] which detects differences between two versions of a procedure and uses program analysis techniques to summarize the semantic differences. More recent and modern examples of differencing tools are *DeltaDoc* [18] and *Commit 2.0* [30] that (1) describe source code modifications using symbolic execution with summarization techniques and (2) augment commit logs with a visual context of the changes, respectively. However, most of code change summarization approaches proposed in the literature [28, 82] are based on a specific, well-known differencing tool called *Change Distiller*, implemented by Fluri et al. [43], which extracts fine-grained source code changes based on a specialized tree differencing algorithm. Thus, Change Distiller generates a list of classified changes based on the operation type performed by the developers in the analyzed commit, that is, *insertion*, *deletion*, or *modification*. On top of such change types information, it generates the corresponding customized abstract syntax tree.

Hence, information coming from Change Distiller tools have been exploited, for example, by researchers to automatically generate high-quality (1) commit messages [28] and (2) release notes [82]. Specifically, the approach for generating commit messages, called Change Scribe, conceived by Cortes-Coy et al. [28] takes as input two consecutive versions of a Java project; then it (1) uses Change Distiller to extract the source code changes occurred between the two versions of the project (changes related to addition, removal, or modification types); (2) detects responsibilities of methods within each Java class using the concept of method stereotypes; (3) characterizes the change set using commit stereotypes; (4) estimates the impact set for the changes in the commit; (5) performs the selection of the content considering the threshold values defined by the developer; and (6) finally generates the change descriptions for the analyzed commit. The tool proposed by Moreno et al. [82], called ARENA, extended the work by Cortes-Coy et al. [28], extracting the information about the change types from two different sources of information, namely, the versioning system and the source archives of the releases to be com- pared. ARENA and Change Scribe achieved high accuracy in generating high-quality commit messages and release notes. Indeed, in some cases, according to the involved study participants, they were often preferred to the one written by the original developers.

6.2.2   Summarization Techniques for Testing and Code Reuse

As discussed previously, most of previous works on source code and code change summarization have been evaluated by simply surveying developers about the general quality of the provided summaries [14, 56, 75, 81, 115, 116]. However, recent work proposed summarization techniques to support developers during bug fixing and/or testing tasks [65, 94], demonstrating their practical usefulness in performing such tasks.

Specifically, since *Waterfall* up until *Agile*, Software Testing has been playing an essential role in any software development methodology to detect the defects of software products in different target environments. However, developers perceived testing as a time-consuming task because it requires a quarter of their working time engineering tests [13] and up to 50% of the overall project effort [15]. In this scenario, automated test generation tools [46, 47] in software development pipelines could potentially reduce the time spent by developers in writing test cases. The main advantages of such tools include the generation of tests achieving higher code coverage when compared to the coverage obtained through manual testing [47] and to find violations of undeclared exceptions [46].

Despite such undisputed advantages, nowadays, automated test generation tools are still not used in practice. The main reason is that the generated tests are too hard to understand and difficult to maintain [29, 94]. As a consequence, generated tests do not improve the ability of developers to detect faults when compared to manual testing [20, 47]. Thus, to foster the adoption of automated testing tools, Panichella et al. [94] presented *TestDescriber*, a tool that summarizes both automatically generated or manually written JUnit test cases. Specifically, taking as input the JUnit test and the corresponding class under test (CUT), TestDescriber (i) runs each test method tracing statements and branches exercised in the CUT and (iii) augments the JUnit test with summaries that, at different abstraction levels, provides a dynamic view of the CUT.

Having TestDescriber at their disposal, Panichella et al. [94] performed an empirical study [94] to investigate the usefulness of the proposed tool when used in a concrete scenario of use: a Java class has been modified or developed and must be tested using generated test cases with the purpose of identifying and fixing eventual bugs affecting the production code. Thus, the goal of the study was to determine the impact of the generated test summaries on the number of bugs actually fixed by developers when assisted by automated test generation tools. The results of our study show that participants without TestDescriber summaries were able to remove only 40% of bugs present on the considered classes. Instead, when relying on test case with summaries, TestDescriber improved the bug fixing performance of the participants from 50% up to 100%. The results of the Wilcoxon test highlighted that the result was statistically significant (with p-values always <0.05).

Thus, differently from most work in the literature, the work by Panichella et al. [94] is the first that deals with the defect or bug detection. Indeed, it is important to mention that other recent work in the literature proposed the use of NLP templates and/or summarization techniques mostly to document undocumented part of source code, without addressing the problem of bug detection [80, 86]. Following this line of research, Zhou et al. [130] proposed an approach based on NLP templates, able to detect *API defects* in Java Libraries. Specifically, application programming interfaces (APIs) represent the most adopted tools for developers to build complex software systems nowadays. However, several studies have revealed that also major API providers tend to have an incomplete or inconsistent API documentation. This severely hampers the API comprehension and the quality of software built on it. Thus, Zhou et al. [130] proposed DRONE, a framework to automatically detect and repair defects affecting API documents by leveraging techniques from program analysis, natural language processing, and constraint solving. The research evaluation involving part of well-documented JDK 1.8 APIs has shown that DRONE is able to detect API defects with an average F-measure of 79.9%, 71.7%, and 81.4%, respectively, demonstrating its usefulness.

6.3   Summarization of Textual User Feedback

In the current software industry, developers are involved in a fierce competition to acquire and retain users. Thus, in this competitive market, understanding the factors affecting users' experience and satisfaction and how these factors are related to software quality represents a valuable benefit for developers interested to evolve their software applications. In this context, app stores, such as Google Play or the Apple Store, allow users to provide feedback on apps by posting review comments and giving star ratings. The experience an end user has with apps reported in user reviews is a key concern when creating and maintaining any successful application. For this reason, mobile developers are interested to exploiting opinions and/or feedback of end users during the evolution of their software [24, 125].

As discussed previously, automatically generated summaries can be either *indicative*, *informative*, or *critical* [55]. Specifically, a **critical summary (or review)** reports or selects the main opinions or statements related to a specific discussed topic; thus, it brings the most relevant feedback, both positives and negatives, about a given subject discussed in the source document. Thus, the peculiarity of critical summaries has pushed researchers to conceive tools for automatically extracting user feedback from user review, relevant for software evolution [24, 27, 53, 54, 63, 74, 92, 93]. For instance, Chen et al. presented a computational framework which automatically groups, prioritizes, and visualizes informative reviews [24]. However, most of proposed tools only perform a simple classification of user reviews according to specific topics [53, 54, 63, 88, 92, 92], without reducing the amount of reviews developers have to deal with, which is very large for popular apps.

A more recent work by Ciurumelea et al. [27] proposed an approach that classifies reviews according to more fine-grained topics addressed by users in app reviews, which uses machine learning to classify reviews according to such topics. In addition, to deal with such an amount of user review data, Di Sorbo et al. [37, 38] proposed an approach called SURF, which at the same time (1) determines the specific topic discussed in the review (e.g., UI improvements, security issues, etc.), (2) identifies the maintenance task to perform for addressing the request stated in the review (e.g., bug fixing, feature enhancement, etc.), and (3) presents such information to developers as an actionable *condensed, interactive, and structured agenda of recommended software changes*. The approach relies on a conceptual model of the user requests reported by app reviews; then it uses sophisticated summarization approaches, based on machine learning and NLP techniques, for summarizing thousands of reviews. Di Sorbo et al. [37, 38] performed an end-to-end evaluation of the proposed approach on user reviews of 17 mobile apps involving 23 developers. Results demonstrate high accuracy of SURF in summarizing reviews containing feedback for planning future software changes, substantially reducing the time and effort required for manually analyzing user review content.

6.4 Future Research

Recent research in SE observed an increasing adoption of summarization techniques for accomplishing simple or more complex development, maintenance, and testing tasks. However, their adoption in industrial contexts requires substantial novel and advanced research to make them applicable in any industrial or open-source organizations. Thus, future research in the field is devoted to fill the existing gap between industrial needs and current provided research prototypes:

- *Summarization of heterogeneous data*: current summarization approaches are mostly conceived for analyzing one or two sources of information. However, when performing development, maintenance, and testing tasks, developers access various types of heterogeneous data. Thus, future summarization techniques should be designed with advanced mechanisms able to distill, in a simultaneous manner, the relevant knowledge present in different sources of information, presenting it in a unified manner, depending on the specific task the developer is performing.
- *Scalability and integration in the CD/CI process*: current summarization approaches are able to proficiently distill relevant information from various kinds of software artifacts. However, they are usually computationally expensive and thus not applicable in real working contexts. Moreover, most of such tools are difficult to integrate in the current continuous delivery software development process. Hence, future research should be devoted on designing tools able to analyze, with substantial low computational cost, the huge amount of available heterogeneous data, integrating the summarized information in the various development phases composing the CD pipeline applied in a software organization.
- *Visualization of software summaries*: most of the generated software summaries are presented as a set of textual fragments that share similar concepts. Thus, part of the future research related to the application of source code and code change summarization needs to be devoted to the definition of proper visualization metaphors that actually present the information provided by the generated summaries in a more structured manner.

7 Summary

Today's software development is about data and processes. Environments and tools are cornerstones for any successful project. At the same time, we need to adopt new techniques from research to deal with this sheer amount of information that ranges from requirements to code, to tests, and to deployment and experimentation.

We discussed several techniques and their potential for these data-driven decisions and actions that are ready for use in practice. The techniques that we presented originate mostly from our own research and provide new solutions to recommender systems, automated test case generation, performance testing, continuous integration and continuous deployment, evolution analysis feedbacks, and summarization techniques for code or tests.

The next step is to adopt and integrate these and other techniques in the daily development activities and engineering processes. We showed some of the great potential of these technologies in dealing with the large amount of data that is available in any process step of software development.

New development environments are rising that support live development (in the cloud). Such tools require data that is beyond static code or test data; we need to build active feedback loops into the programming environments that employ proper data analytics customized for each development step. Tools such as live programming or programming in the cloud will then be eased and be put on a much more stable basis. With the increasing speed of software delivery to customers, these links between the developer and the customer need to become seamless and active, building on the data aggregated, accumulated, and analyzed for recommendations, summarizations, or testing in various dimensions.

References

1. Alcocer, J.P.S., Bergel, A., Valente, M.T.: Learning from source code history to identify performance failures. In: Proceedings of the 7th ACM/ SPEC International Conference on Performance Engineering (ICPE), pp. 37–48 (2016)
2. Alexandru, C.V., Panichella, S., Gall, H.: Reducing redundancies in multi-revision code analysis. In: IEEE International Conference on Software Analysis, Evolution and Reengineering (SANER), Klagenfurt (2017)
3. Ali, S., Briand, L.C., Hemmati, H., Panesar-Walawege, R.K.: A systematic review of the application and empirical investigation of search-based test case generation. IEEE Trans. Softw. Eng. **36**(6), 742–762 (2010)
4. Allamanis, M., Sutton, C.: Mining source code repositories at massive scale using language modeling. In: Proceedings of the 10th Working Conference on Mining Software Repositories, MSR '13, pp. 207–216. IEEE Press, Piscataway (2013)
5. Allamanis, M., Barr, E.T., Bird, C., Sutton, C.: Learning natural coding conventions. In: Proceedings of the 22nd ACM SIGSOFT International Symposium on Foundations of Software Engineering, FSE 2014, pp. 281–293. ACM, New York (2014)
6. Allamanis, M., Barr, E.T., Bird, C., Sutton, C.: Suggesting accurate method and class names. In: Proceedings of the 2015 10th Joint Meeting on Foundations of Software Engineering, ESEC/FSE 2015, pp. 38–49. ACM, New York (2015)
7. Allamanis, M., Barr, E.T., Devanbu, P., Sutton, C.: A Survey of Machine Learning for Big Code and Naturalness. arXiv e-prints, September 2017
8. Amann, S., Proksch, S., Nadi, S.: FeedBaG: an interaction tracker for visual studio. In: International Conference on Program Comprehension. IEEE, Piscataway (2016)
9. Amann, S., Proksch, S., Nadi, S., Mezini, M.: A study of visual studio usage in practice. In: International Conference on Software Analysis, Evolution, and Reengineering. IEEE, Piscataway (2016)
10. Bacchelli, A., Sasso, T.D., D'Ambros, M., Lanza, M.: Content classification of development emails. In: 34th International Conference on Software Engineering, ICSE 2012, June 2–9, Zurich, pp. 375–385 (2012)

11. Barr, E.T., Harman, M., McMinn, P., Shahbaz, M., Yoo, S.: The oracle problem in software testing: a survey. IEEE Trans. Softw. Eng. **41**(5), 507–525 (2015)
12. Beizer, B.: Software Testing Techniques, 2nd edn. Van Nostrand Reinhold Co., New York (1990)
13. Beller, M., Gousios, G., Panichella, A., Zaidman, A.: When, how, and why developers (do not) test in their IDEs. In: Proceedings of the 10th Joint Meeting of the European Software Engineering Conference and the ACMSIGSOFT Symposium on the Foundations of Software Engineering (ESEC/FSE). ACM, New York (2015)
14. Binkley, D., Lawrie, D., Hill, E., Burge, J., Harris, I., Hebig, R., Keszocze, O., Reed, K., Slankas, J.: Task-driven software summarization. In: Proceedings of the International Conference on Software Maintenance (ICSM), pp. 432–435. IEEE, Piscataway (2013)
15. Brooks, F.P.Jr.: The Mythical Man-Month. Addison-Wesley, Reading (1975)
16. Bruch, M., Monperrus, M., Mezini, M.: Learning from examples to improve code completion systems. In: Proceedings of the 7th Joint Meeting of the European Software Engineering Conference and the ACM SIGSOFT Symposium on the Foundations of Software Engineering, pp. 213–222. ACM, New York (2009)
17. Bulej, L., Bureš, T., Horký, V., Kotrč, J., Marek, L., Trojánek, T., Tůma, P.: Unit testing performance with stochastic performance logic. Autom. Softw. Eng. **24**(1), 139–187 (2017)
18. Buse R.P.L., Weimer, W.R.: Automatically documenting program changes. In: Proceedings of the IEEE/ACM International Conference on Automated Software Engineering, ASE '10, pp. 33–42. ACM, New York (2010)
19. Campbell, J.C., Hindle, A., Amaral, J.N.: Syntax errors just aren't natural: improving error reporting with language models. In: Proceedings of the 11th Working Conference on Mining Software Repositories, MSR 2014, pp. 252–261. ACM, New York (2014)
20. Ceccato, M., Marchetto, A., Mariani, L., Nguyen, C.D., Tonella, P.: Do automatically generated test cases make debugging easier? An experimental assessment of debugging effectiveness and efficiency. ACM Trans. Softw. Eng. Methodol. **25**(1), 5:1–5:38 (2015)
21. Chang, K.H., Cross II, J.H., Carlisle, W.H., Liao, S.-S.: A performance evaluation of heuristics-based test case generation methods for software branch coverage. Int. J. Softw. Eng. Knowl. Eng. **6**(04), 585–608 (1996)
22. Chen, L.: Continuous delivery: huge benefits, but challenges too. Softw. IEEE **32**(2), 50–54 (2015)
23. Chen, L.: Continuous delivery: overcoming adoption challenges. J. Syst. Softw. **128**, 72–86 (2017)
24. Chen, N., Lin, J., Hoi, S.C.H., Xiao, X., Zhang, B.: Ar-miner: mining informative reviews for developers from mobile app marketplace. In: Proceedings of the 36th International Conference on Software Engineering, ICSE 2014, pp. 767–778. ACM, New York (2014)
25. Cito, J., Leitner, P., Fritz, T., Gall, H.C.: The making of cloud applications: an empirical study on software development for the cloud. In: Proceedings of the 2015 10th Joint Meeting on Foundations of Software Engineering (ESEC/FSE), pp. 393–403. ACM, New York (2015)
26. Cito, J., Schermann, G., Wittern, J.E., Leitner, P., Zumberi, S., Gall, H.C.: An empirical analysis of the docker container ecosystem on github. In: Proceedings of the 14th International Conference on Mining Software Repositories, MSR '17, pp. 323–333. IEEE Press, Piscataway (2017)
27. Ciurumelea, A., Schaufelbühl, A., Panichella, S., Gall, H.: Analyzing reviews and code of mobile apps for better release planning. In: 2017 IEEE 24th IEEE International Conference on Software Analysis, Evolution, and Reengineering (SANER), pp. 91–102 (2017)
28. Cortes-Coy, L.F., Vásquez, M.L., Aponte, J., Poshyvanyk, D.: On automatically generating commit messages via summarization of source code changes. In: Proceedings of the International Working Conference on Source Code Analysis and Manipulation (SCAM), pp. 275–284. IEEE, Piscataway (2014)
29. Daka, E., Campos, J., Fraser, G., Dorn, J., Weimer, W.: Modeling readability to improve unit tests. In: Proceedings of the 10th Joint Meeting of the European Software Engineering Conference and the ACMSIGSOFT Symposium on the Foundations of Software Engineering (ESEC/FSE). ACM, New York (2015)

30. D'Ambros, M., Lanza, M., Robbes, R.: Commit 2.0. In: Proceedings of the 1st Workshop on Web 2.0 for Software Engineering, Web2SE '10, pp. 14–19. ACM, New York (2010)
31. D'Ambros, M., Lanza, M., Robbes, R.: Evaluating defect prediction approaches: a benchmark and an extensive comparison. Empir. Softw. Eng. **17**(4–5), 531–577 (2012)
32. Damevski, K., Shepherd, D., Schneider, J., Pollock, L.: Mining sequences of developer interactions in visual studio for usage smells. IEEE Trans. Softw. Eng. **43**(4), 359–371 (2016)
33. De Lucia, A., Di Penta, M., Oliveto, R., Panichella, A., Panichella, S.: Using IR methods for labeling source code artifacts: is it worthwhile? In: IEEE 20th International Conference on Program Comprehension, ICPC 2012, Passau, June 11–13, 2012, pp. 193–202 (2012)
34. De Lucia, A., Di Penta, M., Oliveto, R., Panichella, A., Panichella, S.: Labeling source code with information retrieval methods: an empirical study. Empir. Softw. Eng. **19**(5), 1383–1420 (2014)
35. de Oliveira, A.B., Fischmeister, S., Diwan, A., Hauswirth, M., Sweeney, P.: Perphecy: performance regression test selection made simple but effective. In: Proceedings of the 10th IEEE International Conference on Software Testing, Verification and Validation (ICST), Tokyo (2017)
36. Di Sorbo, A., Panichella, S., Visaggio, C.A., Di Penta, M., Canfora, G., Gall, H.C.: Development emails content analyzer: intention mining in developer discussions. In: 2015, 30th IEEE/ACM International Conference on Automated Software Engineering (ASE), pp. 12–23. IEEE, Washington (2015)
37. Di Sorbo, A., Panichella, S., Alexandru, C., Shimagaki, J., Visaggio, C.A., Canfora, G., Gall, H.C.: What would users change in my app? summarizing app reviews for recommending software changes. In: 2016 ACM SIGSOFT International Symposium on the Foundations of Software Engineering (FSE), pp. 499–510 (2016)
38. Di Sorbo, A., Panichella, S., Alexandru, C.V., Visaggio, C.A., Canfora, G.: Surf: summarizer of user reviews feedback. In: Proceedings of the 39th International Conference on Software Engineering Companion, pp. 55–58. IEEE Press, Piscataway (2017)
39. Dias, M., Cassou, D., Ducasse, S.: Representing code history with development environment events. In: International Workshop on Smalltalk Technologies (2013)
40. Dyer, R.: Bringing ultra-large-scale software repository mining to the masses with Boa. PhD thesis, Ames (2013). AAI3610634
41. Fabijan, A., Dmitriev, P., Olsson, H.H., Bosch, J.: The evolution of continuous experimentation in software product development. In: International Conference on Software Engineering, ICSE, Buenos Aires (2017)
42. Ferguson, R., Korel, B.: The chaining approach for software test data generation. ACM Trans. Softw. Eng. Methodol. **5**(1), 63–86 (1996)
43. Fluri, B., Wuersch, M., PInzger, M., Gall, H.: Change distilling: tree differencing for fine-grained source code change extraction. IEEE Trans. Softw. Eng. **33**(11), 725–743 (2007)
44. Fraser, G., Arcuri, A.: Evosuite: automatic test suite generation for object-oriented software. In: Proceedings of the 19th ACM SIGSOFT Symposium and the 13th European Conference on Foundations of Software Engineering, ESEC/FSE '11, pp. 416–419. ACM, New York (2011)
45. Fraser, G., Arcuri, A.: Whole test suite generation. IEEE Trans. Softw. Eng. **39**(2), 276–291 (2013)
46. Fraser, G., Arcuri, A.: 1600 faults in 100 projects: automatically finding faults while achieving high coverage with evosuite. Empir. Softw. Eng. **20**(3), 611–639 (2015)
47. Fraser, G., Staats, M., McMinn, P., Arcuri, A., Padberg, F.: Does automated white-box test generation really help software testers? In: Proceedings of the International Symposium on Software Testing and Analysis (ISSTA), pp. 291–301. ACM, New York (2013)
48. Gall, H.C., Fluri, B., Pinzger, M.: Change analysis with evolizer and changedistiller. Software, IEEE **26**(1), 26–33 (2009)
49. Gallagher, M.J., Lakshmi Narasimhan, V: Adtest: a test data generation suite for ada software systems. IEEE Trans. Softw. Eng. **23**(8), 473–484 (1997)

50. Georges, A., Buytaert, D., Eeckhout, L.: Statistically rigorous java performance evaluation. In: Proceedings of the 22nd Annual ACM SIGPLAN Conference on Object-oriented Programming Systems and Applications, OOPSLA '07, pp. 57–76. ACM, New York (2007)
51. Goldberg, D.E.: Genetic Algorithms in Search, Optimization and Machine Learning, 1st edn. Addison-Wesley Longman Publishing Co., Inc., Boston (1989)
52. Grano, G., Di Sorbo, A., Mercaldo, F., Aaron Visaggio, C., Canfora, G., Panichella, S.: Android apps and user feedback: a dataset for software evolution and quality improvement. In: Proceedings of the 2nd ACM SIGSOFT International Workshop on App Market Analytics, WAMA@ESEC/SIGSOFT FSE 2017, Paderborn, September 5, 2017, pp. 8–11 (2017)
53. Guzman, E., Maalej, W.: How do users like this feature? A fine grained sentiment analysis of app reviews. In: 2014 IEEE 22nd International Requirements Engineering Conference (RE), pp. 153–162 (2014)
54. Ha, E., Wagner, D.: Do android users write about electric sheep? Examining consumer reviews in google play. In: Consumer Communications and Networking Conference (CCNC), 2013 IEEE, pp. 149–157 (2013)
55. Hahn, U., Mani, I.: The challenges of automatic summarization. Computer **33**(11), 29–36 (2000)
56. Haiduc, S., Aponte, J., Moreno, L., Marcus, A.: On the use of automated text summarization techniques for summarizing source code. In: Proceedings of the International Working Conference on Reverse Engineering (WCRE), pp. 35–44. IEEE, New York (2010)
57. Hammad, M., Abuljadayel, A., Khalaf, M.: Automatic summarising: the state of the art. Lect. Notes Softw. Eng. **4**(2), 129–132 (2016)
58. Heger, C., Happe, J., Farahbod, R.: Automated root cause isolation of performance regressions during software development. In: Proceedings of the 4th ACM/SPEC International Conference on Performance Engineering, ICPE '13, pp. 27–38. ACM, New York (2013)
59. Hellendoorn, V.J., Devanbu, P.T., Bacchelli, A.: Will they like this? Evaluating code contributions with language models. In: Proceedings of the 12th Working Conference on Mining Software Repositories, MSR '15, pp. 157–167. IEEE Press, Piscataway (2015)
60. Hindle, A., Barr, E.T., Su, Z., Gabel, M., Devanbu, P.: On the naturalness of software. In: Proceedings of the 34th International Conference on Software Engineering, ICSE '12, pp. 837–847. IEEE Press, Piscataway (2012)
61. Huang, P., Ma, X., Shen, D., Zhou, Y.: Performance regression testing target prioritization via performance risk analysis. In: Proceedings of the 36th International Conference on Software Engineering, ICSE 2014, pp. 60–71. ACM, New York (2014)
62. Humble, J., Farley, D.: Continuous Delivery: Reliable Software Releases Through Build, Test, and Deployment Automation. Addison-Wesley Professional, Reading (2010)
63. Iacob, C., Harrison, R.: Retrieving and analyzing mobile apps feature requests from online reviews. In: Proceedings of the 10th Working Conference on Mining Software Repositories, MSR'13, pp. 41–44. IEEE Press, Piscataway (2013)
64. Jin, G., Song, L., Shi, X., Scherpelz, J., Lu, S.: Understanding and detecting real-world performance bugs. In: Proceedings of the 33rd ACM SIGPLAN Conference on Programming Language Design and Implementation, PLDI '12, pp. 77–88. ACM, New York (2012)
65. Kamimura, M., Murphy, G.C.: Towards generating human-oriented summaries of unit test cases. In: Proceedings of the International Conference on Program Comprehension (ICPC), May, pp. 215–218. IEEE, Piscataway (2013)
66. Kerzazi, N., Khomh, F., Adams, B.: Why do automated builds break? An empirical study. In: 30th IEEE International Conference on Software Maintenance and Evolution (ICSME), pp. 41–50. IEEE, Piscataway (2014)
67. Kim, J., You, B., Kwon, M., McMinn, P., Yoo, S.: Evaluating CAVM: a new search-based test data generation tool for C. In: International Symposium on Search-Based Software Engineering (SSBSE 2017) (2017)
68. Ko, A.J., Myers, B.A., Aung, H.H.: Six learning barriers in end-user programming systems. In: 2004 IEEE Symposium on Visual Languages and Human Centric Computing, pp. 199–206. IEEE, Washington (2004)

69. Kocaguneli, E., Menzies, T., Keung, J.W.: On the value of ensemble effort estimation. IEEE Trans. Softw. Eng. **38**(6), 1403–1416 (2012)

70. Kohavi, R., Deng, A., Frasca, B., Walker, T., Xu, Y., Pohlmann, N.: Online controlled experiments at large scale. In: Proceedings of the 19th ACM SIGKDD International Conference on Knowledge Discovery and Data Mining, pp. 1168–1176. ACM, New York (2013)

71. Lahiri, S.K., Hawblitzel, C., Kawaguchi, M., Rebêlo, H.: SYMDIFF: A Language-Agnostic Semantic Diff Tool for Imperative Programs, pp. 712–717. Springer, Berlin (2012)

72. Lakhotia, K., Harman, M., Gross, H. (2013) Austin: an open source tool for search based software testing of C programs. Inf. Softw. Technol. **55**(1), 112–125 (2013)

73. Leitner, P., Bezemer, C.-P.: An exploratory study of the state of practice of performance testing in java-based open source projects. In: Proceedings of the 8th ACM/SPEC on International Conference on Performance Engineering, ICPE '17, pp. 373–384. ACM, New York (2017)

74. Maalej, W., Nabil, H.: Bug report, feature request, or simply praise? On automatically classifying app reviews. In: 2015 IEEE 23rd International Requirements Engineering Conference (RE), August, pp. 116–125 (2015)

75. McBurney, P.W., McMillan, C.: Automatic documentation generation via source code summarization of method context. In: Proceedings of the International Conference on Program Comprehension (ICPC), pp. 279–290. ACM, New York (2014)

76. McCandless, M., Hatcher, E., Gospodnetic, O.: Lucene in Action: Covers Apache Lucene 3.0. Manning Publications Co., Greenwich (2010)

77. McMinn, P.: Search-based software testing: past, present and future. In: Proceedings of the 2011 IEEE Fourth International Conference on Software Testing, Verification and Validation Workshops, ICSTW '11, pp. 153–163. IEEE Computer Society, Washington (2011)

78. Mende, T., Koschke, R.: Revisiting the evaluation of defect prediction models. In: Proceedings of the 5th International Conference on Predictor Models in Software Engineering, PROMISE '09, pp. 7:1–7:10. ACM, New York (2009)

79. Minelli, R., Mocci, A., Robbes, R., Lanza, M.: Taming the ide with fine-grained interaction data. In: International Conference on Program Comprehension (2016)

80. Moreno, L., Marcus, A.: Automatic software summarization: the state of the art. In: Proceedings of the 39th International Conference on Software Engineering, ICSE 2017, Buenos Aires, May 20–28, 2017—Companion Volume, pp. 511–512 (2017)

81. Moreno, L., Aponte, J., Sridhara, G., Marcus, A., Pollock, L., Vijay-Shanker, K.: Automatic generation of natural language summaries for java classes. In: Proceedings of the International Conference on Program Comprehension (ICPC), May, pp. 23–32. IEEE, Piscataway (2013)

82. Moreno, L., Bavota, G., Di Penta, M., Oliveto, R., Marcus, A., Canfora, G.: Automatic generation of release notes. In: Proceedings of the 22nd ACM SIGSOFT International Symposium on Foundations of Software Engineering, (FSE-22), Hong Kong, November 16–22, 2014, pp. 484–495 (2014)

83. Moritz, E., Linares-Vásquez, M., Poshyvanyk, D., Grechanik, M., McMillan, C., Gethers, M.: Export: detecting and visualizing API usages in large source code repositories. In: Proceedings of the 28th IEEE/ACM International Conference on Automated Software Engineering, pp. 646–651. IEEE Press, Piscataway (2013)

84. Murphy, G.C.: Lightweight structural summarization as an aid to software evolution. PhD thesis (1996). AAI9704521

85. Murphy, G.C., Kersten, M., Findlater, L.: How are java software developers using the eclipse IDE? IEEE Softw. **23**(4), 76–83 (2006)

86. Nazar, N., Hu, Y., Jiang, H.: Summarizing software artifacts: a literature review. J. Comput. Sci. Technol. **31**(5), 883–909 (2016)

87. Negara, S., Vakilian, M., Chen, N., Johnson, R.E., Dig, D.: Is it dangerous to use version control histories to study source code evolution? In: European Conference on Object-Oriented Programming, pp. 79–103. Springer, Heidelberg (2012)

88. Palomba, F., Salza, P., Ciurumelea, A., Panichella, S., Gall, H.C., Ferrucci, F., De Lucia, A.: Recommending and localizing change requests for mobile apps based on user reviews. In: Proceedings of the 39th International Conference on Software Engineering, ICSE 2017, Buenos Aires, May 20–28, pp. 106–117 (2017)

89. Panichella, S., Aponte, J., Di Penta, M., Marcus, A., Canfora, G.: Mining source code descriptions from developer communications. In: Proceedings of the International Conference on Program Comprehension, ICPC, pp. 63–72. IEEE, Los Alamitos (2012)

90. Panichella, S., Bavota, G., Di Penta, M., Canfora, G., Antoniol, G.: How developers' collaborations identified from different sources tell us about code changes. In: 30th IEEE International Conference on Software Maintenance and Evolution, Victoria, September 29–October 3, pp. 251–260 (2014)

91. Panichella, A., Kifetew, F.M., Tonella, P.: Reformulating branch coverage as a many-objective optimization problem. In: ICST, pp. 1–10. IEEE Computer Society, Washington (2015)

92. Panichella, S., Di Sorbo, A., Guzman, E., Visaggio, C.A., Canfora, G., Gall, H.C.: How can I improve my app? Classifying user reviews for software maintenance and evolution. In: 2015 IEEE International Conference on Software Maintenance and Evolution (ICSME), pp. 281–290 (2015)

93. Panichella, S., Di Sorbo, A., Guzman, E., Visaggio, C.A., Canfora, G., Gall, G., Gall, H.C.: Ardoc: app reviews development oriented classifier. In: 2016 ACM SIGSOFT International Symposium on the Foundations of Software Engineering (FSE), pp. 1023–1027 (2016)

94. Panichella, S., Panichella, A., Beller, M., Zaidman, A., Gall, H.C.: The impact of test case summaries on bug fixing performance: an empirical investigation. In: Proceedings of the 38th International Conference on Software Engineering, ICSE '16, pp. 547–558. ACM, New York (2016)

95. Ponzanelli, L., Bavota, G., Di Penta, M., Oliveto, R., Lanza, M.: Prompter: a self-confident recommender system. In: 2014 IEEE International Conference on Software Maintenance and Evolution (ICSME), pp. 577–580. IEEE, Victoria (2014)

96. Ponzanelli, L., Mocci, A., Lanza, M.: Summarizing complex development artifacts by mining heterogeneous data. In: Proceedings of the 12th Working Conference on Mining Software Repositories, MSR '15, pp. 401–405. IEEE Press, Piscataway (2015)

97. Proksch, S., Bauer, V., Murphy, G.C.: How to build a recommendation system for software engineering. In: Software Engineering. Springer, Berlin (2015)

98. Proksch, S., Lerch, J., Mezini, M.: Intelligent code completion with Bayesian networks. Trans. Softw. Eng. Methodol. **25**(1), 3 (2015)

99. Proksch, S., Amann, S., Nadi, S., Mezini, M.: Evaluating the evaluations of code recommender systems: a reality check. In: International Conference on Automated Software Engineering. ACM, New York (2016)

100. Proksch, S., Amann, S., Nadi, S.: Enriched event streams: a general dataset for empirical studies on in-IDE activities of software developers. In: International Conference on Mining Software Repositories (accepted Mining Challenge) (2017)

101. Proksch, S., Nadi, S., Amann, S., Mezini, M.: Enriching in-IDE process information with fine-grained source code history. In: International Conference on Software Analysis, Evolution, and Reengineering (2017)

102. Radevski, S., Hata, H., Matsumoto, K.: Towards building api usage example metrics. In: 2016 IEEE 23rd International Conference on Software Analysis, Evolution, and Reengineering (SANER), vol. 1, pp. 619–623. IEEE, Piscataway (2016)

103. Rastkar, S., Murphy, G.C., Murray, G.: Summarizing software artifacts: a case study of bug reports. In: Proceedings of the 32Nd ACM/IEEE International Conference on Software Engineering - volume 1, ICSE '10, pp. 505–514 (2010)

104. Rastkar, S., Murphy, G.C., Murray, G.: Automatic summarization of bug reports. IEEE Trans. Softw. Eng. **40**(4), 366–380 (2014)

105. Ray, B., Hellendoorn, V., Godhane, S., Tu, Z., Bacchelli, A., Devanbu, P.: On the "naturalness" of buggy code. In: Proceedings of the 38th International Conference on Software Engineering, ICSE '16, pp. 428–439. ACM, New York (2016)

106. Robillard, M.P.: What makes APIs hard to learn? Answers from developers. IEEE Softw. **26**(6), 27–39 (2009)
107. Rojas, J.M., Fraser, G., Arcuri, A.: Automated unit test generation during software development: a controlled experiment and think-aloud observations. In: Proceedings of the 2015 International Symposium on Software Testing and Analysis, ISSTA 2015, pp. 338–349. ACM, New York (2015)
108. Saied, M.A., Benomar, O., Abdeen, H., Sahraoui, H.: Mining multi-level api usage patterns. In: 2015 IEEE 22nd International Conference on Software Analysis, Evolution and Reengineering (SANER), pp. 23–32. IEEE, Piscataway (2015)
109. Saied, M.A., Benomar, O., Abdeen, H., Sahraoui, H.: Mining multi-level api usage patterns. In: 2015 IEEE 22nd International Conference on Software Analysis, Evolution and Reengineering (SANER), pp. 23–32. IEEE, Piscataway (2015)
110. Scalabrino, S., Grano, G., Di Nucci, D., Oliveto, R., De Lucia, A.: Search-based testing of procedural programs: iterative single-target or multi-target approach? In: Search Based Software Engineering, October, pp. 64–79. Springer, Cham (2016)
111. Schermann, G., Cito, J., Leitner, P., Gall, H.C.: Towards quality gates in continuous delivery and deployment. In: 2016 IEEE 24th International Conference on Program Comprehension (ICPC), pp. 1–4. IEEE, Piscataway (2016)
112. Schermann, G., Schöni, D., Leitner, P., Gall, H.C.: Bifrost: supporting continuous deployment with automated enactment of multi-phase live testing strategies. In: Proceedings of the 17th International Middleware Conference, pp. 12:1–12:14. ACM, New York (2016)
113. Schermann, G., Cito, J., Leitner, P., Zdun, U., Gall, H.C.: We're doing it live: an empirical study on continuous experimentation. J. Inf. Softw. Technol. (2017, under submission)
114. Spärck Jones, K.: Automatic summarising: the state of the art. Inf. Process. Manage. **43**(6), 1449–1481 (2007)
115. Sridhara, G.: Automatic generation of descriptive summary comments for methods in object-oriented programs. PhD thesis, Newark (2012). AAI3499878
116. Sridhara, G., Hill, E., Muppaneni, D., Pollock, L., Vijay-Shanker, K.: Towards automatically generating summary comments for java methods. In: Proceedings of the International Conference on Automated Software Engineering (ASE), pp. 43–52. ACM, Piscataway (2010)
117. Sridhara, G., Pollock, L., Vijay-Shanker, K.: Automatically detecting and describing high level actions within methods. In: Proceedings of the International Conference on Software Engineering (ICSE), pp. 101–110. IEEE, Piscataway (2011)
118. Sridhara, G., Pollock, L., Vijay-Shanker, K.: Generating parameter comments and integrating with method summaries. In: Proceedings of the International Conference on Program Comprehension (ICPC), pp. 71–80. IEEE, Piscataway (2011)
119. Stefan, P., Horky, V., Bulej, L., Tuma, P.: Unit testing performance in java projects: are we there yet? In: Proceedings of the 8th ACM/SPEC on International Conference on Performance Engineering, ICPE '17, pp. 401–412. ACM, New York (2017)
120. Tu, Z., Su, Z., Devanbu, P.: On the localness of software. In: Proceedings of the 22nd ACM SIGSOFT International Symposium on Foundations of Software Engineering, FSE 2014, pp. 269–280. ACM, New York (2014)
121. VanHilst, M., Huang, S., Mulcahy, J., Ballantyne, W., Suarez-Rivero, E., Harwood, D.: Measuring effort in a corporate repository. In: IRI, pp. 246–252. IEEE Systems, Man, and Cybernetics Society, Piscataway (2011)
122. Vassallo, C., Panichella, S., Di Penta, M., Canfora, G.: Codes: mining source code descriptions from developers discussions. In: Proceedings of the International Conference on Program Comprehension (ICPC), pp. 106–109. ACM, New York (2014)
123. Vassallo, C., Zampetti, F., Romano, D., Beller, M., Panichella, A., Di Penta, M., Zaidman, A.: Continuous delivery practices in a large financial organization. In: 2016 IEEE International Conference on Software Maintenance and Evolution, ICSME 2016, Raleigh, October 2–7, 2016, pp. 519–528 (2016)
124. Vassallo, C., Schermann, G., Zampetti, F., Romano, D., Leitner, P., Zaidman, A., Di Penta, M., Panichella, S.: A tale of ci build failures: an open source and a financial organization perspective (2017)

125. Vithani, T.: Modeling the mobile application development lifecycle. In: Proceedings of the International MultiConference of Engineers and Computer Scientists 2014, vol. I, IMECS 2014, pp. 596–600 (2014)
126. Wong, E., Yang, J., Tan, L.: Autocomment: mining question and answer sites for automatic comment generation. In: Proceedings of the International Conference on Automated Software Engineering (ASE), pp. 562–567. IEEE, Piscataway (2013)
127. Wu, H.C., Luk, R.W.P., Wong, K.F., Kwok, K.L.: Interpreting tf-idf term weights as making relevance decisions. ACM Trans. Inf. Syst. (TOIS) **26**(3), 13 (2008)
128. Xie, T., Pei, J.: Mapo: mining api usages from open source repositories. In: Proceedings of the 2006 International Workshop on Mining Software Repositories, pp. 54–57. ACM, New York (2006)
129. Zagalsky, A., Barzilay, O., Yehudai, A.: Example overflow: using social media for code recommendation. In: Proceedings of the Third International Workshop on Recommendation Systems for Software Engineering, pp. 38–42. IEEE Press, Piscataway (2012)
130. Zhou, Y., Gu, R., Chen, T., Huang, Z., Panichella, S., Gall, H.C.: Analyzing apis documentation and code to detect directive defects. In: Proceedings of the 39th International Conference on Software Engineering, ICSE 2017, Buenos Aires, May 20–28, 2017, pp. 27–37 (2017)

Software Architecture: Past, Present, Future

Wilhelm Hasselbring

1 Introduction

For large, complex software systems, the design of the overall system structure (the software architecture) is an essential challenge. The *architecture* of a software system defines that system in terms of components and connections among those components [55, 58]. It is not the *design* of that system which is more detailed. The architecture shows the correspondence between the requirements and the constructed system, thereby providing some rationale for the design decisions. This level of design has been addressed in a number of ways including informal diagrams and descriptive terms, module interconnection languages, and frameworks for systems that serve the needs of specific application domains. An architecture embodies decisions about quality properties. It represents the earliest opportunity for evaluating those decisions. Furthermore, reusability of components and services depends on how strongly coupled they are with other components in the system architecture. Performance, for instance, depends largely upon the complexity of the required coordination, in particular when the components are distributed via some network. The architecture is usually the first artifact to be examined when a programmer (particularly a maintenance programmer) unfamiliar with the system begins to work on it. Software architecture is often the first design artifact that represents decisions on how requirements of all types are to be achieved. As the manifestation of early design decisions, it represents design decisions that are hardest to change and hence most deserving of careful consideration.

W. Hasselbring (✉)
Kiel University, Kiel, Germany
e-mail: hasselbring@email.uni-kiel.de

© The Author(s) 2018
V. Gruhn, R. Striemer (eds.), *The Essence of Software Engineering*,
https://doi.org/10.1007/978-3-319-73897-0_10

169

In the following, I take a look backwards to the past development of software architecture as a discipline (Sect. 2) and at the present state (Sect. 3) and provide my view on the envisioned future (Sect. 4), before I summarize in Sect. 5.

2 Past: Focus on Architecture Description and Reuse

Long before software architecture emerged as a discipline [55], pioneers such as Parnas [49] and others [19] observed that it is not enough for a software system to produce the correct functions. Other software qualities such as dependability and maintainability are also important and can only be achieved by careful structuring of software systems.

The concept of software architecture as a distinct discipline started to emerge in the 1990s with architecture description languages, formalization, and classification of architectural styles. The study of software architecture has evolved from the seminal work of Perry and Wolf [50], Shaw and Garlan [55], and others. Architecture description languages (ADLs) [42] have emerged to provide formal rigor to architecture representation. The ANSI/IEEE standard, IEEE-Std-1471-2000, aims to codify the best practices and insights of both the systems and software engineering communities in the area of architecture documentation [36].

The structures proven in practice were cataloged and explained as patterns [13]. On the programming level, reuse is usually accomplished by means of high-level programming language constructs, function libraries, or object-oriented class frameworks. On the design level, design patterns and established software architectures are essential. Design patterns [26] are "micro-architectures" while software architectures are more coarse-grained designs. A design pattern describes solutions to a recurring problem. Patterns form larger wholes like pattern languages to provide guidance for solving complex problems. Patterns express the understanding gained from practice in software design and construction. The patterns community catalogs useful design fragments and the context that guides their use.

An architecture description language is a set of notations, languages, standards, and conventions for architectural models. In Sect. 2.1, the formalization of such architectural models is discussed. An architectural model captures part of the knowledge about an architecture for a single system or a family of systems in a domain (i.e., a reference architecture). In Sect. 2.2, the reuse of reference architectures in the context of software product line engineering is discussed.

2.1 Formalization of Architectural Models

In industrial practice, software architectures are usually described informally or semi-formally with diagrams using boxes, circles, and lines together with accompanying prose. The prose explains the diagrams and provides some rationale for

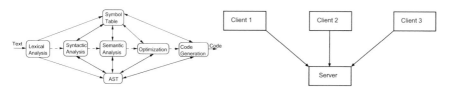

Fig. 1 Typical *pipeline* architecture for the various phases of a compiler (left) and a *client-server* architecture for information systems (right)

the chosen architecture. Typical examples are *pipeline* architectures for the various phases of a compiler or a *client-server* architecture for information systems, as illustrated in Fig. 1. Shaw and Clements called this method "boxology" [54].

Such figures often give an intuitive picture of the system's construction, but the semantics of the components and their connections/interactions may be interpreted by different people in different ways (due to the informality). Thus, such descriptions have been criticized because they lack (formal) semantics. However, they are useful for communication with stakeholders and for project planning. The degree of formality depends on the intended use of architectural models.

The UML is often employed for architecture documentation [40]. However, the UML—as a general object-oriented modeling language—provides only limited support for architecture documentation. For instance, it still lacks basic architectural concepts such as layers.

Formalizations of architecture descriptions developed in parallel with language development [2, 3]. Some specific advantages of formality in software architecture description may be summarized as follows:

- Software architectures become amenable to analysis and evaluation [16]. This helps to evaluate architectures and to guide in the selection of architectural variations as solutions to specific problems.
- Software architectures can be a basis for *design reuse* [24, 53], provided that the individual elements of the architectural descriptions are defined independently and in a precise way. Reusable architectures give designers a *blueprint* in development by helping them avoid typical design errors.
- Software architectures support improved program understanding as a basis for system evolution if its specification is well understood: Retaining the designer's intention about a system organization should help maintainers preserve the system's design integrity [8, 45].
- Formality can allow prototyping for early design evaluation [14].
- Testing may be supported by deriving test plans from formal architectural descriptions [10, 44].
- Proper tool support for designing and analyzing software architectures becomes possible [56].

The recognition that architectural analysis must reconcile multiple views helped to frame the requirements for formalism. An ADL defines a set of notations (e.g., diagrams, formal languages, natural language text fields) for each view that the ADL includes. Architecture models provide one or more views of an architecture. Views highlight certain types of information and hide other types. Examples of well-known architectural views include data-flow control-flow diagrams, state-transition diagrams, data models and entity-relation diagrams, structure charts, and object-oriented hierarchy diagrams.

Formalization of architectural styles aims to allow formal checks of conformance between architecture and implementation, to predict the impact of changes, and to formally reason about a system's architectural description [2]. Various approaches to formalizing architectural styles have been proposed [9, 31, 48]. The formal comparison allows for a detailed analysis of similarities and differences among the architectural variations.

2.2 Software Product Lines for Reusing Software Components

Software architectures usually address the quality attributes for individual systems. Systems in the same domain often have similar architectures that reflect domain concepts. Reference architectures capture architectural commonality of multiple, related systems, that is, systems within the same domain. Reference architectures are central to domain-specific reuse, in that they provide a framework for creating assets and constructing systems within a domain. Domain engineering thus allows for product line development, which seeks to achieve reuse across a family of systems.

A software product line consists of software systems that have some common functionality and some variable functionality [11]. The interest in software product lines emerged from the field of software reuse when developers and managers realized that they could obtain much greater reuse benefits by reusing software architectures instead of only reusing individual software components. The basic philosophy of software product lines is reuse through the explicitly planned exploitation of commonalities of related products and proper management of *variability* in software systems [25].

Product development in software product lines is organized into two stages: domain engineering and application engineering with reuse of software components [29]. The idea behind this approach to application engineering is that the investments required to develop the reusable artifacts during domain engineering are outweighed by the benefits of deriving the individual products during application engineering.

Reference architectures play an important role in domain engineering. *Domain engineering* is an activity for building reusable components, whereby the systematic creation of domain models and architectures is addressed. Domain engineering aims

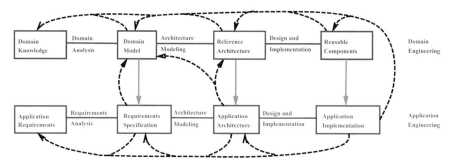

Fig. 2 Domain and application engineering for component-based software product lines [29]. In application engineering, software systems are developed from reusable components created by a domain engineering process. As indicated by the dashed arrows, multifaceted feedback is possible

at supporting *application engineering* which uses the domain models and reference architectures to build concrete systems, as illustrated in Fig. 2 [29]. The domain model characterizes the *problem space*, while the *reference architecture* addresses the *solution space* in domain engineering. The emphasis is on reuse and product lines.

3   Present: Establishment of Domain-Specific Architectures and Focus on Quality Attributes

As discussed in the previous section, the past emphasis was mainly on generic architectural styles such as pipe-and-filter architectures. However, the Domain-Specific Software Architecture (DSSA) engineering process was introduced early in the 1990s to promote a clear distinction between domain and application requirements [57]. A Domain-Specific Software Architecture consists of a domain model and a reference architecture. DSSA was promoted for domains such as avionics.

Meanwhile, various architectures are established for many domains and applications. Where total architectural solutions do not yet exist, partial ones certainly do in the form of catalogs of architectural patterns that help solve many problems and achieve various quality attributes. Various domain-specific architectures emerged, particularly from industrial practice. Examples are data warehouse architectures [60] for business analytics and, more recently, microservice architectures [46] for Internet services. Exemplary, we will take a closer look at recent microservice architectures in Sect. 3.1. Many present architecture approaches focus on quality requirements, which are discussed in Sect. 3.2.

3.1 Example: Microservice Architectures

Microservices [41, 46] are an architectural style for software which currently receives a lot of attention in both industry and academia. Especially so-called Internet-scale systems use them to satisfy their enormous scalability requirements and to rapidly deliver new features to their users. As the name implies, services are the building blocks and main means of modularization in microservice architectures. Services run in separate process contexts and can be individually deployed, replaced, and retired. The services are built around business capabilities by cross-functional teams, which are responsible for every aspect of the service from development to productive operation.

Traditionally, information system integration aims at achieving high data coherence among heterogeneous information sources [28, 30]. However, a great challenge with integrated databases is the inherently limited horizontal scalability of transactional database management [1]. One of the intentions of microservice architectures is to overcome the limited scalability of such monolithic architectures [32]. A system has a microservice architecture when that system is composed of many collaborating microservices, typically without centralized control [46]. Microservices are built around business capabilities and take a full-stack implementation of software for that business area, including individual data stores.

Microservice architectures provide small services that may be deployed and scaled independently of each other and may employ different middleware stacks for their implementation. Microservice architectures intend to overcome the shortcomings of monolithic architectures where all of the application's logic and data are managed in one deployable unit.

A vertical decomposition into self-contained systems (scs-architecture.org) along business services is recommended. Besides scalability, an appropriate modular structure supports program comprehension, resilience (inhibiting error propagation), and autonomous teams with good knowledge of their vertical domain. Microservice architectures facilitate scalability [32], as well as agility and reliability [33].

An example vertical decomposition of an e-commerce system into self-contained services is illustrated in Fig. 3. A vertical microservice is a part of the platform that is responsible for a single bounded context in a business domain [20]. Verticals could be as small as a microservice, but most of the time, they are more coarse grained. The trade-off between many small components and a few large components must be considered in service and system design [29].

Microservices should follow the "Shared Nothing" principle: They do not share state, no infrastructure component, no database, or other shared resources. The big advantages of shared-nothing architectures are horizontal scalability and improved fault tolerance. The reason for this is apparent: If two components are not sharing anything, they are obviously unable to have a negative impact on each other. Small services are easier to deploy and, since they are autonomous, are less likely to cause system failures when they go wrong.

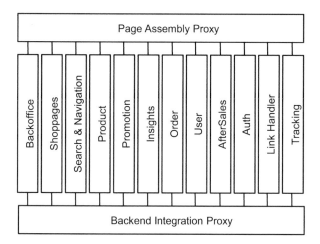

Fig. 3 Example vertical decomposition of an e-commerce system into self-contained microservices [33]

The well-known Conway's law states that organizations which design systems are constrained to produce designs which are copies of the communication structures of these organizations [17]. If the organizational structure is decomposed vertically and according to the microservices structure into cross-functional feature teams, scaling development capacities according to changing business requirements is enabled. The feature teams should be highly independent, having members of all roles and skills that are required to build and maintain their microservices. Microservices reinforce modular structure, which is particularly important for larger teams. Decoupling teams is as relevant as decoupling software modules.

Being a highly distributed architecture, microservices are particularly susceptible to partial failures. Therefore, microservices must be designed to cope gracefully with the unavailability of required services to prevent cascading failures. Several patterns have emerged for this purpose [47], such as the circuit-breaker pattern. In this pattern, dependencies such as other services are wrapped in a so-called circuit-breaker object, which serves as a proxy for the dependency and monitors its availability. If the dependency becomes unavailable or unresponsive, the circuit breaker trips and takes appropriate measures, such as immediately returning cached data or default values. After some time, the circuit breaker may check whether the dependency is available again, and if so, return to proxy mode.

Decentralizing responsibility for data across microservices has implications for managing updates. The traditional approach to dealing with updates is to use transactions to guarantee consistency when updating multiple resources. This approach is often used within monoliths. Using transactions this way helps with consistency, but imposes significant coupling, which is problematic across distributed services. Distributed transactions are notoriously difficult to implement, and as a consequence, microservice architectures emphasize transaction-less coordination between services, with explicit recognition that consistency may only be eventual consistency and problems are dealt with by compensating operations.

However, be aware that microservice architectures also come with costs. Maintaining consistency, monitoring, alarming, and fault tolerance are difficult for a distributed system, which means that you have to operate a much more complex system than in monolithic architectures. You need a mature operations team to manage lots of services, which are being redeployed frequently.

3.2   Focus on Quality Requirements

Quality requirements are the most important requirements for architectural work. The study of software architecture recognizes the dependency between an architecture and a software system's quality attributes such as performance, modifiability, and security. Architectural analysis and evaluation emerged connecting quality attributes and architectural design decisions [16]. For the analysis of quality attributes, software architecture models are used to analyze whether the system can meet its nonfunctional requirements [18]. The goals of architectural evaluations are estimations about the effects of architectural decisions, concerning quality attributes of software. Scenario-based software architecture evaluation methods, for instance, usually assess maintainability [4]. Architectural evaluation for software design helps to understand the consequences of design decisions, enables substantiated design decisions, helps to identify trade-offs, helps to check compliance, and supports managing risks.

Quality can be addressed by a model-based or a measurement-based approach. Model-based quality analysis provides information at an early stage, that is, before the system is implemented [51]. This approach may identify problems early and may reduce rework costs. However, developing the appropriate models requires additional effort and time. Measurement-based approaches to quality perform real measurements [62]. However, this is only applicable when the system is implemented, but can provide real-life data.

Nonfunctional attributes, such as scalability and fault tolerance for high availability, are addressed by microservice architectures (Sect. 3.1). A consequence of using microservices is that applications need to be designed such that they can tolerate the failure of individual services. Since services can fail at any time, it is important to be able to detect the failures quickly and, if possible, automatically restore services. Thus, microservice applications put a lot of emphasis on real-time monitoring of the application, checking both technical metrics (e.g., how many requests per second is the database getting) and business-relevant metrics (such as how many orders per minute are received). Monitoring [62] can provide an early warning system of something going wrong that triggers development teams to follow up.

Quality does not just happen. It needs to be thought about and carefully considered. If you do not pay attention to system qualities, they can be hard to achieve at the last moment.

4 Future: Proper Integration of Architecture Work into Agile Software Development

The tension between the agile and architecture communities still is fairly high. Ford is often cited for his statements "Architecture is the stuff that's hard to change later" and "By deferring important architectural and design decisions until the last responsible moment, you can prevent unnecessary complexity from undermining your software projects" [23]. However, software architecture should be recognized as a key foundation to agile software development, despite the fact that it is often ignored by the agile community who has nicknamed it BUFD (big up-front design).

Meanwhile, the agile community observes a renaissance with innovation in software architecture [59]: Organizations have accepted that "cloud" is the de facto platform of the future, and the benefits and flexibility it brings have ushered in a "renaissance" in software architecture. The disposable infrastructure of cloud has enabled the first "cloud native" architecture, namely, microservices. Continuous delivery, a technique that is radically changing how tech-based businesses evolve, amplifies the impact of cloud as an architecture. ThoughtWorks [59] expect architectural innovation to continue, with trends such as containerization and software-defined networking providing even more technical options and capabilities.

As observed by Keeling [37], promoting business agility requires sound architecture design. The question is how best to achieve agility through architecture. Highly modular architectures that allow for rapid experimentation are critical to a successful integration of architecture work into agile software development. Lightweight, agile methods are promising because they enable teams to learn fast, fail fast, change fast, and communicate effectively. These factors are essential for self-organizing teams, which in turn enable better designs to emerge [37].

Section 4.1 introduces the envisioned role of architecture owner in agile teams, before the relationship between software development and operations is discussed in Sect. 4.2. Achieving reliability with agile development, runtime adaptivity, and keeping architecture knowledge up to date for long-living software systems are discussed in Sects. 4.3–4.5.

4.1 Integrating Architecture Owners into Agile Teams

Treating architecture as a phase ignores its foundational role in software development. Architecture work should be integrated with all software development activities. With agile development, you may have an "Architecture Owner" role, who should involve the entire team to make informed and accepted architectural decisions. The big question is, how many architectural and design decisions upfront (before Sprint 1)? A promising approach is to create an architecture *vision* in Sprint "zero." You need to accept constraints, identify and promote desired quality attributes, assign functional responsibilities to elements, and guide the design with patterns. Try to establish a clear architecture vision.

With agile software development, you can design the architecture through stories and use cases, so driven by requirements. Use case scenarios describe specific interactions between the user of an application system and the system itself. We should test the architecture against the scenarios that are associated with the quality attribute requirements for the system, such as performance. You can add backlog items for technical debt and quality-related architecture work. Quality-related acceptance criteria can be attached to user stories. You should monitor system qualities, for instance, via an operational dashboard. Do not worry about getting your architecture right on the first day. Model and implement incrementally. Prioritize the architecture features and mitigate the key risks.

Architecture validations encourage communication among project stakeholders. Continuously validating the architecture tells us whether we still have the right team structure. Fixing defects early is the best approach. Communication and collaboration aspects of architecture are just as important as developing it. Architecture evaluations help significantly with collaboration and communication. The architecture owner should provide architecture leadership in a collaborative manner and help the team members enhance their capabilities in understanding architectural principles and trade-offs involved. The architecture owner should be integrated with day-to-day development and pay attention to details.

Some decisions are too important to leave until the *last* responsible moment, so choose the *most* responsible moment. Choose an architecture, before it chooses you, as may otherwise happen with *emergent* architectures.

4.2   Integrating Software Development and Operations: DevOps

The DevOps movement continues what agile started. The DevOps movement intends to improve communication, collaboration, and integration between software developers (Dev) and IT operations professionals (Ops). Automation is key to DevOps success: automated building of systems out of version management repositories; automated execution of unit tests, integration and system tests; automated deployment in test and production environments; including performance benchmarks [64]. DevOps is a set of practices intended to reduce the time between committing a change to a system and the change being placed into normal production, while ensuring high quality [6, 12].

The deployment pipeline is the place where the architectural aspects and the process aspects of DevOps intersect [6]. Architectural choices need to facilitate continuous delivery. Microservice architecture is designed for minimizing coordination needs and allowing independent deployment. Multiple simultaneous versions may be managed with feature toggles and backward/forward compatibility. Feature toggles support rollback, canary testing, and A/B testing. Microservices leverage continuous integration [43] and continuous deployment [52] to promote DevOps. Microservice architectures and DevOps benefit from each other [5].

4.3   Achieving Reliability with Agile Software Development

For large software systems, a major difficulty for automated regression testing is caused by the high computational costs of tests. To ensure high code coverage, a potentially exponential set of test configurations must be executed. A solution to this challenge could be a proper modularization of the software such that the software components become testable in isolation. Modularization approaches such as microservices may also facilitate automated regression testing of large software systems. Tooling and automation is needed to satisfy quality assurance needs. The combination of modular microservice architectures with automated quality assurance allows to retain reliability with agile software development [33].

Many agile teams only focus on functional testing, but there is a lot more to test, for instance, performance. Performance tests may be automated in continuous integration setting via regression benchmarking [64]. A strong model of architecture-based testing, backed by formal reasoning and appropriate tooling, could have a major economic impact on software system development.

4.4   Using Architecture Models for Runtime Adaptability

Scalable systems should allow to react to changing workloads automatically via elastic capacity management [63], as offered by cloud infrastructures [35]. With microservice architectures, you can dynamically replicate those microservices to cloud infrastructures that are under heavy load. It is not necessary to scale the complete system, as it would be required with a monolithic system.

Fault tolerance is intended to ensure the delivery of the correct services in the presence of active faults. It is implemented by error detection and subsequent system recovery. Error detection finds an erroneous system state. The following system recovery transforms the system state that contains one or more errors into a state without detected errors. A possible solution is given by dynamic adaptation. In the case of errors, dynamic adaptation can ensure that the best possible system functionality is achieved and that critical functions are kept alive (survivability). Realizing survivability instead of fault tolerance provides an immense potential for saving costs, for ensuring the safety of the system, and for achieving acceptable availability. The abovementioned circuit-breaker pattern provides such properties.

To enable such runtime adaptability, we need architecture information in the running system: architecture description as an executable deliverable, also called models@runtime [7].

4.5   Keeping Architecture Knowledge up to Date for Long-Living Software Systems

The highest costs in software development are generally in system maintenance and the addition of new features. If done early on, architectural evaluation can reduce that cost by revealing a design's implications [16]. This, in turn, can lead to an early detection of errors and to the most predictable and cost-effective modifications to the system over its life cycle. Software architecture captures and preserves designers' intentions about system structure and behavior, thereby providing a defense against design decay as a system ages [38]. The quality and longevity of a software-reliant system is largely determined by its architecture. Technical debt [39] should be avoided. Bad architectural decisions are a major contributor to technical debt.

Architecture knowledge is often lost as we move to code. The best architecture is worthless if the code does not follow it [15]. For such long-living software, it is important to keep the documentation and knowledge about the software up to date [27]. Without conformance between architecture documentation and code, the architecture documentation becomes irrelevant. We might establish conformance by construction—via model-driven software engineering—or by reverse engineering (analyzing an artifact statically or dynamically to determine its architecture). Software system comprehension with reverse engineered architecture models is helpful in this context [21, 22].

Successful, large systems have a long lifetime. They must evolve to meet changing requirements. Existing systems which must be maintained are sometimes called legacy systems. Modernization of legacy software systems is required [34, 61]. When a software system evolves, ideally its prescriptive architecture is modified first. In practice, however, the system—and thus its descriptive architecture—is often directly modified. This happens because of perception of short deadlines, need for code optimizations, inadequate tool support, etc.

Understanding the relationship between architectural decisions and a system's quality attributes reveals software architecture evaluation as a useful risk-reduction strategy. Decisions are the main deliverable of (agile) architecture work, while keeping a backlog of architectural concerns. Managing cost and risks is the primary business goal and prioritizing factors for architecture owners. For longevity, decide at the most responsible moment, not the last possible moment.

5   Summary

Software architectures are essential to develop and maintain large-scale, long-living software systems. The understanding of these systems is improved by a high-level abstract view on a system. Architecture supports the reuse of components and frameworks. Architecture makes expected evolution explicit and separates functionality and connection mechanisms of components and services, so that they can evolve individually. Full automation of quality assurance and software deployment allows for early fault and error detection, thus reducing repair times both during development and during operations.

Finding the right balance for architecture work is the art of agile architecture ownership. We can expect a coalescence of architecture work and agile software development practices. Architecture owners should decide at the *most responsible* moment, not the *last possible* moment.

References

1. Abbott, M., Fisher, M.: The Art of Scalability, 2nd edn. Addison-Wesley, Reading (2015)
2. Abowd, G., Allen, R., Garlan, D.: Formalizing style to understand descriptions of software architecture. ACM Trans. Softw. Eng. Methodol. **4**(4), 319–364 (1995)
3. Allen, R., Garlan, D.: A formal basis for architectural connection. ACM Trans. Softw. Eng. Methodol. **6**(3), 213–249 (1997)
4. Babar, M., Gorton, I.: Comparison of scenario-based software architecture evaluation methods. In: Proceedings of the 11th Asia-Pacific Software Engineering Conference, pp. 600–607 (2004)
5. Balalaie, A., Heydarnoori, A., Jamshidi, P.: Microservices architecture enables DevOps: migration to a cloud-native architecture. IEEE Softw. **33**(3), 42–52 (2016)
6. Bass, L., Weber, I., Zhu, L.: DevOps: A Software Architect's Perspective. Addison-Wesley, Reading (2015)
7. Bencomo, N., France, R., Cheng, B.H.C., Aßmann, U. (eds.): Models@run.time. Lecture Notes in Computer Science, vol. 8378. Springer, Cham (2014)
8. Bennett, K.H., Rajlich, V.T.: Software maintenance and evolution: a roadmap. In: Proceedings of the Conference on The Future of Software Engineering, ICSE '00, pp. 73–87. ACM, New York (2000)
9. Bernardo, M., Inverardi, P. (eds.): Formal Methods for Software Architectures. Lecture Notes in Computer Science, vol. 2804. Springer, Berlin (2003)
10. Bertolino, A., Corradini, F., Inverardi, P., Muccini, H.: Deriving test plans from architectural descriptions. In: Proceedings of the 22th International Conference on Software Engineering, pp. 220–229. IEEE Computer Society Press, Limerick (2000)
11. Bosch, J.: Design & Use of Software Architectures: Adopting and Evolving a Product-Line Approach. Addison-Wesley, Harlow (2000)
12. Brunnert, A., van Hoorn, A., Willnecker, F., Danciu, A., Hasselbring, W., Heger, C., Herbst, N., Jamshidi, P., Jung, R., von Kistowski, J., Koziolek, A., Kroß, J., Spinner, S., Vögele, C., Walter, J., Wert, A.: Performance-oriented devOps: a research agenda. Technical report, Standard Performance Evaluation Corporation (SPEC) (2015)
13. Buschmann, F., Henney, K., Schmidt, D.C.: Pattern-Oriented Software Architecture: On Patterns and Pattern Languages, vol. 5. Wiley, Chichester (2007)
14. Christensen, H.B., Hansen, K.M.: An empirical investigation of architectural prototyping. J. Softw. Syst. **83**(1), 133–142 (2010)
15. Clements, P., Shaw, M.: The golden age of software architecture revisited. IEEE Softw. **26**(4), 70–72 (2009). https://doi.org/10.1109/MS.2009.83
16. Clements, P., Kazman, R., Klein, M.: Evaluating Software Architectures: Methods and Case Studies. Addison-Wesley, Reading (2001)
17. Conway, M.E.: How do committees invent? Datamation **14**(4), 28–31 (1968)
18. Crnkovic, I., Larsson, M., Preiss, O.: Concerning predictability in dependable component-based systems: classification of quality attributes. In: Architecting Dependable Systems II. Lecture Notes in Computer Science, vol. 3549. Springer, Berlin (2005)

19. Dahl, O.J., Dijkstra, E.W., Hoare, C.A.R.: Structured Programming. Academic, London (1972)
20. Evans, E.: Domain-Driven Design. Addison-Wesley, Reading (2004)
21. Fittkau, F., Roth, S., Hasselbring, W.: ExplorViz: visual runtime behavior analysis of enterprise application landscapes. In: 23rd European Conference on Information Systems (ECIS 2015 Completed Research Papers), pp. 1–13. AIS Electronic Library (2015)
22. Fittkau, F., Krause, A., Hasselbring, W.: Software landscape and application visualization for system comprehension with ExplorViz. Inf. Softw. Technol. **87**, 259–277 (2017)
23. Ford, N.: Evolutionary architecture and emergent design: environmental considerations for design, part 2 (2010). https://www.ibm.com/developerworks/java/library/j-eaed18/index.html
24. Frakes, W.B., Kang, K.: Software reuse research: status and future. IEEE Trans. Softw. Eng. **31**(7), 529–536 (2005)
25. Galster, M., Weyns, D., Tofan, D., Michalik, B., Avgeriou, P.: Variability in software systems – a systematic literature review. IEEE Trans. Softw. Eng. **40**(3), 282–306 (2014)
26. Gamma, E., Helm, R., Johnson, R., Vlissides, J.: Design Patterns – Elements of Reusable Object-Oriented Software. Addison Wesley, Reading (1995)
27. Goltz, U., Reussner, R., Goedicke, M., Hasselbring, W., Märtin, L., Vogel-Heuser, B.: Design for future: managed software evolution. Comput. Sci. Res. Dev. **30**(3), 321–331 (2015)
28. Hasselbring, W.: Information system integration. Commun. ACM **43**(6), 32–36 (2000)
29. Hasselbring, W.: Component-based software engineering. In: Handbook of Software Engineering and Knowledge Engineering, pp. 289–305. World Scientific Publishing, Singapore (2002)
30. Hasselbring, W.: Web data integration for E-commerce applications. IEEE Multimedia **9**(1), 16–25 (2002)
31. Hasselbring, W.: Formalization of federated schema architectural style variability. J. Softw. Eng. Appl. **8**(2), 72–92 (2015)
32. Hasselbring, W.: Microservices for scalability: keynote talk abstract. In: Proceedings of the 7th ACM/SPEC on International Conference on Performance Engineering (ICPE 2016), pp. 133–134. ACM, New York (2016)
33. Hasselbring, W., Steinacker, G.: Microservice architectures for scalability, agility and reliability in e-commerce. In: Proceedings 2017 IEEE International Conference on Software Architecture Workshops (ICSAW), pp. 243–246. IEEE, Gothenburg (2017)
34. Hasselbring, W., Reussner, R., Jaekel, H., Schlegelmilch, J., Teschke, T., Krieghoff, S.: The Dublo architecture pattern for smooth migration of business information systems. In: Proceedings of the 26th International Conference on Software Engineering (ICSE 2004), pp. 117–126. IEEE Computer Society Press, Edinburgh (2004)
35. Heinrich, R., Schmieders, E., Jung, R., Rostami, K., Metzger, A., Hasselbring, W., Reussner, R., Pohl, K.: Integrating run-time observations and design component models for cloud system analysis. In: Proceedings of the 9th Workshop on Models@run.time, Workshop Proceedings, vol. 1270, pp. 41–46. CEUR, Aachen (2014)
36. IEEE recommended practice for architectural description of software-intensive systems (2000). (also ISO/IEC DIS 25961 (2006))
37. Keeling, M.: Lightweight and flexible: emerging trends in software architecture from the SATURN conferences. IEEE Softw. **32**(3), 7–11 (2015)
38. Kruchten, P., Obbink, H., Stafford, J.: The past, present, and future of software architecture. IEEE Softw. **23**(2), 22–30 (2006)
39. Kruchten, P., Nord, R.L., Ozkaya, I.: Technical debt: from metaphor to theory and practice. IEEE Softw. **29**(6), 18–21 (2012)
40. Lange, C.F.J., Chaudron, M.R.V., Muskens, J.: In practice: UML software architecture and design description. IEEE Softw. **23**(2), 40–46 (2006)
41. Lewis, J., Fowler, M.: Microservices (2014). http://martinfowler.com/articles/microservices.html
42. Medvidovic, N., Taylor, R.N.: A classification and comparison framework for software architecture description languages. IEEE Trans. Softw. Eng. **26**(1), 70–93 (2000)
43. Meyer, M.: Continuous integration and its tools. IEEE Softw. **31**(3), 14–16 (2014)

44. Muccini, H., Bertolino, A., Inverardi, P.: Using software architecture for code testing. IEEE Trans. Softw. Eng. **30**(3), 160–171 (2004)
45. Müller, H., Wong, K., Tilley, S.: Dimensions of software architecture for program understanding. In: Proceedings of the International Workshop on Software Architecture (IWSA '95), Dagstuhl (1995)
46. Newman, S.: Building Microservices. O'Reilly, Sebastopol (2015)
47. Nygard, M.T.: Release It! – Design and Deploy Production-Ready Software. The Pragmatic Bookshelf, Raleigh (2007)
48. Pahl, C., Giesecke, S., Hasselbring, W.: Ontology-based modelling of architectural styles. Inf. Softw. Technol. **51**(12), 1739–1749 (2009)
49. Parnas, D.: On the criteria to be used in decomposing systems into modules. Commun. ACM **15**(12), 1053–1058 (1972)
50. Perry, D., Wolf, A.: Foundations for the study of software architecture. ACM SIGSOFT Softw. Eng. Notes **17**(4), 40–52 (1992)
51. Reussner, R.H., Becker, S., Happe, J., Heinrich, R., Koziolek, A., Koziolek, H., Kramer, M., Krogmann, K.: Modeling and Simulating Software Architectures: The Palladio Approach. MIT Press, Cambridge (2016)
52. Rodriguez, P., Haghighatkhah, A., Lwakatare, L.E., Teppola, S., Suomalainen, T., Eskeli, J., Karvonen, T., Kuvaja, P., Verner, J.M., Oivo, M.: Continuous deployment of software intensive products and services: a systematic mapping study. J. Syst. Softw. **123**, 263–291 (2017)
53. Shaw, M.: Architectural issues in software reuse: it's not just the functionality, it's the packaging. Softw. Eng. Notes **20**, 3–6 (1995)
54. Shaw, M., Clements, P.: A field guide to boxology: preliminary classification of architectural styles for software systems. In: Proceedings of the Twenty-First Annual International Computer Software and Applications Conference (COMPSAC 1997), pp. 6–13 (1997)
55. Shaw, M., Garlan, D.: Software Architecture: Perspectives on an Emerging Discipline. Prentice Hall, Upper Saddle River (1996)
56. Shaw, M., DeLine, R., Klein, D., Ross, T., Young, D., Zelesnik, G.: Abstractions for software architecture and tools to support them. IEEE Trans. Softw. Eng. **21**(4), 314–335 (1995)
57. Taylor, R., Tracz, W., Coglianese, L.: Software development using domain-specific software architectures. ACM SIGSOFT Softw. Eng. Notes **20**(5), 27–38 (1995)
58. Taylor, R.N., Medvidovic, N., Dashofy, E.M.: Software Architecture: Foundations, Theory, and Practice. Wiley, Hoboken (2009)
59. ThoughtWorks Inc.: Technology Radar (2015). http://www.thoughtworks.com/radar
60. Vaisman, A., Zimányi, E.: Data Warehouse Systems: Design and Implementation. Springer, Berlin (2014)
61. van Hoorn, A., Frey, S., Goerigk, W., Hasselbring, W., Knoche, H., Köster, S., Krause, H., Porembski, M., Stahl, T., Steinkamp, M., Wittmüss, N.: Dynamod project: dynamic analysis for model-driven software modernization. In: Proceedings of the 1st International Workshop on Model-Driven Software Migration (MDSM 2011), vol. 708, pp. 12–13. CEUR, Aachen (2011)
62. van Hoorn, A., Waller, J., Hasselbring, W.: Kieker: a framework for application performance monitoring and dynamic software analysis. In: Proceedings of the 3rd ACM/SPEC International Conference on Performance Engineering (ICPE 2012), pp. 247–248. ACM, New York (2012)

63. von Massow, R., van Hoorn, A., Hasselbring, W.: Performance simulation of runtime recon-figurable component-based software architectures. In: Crnkovic, I., Gruhn, V., Book, M. (eds.) Software Architecture (Proceedings ECSA 2011). Lecture Notes in Computer Science, vol. 6903, pp. 43–58. Springer, Heidelberg (2011)
64. Waller, J., Ehmke, N.C., Hasselbring, W.: Including performance benchmarks into continuous integration to enable DevOps. SIGSOFT Softw. Eng. Notes **40**(2), 1–4 (2015)

Software Product Lines

Klaus Pohl and Andreas Metzger

1 Introduction

Software product line engineering (SPLE) has proven to empower industry to develop a diversity of similar systems at lower cost, in shorter time, and with higher quality when compared with the development of single systems [1, 2]. A software product line (also sometimes called software product family) is "a set of software-intensive systems that share a common, managed set of features satisfying the specific needs of a particular market segment or mission and that are developed from a common set of core assets [artifacts] in a prescribed way" [3].

SPLE exploits the commonalities of the different systems (typically called *applications*) belonging to the product line and systematically handles the variation (i.e., the differences) among those applications. *Commonality* is invariant for (i.e., shared by) all product line applications [4]; for example, all mobile phones allow users to make calls. Product line *variability* defines how the different applications of the product line may vary [5]. Product line applications may differ in terms of features and functional and quality requirements they fulfill; for example, some tablet computers may include mobile broadband connectivity, while others may not.

The SPLE paradigm has a strong track record of success in industry. Success stories can be found in textbooks (such as [1, 3, 6]) or in the product line hall of fame of the leading international software product line conference (http://splc.net/fame.html). Reported benefits of SPLE include improved productivity by as much as a factor of 10, increased quality by as much as a factor of 10, decreased cost by as much as 60%, decreased labor needs by as much as 87%, decreased time to market by as much as 98%, and ability to move into new markets in months, not years.

K. Pohl (✉) · A. Metzger
Paluno (The Ruhr Institute for Software Technology), University of Duisburg-Essen, Essen, Germany
e-mail: andreas.metzger@paluno.uni-due.de; klaus.pohl@paluno.uni-due.de

© The Author(s) 2018
V. Gruhn, R. Striemer (eds.), *The Essence of Software Engineering*,
https://doi.org/10.1007/978-3-319-73897-0_11

In this chapter, we describe the key differences between software product line engineering and the development of single software systems (Sect. 2). In particular, we provide an overview of the activities and techniques used in the two development processes of SPLE (Sects. 3 and 4) and discuss different ways for modeling the variability of software product lines (Sect. 5). Finally, we provide some examples of using variability modeling techniques in non-SPLE settings (Sect. 6).

2   Differences Between SPLE and Single System Development

Figure 1 depicts a well-established SPLE framework defined in the European SPLE research projects ESAPS, CAFÉ, and FAMILIES. The framework was adopted as part of the ISO/IEC standard #26550 ("Software and systems engineering: Reference model for product line engineering and management"). It is described in detail in [1].

The SPLE framework highlights the main differences between the development of single systems and software product line engineering: the two complementary development processes ("domain engineering" and "application engineering") as well as the explicit modeling and management of product line variability ("domain variability model" and "application variability model").

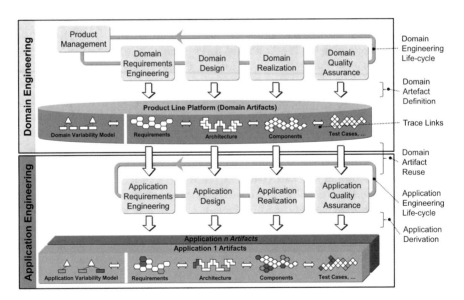

Fig. 1 SPLE framework (adapted from [1])

2.1   Two Development Processes

SPLE differentiates between the following two complementary development processes.

Domain Engineering   The domain engineering process (shown in the upper half of Fig. 1) is responsible for defining the commonality and the variability of the product line, as well as for developing the *domain artifacts*. Domain artifacts "realize" commonality and variability. They include, among others, requirements artifacts (e.g., use case diagrams, requirements models), architectural artifacts (e.g., component models, class diagrams), implementation artifacts (e.g., source code files, libraries), and test artifacts (e.g., test cases, test data). The *product line platform* encompasses the domain artifacts of the product line. Important parts of the product line platform are the domain requirements and the product line architecture. The product line architecture is often called the *reference architecture* of the product line [1, 6]. We elaborate on the development activities executed during domain engineering in Sect. 3.

Application Engineering   The application engineering process (shown in the lower half of Fig. 1) is responsible for deriving concrete applications from the domain artifacts. During application engineering, the variability of the domain artifacts is exploited and bound (resolved) according to the needs and requirements of the particular application. Thereby, invariant and variant domain artifacts are reused. We elaborate on the activities during application engineering in Sect. 4.

2.2   Product Line Variability

Product line variability is the key, crosscutting concern in SPLE [1, 3]. Product line variability defines how applications of a software product line can differ, for example, in terms of properties, features offered, functions, or qualities offered. Whether a given property is invariant (common) or variable for the applications of the software product line is determined by explicit management decisions, typically made by product management [1, 5]. Product line variability is documented in so-called variability models. The SPLE framework in Fig. 1 differentiates between two types of variability models: domain variability models and application variability models [7].

During domain engineering, the variability of the product line is defined and documented in the domain variability model. In application engineering, the variability defined in the domain variability model is bound in order to fulfill the application-specific requirements. The variability bindings for a specific application are documented in the application variability model.

Product line variability is preplanned in order to fulfill different market and stakeholder needs. Still, application engineers may face the problem that individual customer- or market-specific needs cannot be satisfied by reusing common and variable domain artifacts. In this case, customer- or market-specific extensions or adjustments of the common and variable artifacts are required. The adjustment required can be enabled by initiating a product line evolution (e.g., by introducing additional product line variability) or by adapting the application artifacts and document such adaptation in the application variability model [7]. An application variability model thus documents both the variability bound for the specific application and the application-specific adaptations.

2.3   Software Variability Versus Product Line Variability

Software variability refers to the ability of software systems or artifacts to be efficiently extended, changed, customized, or configured [8]. Most modeling and programming languages provide mechanism for software variability. Examples include abstract superclasses allowing different specializations, interfaces facilitating different implementations, or conditional compilation (e.g., using #ifdefs) facilitating the inclusion of different code fragments.

In contrast to software variability, product line variability defines how the applications of a product line can differ. Together with the commonalities, product line variability defines the scope of a product line (see Sect. 3.1). Product line variability is preplanned. Defining whether a given feature, functional or quality requirement is product line variability or not requires explicit decisions from product management or other stakeholders.

Software variability can represent both product line variability as well as commonality. As an example for software variability, take the abstract superclass *Communication* with two concrete subclasses, *WiFi* and *MobileBroadband*, documented in a UML class diagram. Clearly, the superclass together with the subclasses documents software variability. In principle, any of the two or even both subclasses could be used in place of the superclass.

This software variability, on the one hand, can represent a commonality if the stakeholders, for instance, had decided that all product line applications must include both subclasses *WiFi* and *MobileBroadband*—in other words, if the stakeholders have decided that the product line applications cannot differ in terms of the communication used. In such cases, software variability documents commonality of the product line and not product line variability. On the other hand, this software variability could also document product line variability. For example, if the stakeholders had decided that for each application of the product line the engineer has to choose at least one of the two communication subclasses, the applications could differ in terms of the subclasses they include for communication.

Consequently, product line variability cannot be automatically derived from software variability. In other words, product line variability cannot be identified by analyzing software variability documented in existing software artifacts or models. Thus, defining and modeling product line variability requires additional modeling concepts (see Sect. 5).

3 Domain Engineering

3.1 Product Management

The main task of product management in SPLE is product line scoping [9]. One facet of product line scoping is the definition of the product portfolio, that is, the set of applications offered for a certain market segment by a particular business unit or company. Further facets commonly include the definition of which set of features as well as which set of domain artifacts can be economically reused. If the scope of a software product line is too broad, domain artifacts may become too generic and the effort of realizing them may become too high. In this case, the product line may not be economically viable. On the other hand, if the scope is defined too narrow, required features as well as functional and quality requirements of many customers may not be covered and thus only very few applications might be derived from the product line. Again, the product line may not be economically viable. Therefore, product line scoping techniques need to include cost estimations and benefits as well as business and technical experts.

3.2 Domain Requirements Engineering

Domain requirements engineering encompasses the typical requirements engineering activities [10], such as elicitation, negotiation, documentation, validation, and management, but in this case for the common and variable requirements for the product portfolio envisioned by product management. To identify all relevant common and variable requirements, product line requirements engineers have to involve a larger number of stakeholders than for single systems and have to consider additional requirements sources and constraints [1]. For example, a product line may address multiple customer groups and thus requirements engineers need to involve representatives of those groups, which requires support for the elicitation and documentation of common and variable requirements [11].

The amount of commonality and variability defined in domain requirements engineering has a huge impact on all other product line engineering activities, both in domain and application engineering. A high percentage of common features and common domain requirements in a product line typically require lower effort for designing and realizing the product line. Moreover, common requirements and domain artifacts are essential to engineering a product line platform that is stable yet flexible enough. On the other hand, the extent of variable requirements determines the potential number of different applications that can be derived from the product line and thus has significant impact on whether all goals and needs of the envisioned customers and/or market segments may be satisfied [1]. If a set of differing but related requirements is identified, two principal ways to treat those requirements exist. Those requirements may be defined as variable in the domain requirements.

Or those requirements may be harmonized or generalized and thereby defined as a common domain requirement. Determining how to treat those requirements is clearly a trade-off decision that has to be made in concert with product management and scoping.

3.3 Domain Design

Domain design encompasses all activities for defining the reference architecture of the product line. Numerous SPLE design methods have been advocated and targeted techniques for modeling variability in the architecture are available.

Traditionally, product line architecture approaches have been *component based*. In such a setting, variability is realized as component compositions and/or by introducing variation points into the components themselves. More recently, *aspect-oriented architectures* have been proposed to better address crosscutting features. Crosscutting features are encapsulated into modular units, the aspects, and composed by means of aspect-oriented mechanisms such as advices, join-points, and point-cuts [12]. Most recently, *service-oriented architectures* have been considered as part of SPLE [13]. In contrast to a component, which represents a comprehensive piece of software that is part of the software product line, a service represents functionality with associated quality characteristics (typically defined in a service-level agreement) offered by a service provider via a service interface [14]. The service itself or the service provider can change as long as the functionality and the service-level agreement remain the same.

3.4 Domain Realization

Domain realization deals with the detailed design and the implementation of the domain artifacts, for example, as reusable components or services. Variability can be realized using the capabilities of existing programming languages, compilers, and linkers [15]. Approaches include the use of inheritance (e.g., implementing alternative subclasses for an abstract superclass), aspect-oriented programming (e.g., the weaving of alternative code), conditional compilation (e.g., using preprocessor directives such as #ifdef), and binary replacement (e.g., providing the linker with alternative implementations of libraries).

To explicitly handle feature modularity and feature dependencies (or interactions) at the language level, new types of programming languages have been proposed that consider features and variability as first-class concepts. *Feature-oriented programming* supports the flexible and modular composition of systems from individual features. In FOP, "a feature module encapsulates changes that are made to a program in order to add a new capability or functionality" [16]. In *delta-oriented programming*, a compositional programming language, a product line is realized by a core module and a set of delta modules. The core module implements a valid application developed with single system development techniques. Delta modules specify changes to be applied to the core module to implement additional applications. Changes to the core model include the adding of additional code (as in FOP), but also removing and even the modification of code [17].

3.5 Domain Quality Assurance

Quality assurance of domain artifacts is essential for successful product line engineering. A fault in a domain artifact may affect all applications of the product line in which this artifact is reused. Quality assurance techniques from single-system engineering cannot be directly applied to domain artifacts. As an example, a domain requirements specification can define a variable requirement r, that is related to variant v_1, and a variable requirement $\neg r$ related to variant v_2. Performing a consistency check of the domain requirements specification $R = \{r, \neg r\}$ using quality assurance techniques from single system development would identify a contradiction between r and $\neg r$. Yet, if the variants v_1 and v_2 are defined to be mutually exclusive, the contradicting requirements can never be implemented together in the same application. Thus, the two requirements will never cause an inconsistency. A central challenge for quality assurance techniques in domain engineering is thus the consideration of product line variability [18].

Quality Assurance of Domain Artifacts Quality assurance of domain artifacts calls for quality assurance techniques that work in the presence of variability, including formal verification and testing. For the *formal verification* of product line artifacts, prominent verification techniques from single systems engineering have been adapted to the software product line setting, including type checking, model checking, and theorem proving. To handle variability during verification, various strategies have been followed, such as checking representative applications, checking features in isolation, or aiming to check all potential applications of the product line [18].

As in the development of single systems, *testing* in SPLE aims to execute the software to uncover the evidence of defects. One class of domain testing techniques includes techniques for developing reusable test cases in domain engineering and reusing and executing these test cases in application engineering [19]. In addition, domain testing aims to uncover evidence of defects in domain artifacts before these artifacts are reused in application engineering. Due to the variability defined in the domain artifacts, testing all potential product line applications (i.e., all potential combination of the common and variable artifacts) during domain engineering is impossible [20]. Typical domain testing strategies thus reduce the number of artifact combinations by using pairwise or *t*-wise testing strategies, or by focusing on important features and feature combinations.

Variability Analysis The consistency of the variability model is often a prerequisite for the analysis of domain artifacts. Variability analysis techniques help to ensure this consistency. Variability analysis aims to check and ensure whether certain properties for a given variability model hold. Examples for properties checked are satisfiability (i.e., whether at least one application can be derived from the variability model), membership (i.e., whether a given configuration is consistent with the variability model and thus represents a valid application of the product line), commonality (i.e., the set of "features" that appear in all applications), and "dead" features (i.e., features that cannot be selected for any application).

Manual analysis of variability models is error prone and infeasible when facing large-scale variability models. A broad spectrum of automated variability analysis techniques has been proposed which can be categorized in three main classes [21]: propositional-logics-based (using SAT or BDD solvers), constraint-programming-based (using CSP solvers), and description-logics-based (using DL reasoners). In general, variability model analyses exhibit an exponential worst-case execution time. Yet, research results indicate that in most cases variability model analysis can be mastered quite successfully using powerful solvers [22].

4   Application Engineering

4.1   Application Requirements Engineering

During application requirements engineering, the requirements for a specific application are defined. In general, the application-specific requirements should be satisfied by exploiting the variability and using the commonality defined for the software product line. The application-specific binding of the variability is defined in the application variability model [1, 7].

In SPLE research, many publications convey the impression that an application can be derived from the domain artifacts by binding the defined variability of the product line and thus application derivation is seen purely as a feature selection process. For example, decision models define the decisions to be taken to derive an application of the product line [23]. To guide users to make those decisions, specific tools have been suggested. In the extreme, fully automated approaches have been devised that aim at optimal feature selection, for example, using search-based techniques.

In practice, customer- or market-specific applications often cannot be fully realized by reusing domain artifacts alone [7]. Often, there are application-specific requirements that cannot be satisfied by reusing domain requirements and thus require application-specific extensions to satisfy them. In order to handle such application-specific deviations from product line requirements, these application-specific extensions should be modeled as application-specific variation and documented, in addition to the variability bindings, in the application variability model [7].

4.2   Application Design

Based on the application requirements, the application-specific architecture is derived from the domain architecture. The application architecture is typically a specialization of the reference architecture of the product line [1].

During application design, the design alternatives documented as variability in the domain architecture are assessed. The alternatives that fit the application requirements best are selected. Yet, in the case of application-specific deviations (see above), additional design decisions may have to be taken in order to derive an architecture that satisfies the application-specific requirements. Or even the architecture might have to be extended or adjusted, or the evolution of the product line architecture might be triggered.

4.3   Application Realization

During application realization, code artifacts developed during domain engineering are derived and adjusted based on the application architecture and the application-specific requirements. For example, by parameterizing code modules using software configuration techniques, code modules can be adapted to fit a particular application. Application realization techniques facilitate such adaptations. An alternative approach to software configuration is code generation. Code generation techniques for product line applications have mainly adapted techniques from model-driven development and domain-specific languages.

Generative software product lines, a subclass of software product lines, support the derivation of individual applications without programming glue code or modifying the domain components. Yet, such an ideal approach is often not possible in practice (see above). In other words, application-specific coding and adjustments are usually required.

4.4   Application Quality Assurance

Due to the variability of the reusable artifacts, it is impossible—except for trivial product lines—to comprehensively test all potential product line applications during domain engineering. Moreover, if based on concrete application requirements, specific variants are developed or application-specific extensions are made (e.g., see the discussion in Sect. 4.1), such variants and extensions can only be tested during application engineering.

Application testing techniques support the derivation of application-specific test cases from reusable domain test artifacts [19, 24]. Some application testing techniques aim to minimize the retesting of application parts already been tested for another application of the product line, thereby representing a special case of regression testing [25].

5 Modeling Product Line Variability

As explained in Sect. 2.3, product line variability differs significantly from software variability. Product line variability needs to be explicitly defined to empower and support the communication, discussion, management, and analysis of product line variability. Here, we introduce key constructs and two different approaches for modeling product line variability.

5.1 Key Modeling Constructs

There are few, simple modeling constructs required for modeling product line variability:

- A *variation point* documents a variable item and thus defines "what can vary" (without saying how it can vary). As an example, the color of a car may vary.
- A *variant* documents a concrete variation and is related to a variation point. A variant thus defines "how something can vary." As an example, colors for a car may include black, red, and white.
- A *variability constraint* defines restrictions about the variability, for example, to define permissible combinations of variants in an application or to define that the selection of one variant requires or excludes the selection of another variant. As an example, only one single color may be chosen for any concrete car.

5.2 Integrated Versus Orthogonal Modeling of Variability

There are two principal ways in SPLE research and practice to explicitly document product line variability: integrated and orthogonal documentation.

Integrated Variability Modeling To support the integrated documentation of product line variability, dedicated or specialized modeling and documentation concepts are introduced into existing modeling languages or document templates. An example for the integrated documentation of product line variability is depicted in Fig. 2a. The figure shows a UML class diagram extended by two stereotypes, "VariationPoint" and "Variant." The stereotypes are used to explicitly document the product line variability. This example models a product line, in which communication is defined as product line variability (documented by *Communication* being a variation point and *WiFi* and *MobileBroadband* being variants).

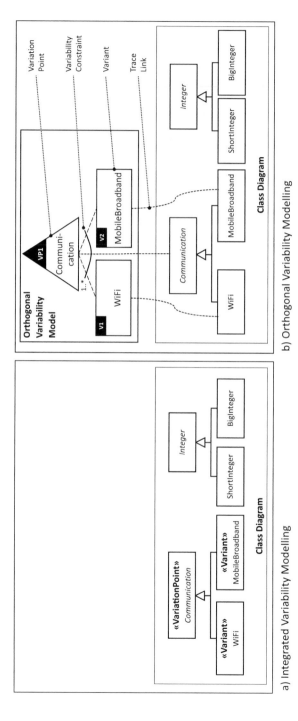

a) Integrated Variability Modelling

b) Orthogonal Variability Modelling

Fig. 2 Illustration of integrated vs. orthogonal variability modeling

Feature models are a commonly used form of integrated variability modeling (e.g., see [15]). A feature model is a tree or a directed acyclic graph of features. A feature model is organized hierarchically. A feature can be decomposed into sub-features. A mandatory feature has to be selected if its parent feature is mandatory or if its parent feature is optional and has been selected. Mandatory features define commonalities. Mandatory features have to be selected for all applications of the product line. Optional, alternative, and "or" features define variability in feature models. As a result, a feature model is a compact representation of all mandatory and optional features of a software product line. Each valid combination of features represents a potential product line application.

Orthogonal Variability Modeling To support the orthogonal documentation of product line variability, product line variability is documented in a dedicated model. In other words, the documentation of product line variability is separated from the documentation of the software development artifacts. Thereby, the variability of the product line is treated as a first-class product line artifact. By relating the product line variability defined in the orthogonal variability model with the software artifacts defined in the artifact models, the realization of product line variability within the software artifacts is documented. Figure 2b sketches an example of an orthogonal documentation of product line variability and its relation to software development artifacts. As depicted in the figure, the documentation of product line variability is clearly separated from the documentation of other software development aspects. Note that the orthogonal variability model only defines product line variability. It does not define product line commonalities.

Integrated Versus Orthogonal Variability Modeling Integrated variability modeling increases the complexity of the software artifact models and documentations due to the additional documentation of product line variability within those artifacts. Moreover, product line variability is redundantly defined in different development artifacts such as requirements models, component diagrams, code, or test cases. As a result, understanding and tracing product line variability between different artifact models becomes difficult. First, different modeling constructs are used to represent the variability in the different models. As a consequence, product line variability is represented differently in the various models. Second, dependencies between the variability defined in the different artifact models are typically not documented explicitly. Third, it is difficult, if not impossible, to keep the variability defined in the different models consistent.

Orthogonal variability modeling avoids those three significant drawbacks of integrated variability modeling. In an orthogonal variability model, *only* the variability of a product line is defined. Commonalities of the product line are only documented in the base models—a key difference from "traditional" feature models, which define both commonalities and variability. The explicit differentiation between variation point and variant marks a second key difference from feature models, which do not provide explicit modeling concepts for variation points. As a third key difference, the variability definition in an orthogonal variability model is free from realization concerns. Therefore, orthogonal variability models provide a clear separation between product line variability (documented in an orthogonal variability model) and software variability (specified in the base models). When using feature models, the separation between product line variability and software variability often gets blurred [5]. Defining the variability in a dedicated, orthogonal variability model avoids this problem.

Product line variability defined in variability models must be interrelated with the software development artifacts defined in the base models. Establishing and maintaining trace links between variability models and the base models is not trivial. A solution for the interrelation is to parameterize the base models to indicate which base model elements link to which feature. However, this solution violates the key principle of keeping product line variability separate from base models. More recent solutions argue for dedicated mapping specifications, which define mappings from variation points and variants to MOF-compliant base models.

6   Variability Modeling in Non-Product-Line Settings

Explicit variability modeling and management can also support the development of software-intensive systems in non-SPLE settings. In this section, we briefly describe some examples.

Clone-and-Own Development   There are cases in which a strategic and planned definition of a product line is not economically viable or not even possible. Beyond the investment in technical design and development of domain artifacts, the introduction of SPLE usually requires a change of processes and organization structure and thus requires significant investments. Therefore, and for many other reasons, instead of following an SPLE approach, software systems are quite often created by "cloning" existing ones (e.g., by copying and modifying requirements, architecture, and code of preceding systems). We strongly believe that the use of the "copy-and-modify" (aka "clone-and-own") approach will increase. Reasons for this increase are, among others, the need to adapt the applications to new technology and service offerings at run time and the rapid changes of the system context and the system requirements. Increasing change demands make a prediction of the scope of a potential product line much harder if not impossible.

Still, even if the SPLE approach is not followed to its full extent in these settings, principles and techniques from variability management facilitate addressing key challenges faced.

As an example, software configuration management tools may be extended with explicit variability management facilities (e.g., see [26]). Thereby, variability is identified (e.g., by deriving variability information based on "copy-and-modify" activities executed by the engineers) and managed in a non-product-line setting.

As another example, the German BMBF projects SPES 2020 and SPES XT (http://spes2020.informatik.tu-muenchen.de/) incorporated variability management into the engineering process of embedded systems [27]. Here, variability modeling principles and techniques facilitate the management of variability of related, single applications.

Cloud Computing Cloud computing aims to provide seamless reconfiguration of the infrastructure in real time based on measuring infrastructure usage and system execution parameters in real time. When combined with the Internet of Things [28], system execution data is enriched with data about the system context obtained by thousands of sensors. Big data analytics facilitates turning all this data into potential actionable insights with very low latency.

Together, these emerging technologies empower software developers and operators (DevOps) to continuously adjust the system based on instantaneous feedback obtained from system execution and the system context [29]. As a consequence, the tension between upfront investment and planning of a software product line and the increased agility fostered by instantaneous feedback and continuous deployment must be reconciled.

As an example, the EU FP7 project CloudWave (http://cloudwave-fp7.eu/) addressed this challenge by employing variability models to structure feedback about the dynamic reconfiguration of the cloud and in turn drive future reconfigurations [30]. An interesting opportunity is inferring the changes of product line variability and commonalities from analyzing operational and contextual data from cloud operations.

Adaptive Systems Driven by the Internet of Services, the Internet of Things, and the emergence of new highly distributed systems, such as cyber-physical systems and ultra-large-scale systems, the need for software to live in an *open* and highly dynamic world is becoming mandatory. Traditionally, software development rests on a closed world assumption. The closed world assumption roughly means that the boundary between the system and its context is known during system development and that the boundary does not change during system execution [31]. In contrast, open world systems cannot be specified completely during design time due to incomplete knowledge about, for instance, services and their actual quality provided during run time, sensors available during system operation to obtain environment information, the availability of other systems to interact and cooperate with, or the quality of data obtained. Such systems must frequently adapt to the dynamic changes faced during run time [14, 32].

As an example, variability models have been used to define the configuration space of a system (i.e., the set of all valid system configurations), thereby describing possible and permissible run-time adaptations of the system [33]. Variability models and mechanisms are well suited to deal with run-time adaptations by considering features as the unit of adaptation.

Oftentimes, foreseeing future context conditions and defining appropriate adaptation options during design time is not possible, and thus defining a variability model completely during design time is not feasible. A possible solution is to apply learning and reasoning techniques to variability models, thereby dealing with unknown situations [34]. For example, the DFG Priority Programme projects iObserve and iObserve 2 (https://www.iobserve-devops.net/) used such principles to update variability models to unknown situations during run time. In the iObserve approach, reinforcement learning is employed to improve the self-adaptive systems adaptation knowledge expressed in terms of variability models [35].

7   Summary

Software product line engineering has proven to facilitate the development of a diversity of similar software-intensive systems at lower cost, in shorter time, and with higher quality when compared with the development of single systems. We have described the main principles and techniques of software product line engineering. Moreover, we sketched how product line engineering principles can facilitate managing variability in non-product-line settings.

References

1. Pohl, K., Böckle, G., van der Linden, F.: Software product line engineering: foundations, principles, and techniques. Springer, Berlin (2005)
2. Metzger, A., Pohl, K.: Software product line engineering and variability management: achievements and challenges. In: International Conference on Software Engineering (ICSE) – Future of Software Engineering Track (FOSE 2014), Hyderabad, India (2014)
3. Clements, P., Northrop, L.: Software product lines: practices and patterns, reading. Addison-Wesley, Upper Saddle River, NJ (2001)
4. Coplien, J., Hoffmann, D., Weiss, D.: Commonality and variability in software engineering. IEEE Soft. **15**(6), 37–45 (1998)
5. Metzger, A., Heymans, P., Pohl, K., Schobbens, P.-Y., Saval, G.: Disambiguating the documentation of variability in software product lines: a separation of concerns, formalization and automated analysis. In: 15th Int'l Requirements Engineering Conference (RE 2007), New Delhi, India (2007)
6. van der Linden, F., Schmid, K., Rommes, E.: Software product lines in action. Springer, Berlin (2007)
7. Halmans, G., Pohl, K., Sikora, E.: Documenting application-specific adaptations in software product line engineering. In: 20th Int'l Conference on Advanced Information Systems Engineering (CAiSE 2008), Montpellier, France (2008)
8. Galster, M., Weyns, D., Tofan, D., Michalek, B. and Avgeriou, P.: Variability in software systems: a systematic literature review. In: IEEE Transactions on Software Engineering. available online (2013)
9. Helferich, A., Schmid, K., Herzwurm, G.: Product management for software product lines: an unsolved problem? Commun. ACM. **49**(12), 66–67 (2006)
10. van Ommering, R., Bosch, J.: Widening the scope of software product lines: from variation to composition. In: 2nd Int'l Software Product Line Conference (SPLC), San Diego, USA (2002)
11. Bühne, S., Lauenroth, K., Pohl, K., Weber, M.: Modelling features for multi-criteria product-lines in the automotive industry. In: ICSE Workshop on Software Engineering for Automotive Systems (SEAS 2004), Edinburgh, UK (2004)

12. Pohl, K.: Requirements engineering: fundamentals, principles, and techniques. Springer, Heidelberg (2010)
13. Niu, N., Easterbrook, S.: Extracting and modeling product line functional requirements. In: 16th Int'l Requirements Engineering Conference (RE 2008), Barcelona, Spain (2008)
14. Figueiredo, E., Cacho, N., Sant'Anna, C., et al.: Evolving software product lines with aspects: an empirical study on design stability. In 30th Int'l Conference on Software Engineering (ICSE 2008), Leipzig, Germany (2008)
15. Mohabbati, B., Asadi, M., Gasevic, D., Hatala, M., Müller, H.: Combining service-orientation and software product line engineering: a systematic mapping study. Inf. Soft. Technol. **55**(11), 1845–1859 (2013)
16. Di Nitto, E., Ghezzi, C., Metzger, A., Papazoglou, M.P., Pohl, K.: A journey to highly dynamic, self-adaptive service-based applications. Autom. Softw. Eng. **15**(3–4), 313–341 (2008)
17. Capilla, R., Bosch, J., Kang, K.-C.: Systems and software variability management. Springer, Heidelberg (2013)
18. Batory, D., Höfner, P., Kim, J.: Feature interactions, products, and composition. In: 10th Int'l Conference on Generative Programming and Component Engineering (GPCE 2011), Portland, USA (2011)
19. Haber, A., Hölldobler, K., Kolassa, C., Look, M., Rumpe, B., Müller, K., Schaefer, I.: Engineering delta modeling languages. In 17th Int'l Software Product Line Conference (SPLC 2013), Tokyo, Japan (2013)
20. Lauenroth, K., Metzger, A., Pohl, K.: Quality assurance in the presence of variability. In: Intentional perspectives on information systems engineering, pp. 319–334. Springer, Heidelberg (2010)
21. Lee, J., Kang, S., Lee, D.: A survey on software product line testing. In 16th Int'l Software Product Line Conference (SPLC 2012), Salvador, Brazil (2012)
22. Pohl, K., Metzger, A.: Software product line testing. Commun. ACM. **49**(12), 78–81 (2006)
23. Benavides, D., Segura, S., Ruiz-Cortés, A.: Automated analysis of feature models 20 years later: a literature review. Inform. Sys. **35**(6), 615–636 (2010)
24. Pohl, R., Stricker, V., Pohl, K.: Measuring the structural complexity of feature models. In 28th Int'l Conference on Automated Software Engineering (ASE 2013), Palo Alto, USA (2013)
25. Dhungana, D., Grünbacher, P., Rabiser, R.: The DOPLER meta-tool for decision-oriented variability modeling: a multiple case study. Autom. Softw. Eng. **18**(1), 77–114 (2011)
26. Engström, E., Runeson, P.: Software product line testing: a systematic mapping study. Inf. Softw. Technol. **53**(1), 2–13 (2011)
27. Stricker, V., Metzger, A., Pohl, K.: Avoiding redundant testing in application engineering. In: 14th Int'l Software Product Line Conference (SPLC 2010), Jeju Island, South Korea (2010).
28. Berger, T., Rublack, R., Nair, D., Atlee, J., Becker, M., Czarnecki, K., Wasowski, A.: A survey of variability modeling in industrial practice. In 7th Int'l Workshop on Variability Modelling of Software-intensive Systems (VaMoS 2013), Pisa, Italy (2013)
29. Rubin, J., Kirshin, A., Botterweck, G., Chechik, M.: Managing forked product variants. In: 16th Int'l Software Product Line Conference (SPLC 2012), Salvador, Brazil (2012)
30. Pohl, K., Broy, M., Daembkes, H., Hönninger, H.: Advanced model-based engineering of embedded systems. Springer, Cham (2016)
31. Atzori, L., Iera, A., Morabito, G.: The internet of things: a survey. Comput. Netw. **54**(15), 2787–2805 (2010)
32. Bosch, J.: Building products as innovation experiment systems. In: 3rd Int'l Conference on Software Business (ICSOB 2012), Cambridge, USA (2012)
33. Cooper, K., Franch, X.: Editorial. J. Syst. Softw. **81**(6), 841–842 (2008)

34. Díaz, J., Pérez, J., Alarcón, P.P., Garbajosa, J.: Agile product line engineering: a systematic literature review. Softw. Pract. Exp. **41**(8), 921–941 (2011)
35. Metzger, A., Bayer, A., Doyle, D., Molzam Sharifloo, A., Pohl, K., Wessling, F.: Coordinated run-time adaptation of variability-intensive systems: an application in cloud computing. In ICSE 2016 1st Int'l Workshop on Variability and Complexity in Software Design (VACE), Austin, Texas (2016)

Enabling Flexible and Robust Business Process Automation for the Agile Enterprise

Manfred Reichert

1 Introduction

In today's dynamic business world, the success of an enterprise increasingly depends on its ability to react to environmental changes in a quick and flexible way. Examples of changes include regulatory adaptations (e.g., Sarbanes-Oxley), market evolution, changes in customer behavior, redesigned business processes, and strategic shifts. Therefore, enterprises have identified *business agility* as a competitive advantage to address business needs like increasing product variability or faster time to market as well as to tightly align business and IT. Improving the efficiency and quality of their *business processes* and optimizing their interactions with partners and customers have become crucial success factors for enterprises [15, 19].

Contemporary enterprise information systems, which are often organized in a data- or function-centric way, lack *process awareness* hindering business agility. In many cases, enterprises prefer abandoning new business initiatives rather than attempting to adapt their enterprise software. To better support their business processes and to manage them in a more flexible manner, however, enterprises are increasingly interested in aligning their information systems in a process-centric way offering the right *business functions* to the right *users* at the right *point in time* along with the needed *information* and *application services* [26]. Along this trend, a new generation of enterprise information systems—so-called *process-aware information systems (PAISs)*—has emerged [19], which aim to overcome this inflexibility.

M. Reichert (✉)
Ulm University, Ulm, Germany
e-mail: manfred.reichert@uni-ulm.de

© The Author(s) 2018
V. Gruhn, R. Striemer (eds.), *The Essence of Software Engineering*,
https://doi.org/10.1007/978-3-319-73897-0_12

Examples of PAISs include workflow management systems, case handling tools, and service orchestration engines [26]. In spite of several success stories on the uptake of PAISs, the latter have not been widely adopted in industry yet [11]. A major reason for their low use is the rigidity enforced by them, which inhibits the ability of enterprises to respond to process changes or exceptions in an agile way [23]. When efforts are taken to improve and automate the flow of business processes, however, in many domains (e.g., healthcare), it is crucial not to restrict staff [13, 17]. For example, first attempts to change the function- and data-centric views on patient treatment processes in hospitals failed whenever rigidity came with them [13, 16]. Variations in the course of a treatment process are inherent to medicine, and to some degree the unforeseen event constitutes a "normal" phenomenon [13]. Hence, a sufficient degree of flexibility is needed to support dynamic process adaptations in case of unforeseen situations. Finally, *PAIS flexibility* is required to accommodate the need for evolving business processes [21, 23].

In general, a PAIS is aligned in a process-centric way, separating process logic from application code (i.e., the implementation of the application services) and, thus, providing an additional architectural layer [4]. In principle, this separation makes PAISs more flexible compared to data- and function-centric information systems. However, it is not yet sufficient to meet the needs of agile enterprises. In particular, traditional PAISs have focused on the support of predictable and repetitive processes, which can be fully described prior to their execution in terms of formal models [27]. Accordingly, such PAISs require complete specifications (i.e., process models) of the business processes to be supported, which are then used as the schemas for process execution. In practice, however, business processes have become increasingly complex and dynamic, demanding for a more agile approach acknowledging that in dynamic environments process models quickly become outdated and, hence, a closer interweaving of modeling and execution is required. Therefore, PAISs not only need to be able to deal with exceptions [20], change the execution of single business cases on the fly [17], efficiently deal with uncertainty [6], and cope with variability [1, 7], but must also support the evolution of implemented business processes over time [19].

The goal of this chapter is to address the flexibility needs emerging in this context and to give insights into technologies addressing them. Emphasis is put on key features enabling process adaptation and evolution. Based on them, PAISs being able to flexibly cope with real-world exceptions, uncertainty, and changes can be realized.

2 Traditional Process-Aware Information Systems

A PAIS targets at the operational support of business processes at the IT level. To accomplish this, the business processes need to be mapped to *executable process models*. Thereby, a *business process* comprises a set of one or more connected *activities* that collectively realize a particular *business goal* [15]. A process is linked to an *organizational structure* defining functional roles and organizational relationships. Furthermore, a business process may take place in a specific department but may also cross departmental borders or even involve different organizations [5]. Examples of business processes include insurance claim processing, order handling, personnel recruitment, product engineering, and patient treatment.

2.1 Business Process Modeling

To provide additional value for the business, any process automation should be preceded by process reengineering and optimization efforts [15]; that is, business processes have to be (re)designed to meet organizational goals in an economic and efficient manner. Goals pursued may include shortening process cycle times, reducing process costs, increasing customer satisfaction, and decreasing error rates.

To discuss alternative designs with stakeholders and to evaluate the designed processes, process knowledge must be captured in *business process models* [2]. The latter describe business processes at a high level of abstraction, serving as a basis for analysis, simulation, and visualization. A business process model comprises the process activities and their attributes (e.g., costs and time) as well as the control and data flow between the activities. Activities may be manual ones without the potential to be automated or system-supported activities requiring human or machine resources for their execution. In general, a distinction has to be made between *business process models* on one hand and their executable counterparts (denoted as *executable process models*) on the other [2]. The latter constitute the key artifacts of a PAIS, realizing the automation of business processes and, in whole or part, the implementation of their models. When interpreting an executable process model, documents, data objects, or activities are passed from one actor to another according to predefined procedural rules [27]. In the following, we focus on executable process models and their flexible support through PAISs.

2.2 Architectural Principles of a PAIS

A PAIS is a specific type of information system that offers advanced process support services. As opposed to data- or function-centric information systems, PAISs enforce a strict separation of process logic and application code. In particular, process logic is described explicitly in terms of *executable process models* providing the schema for process execution. Note that turning away from hard-coded process logic towards explicitly specified process models significantly eases (model-driven) PAIS development and maintenance. The core of the process layer of a PAIS, in turn, is built by a process management system. Its buildtime and runtime components offer generic software services for modeling, implementing, executing, and monitoring business processes as well as for enabling user interactions with them (e.g., through worklists). Workflow management systems (e.g., ADEPT [4, 18],

Staffware [26]) and case handling tools (e.g., FLOWer [26], PHILharmonicFlows [10]) constitute examples of PAISs.

As a basic principle, PAISs foster the splitting of monolithic applications into smaller services, which can then be orchestrated by its *process engine*. Maintainability and traceability are significantly enhanced by this extended architecture. Changes to one layer often can be performed without affecting the other layers. For example, modifying the application service that implements a particular process step (i.e., activity) does usually not imply any change to the process layer as long as interfaces remain stable (i.e., the external observable behavior of the service remains the same). In addition, changing the execution order of activities or adding new activities to the process can, to a large degree, be accomplished without touching the implementation of any application service.

2.3 Process Enactment Based on Executable Process Models

As already mentioned, the business processes or the process parts to be automated by the PAIS need to be captured in *executable process models*. At buildtime, these models are created based on the elements provided by a process meta-model (e.g., BPMN 2.0) using a graphical editor. Basically, an executable process model corresponds to a directed graph that comprises a set of nodes—representing process steps (i.e., activities) or control connectors (e.g., XOR/AND-Split, XOR/AND-Join)—and a set of control edges between them. Control edges specify precedence relations between nodes. Further, the data flow between the activities (i.e., which activities read or write which data elements) needs to be specified and the activities be associated with resources (e.g., user roles). Activities can either be atomic or complex. While an atomic activity is associated with an invokable application service, a complex activity contains a sub-process or, more precisely, a reference to a sub-process model. In turn, this allows for the hierarchical decomposition of process models. Moreover, several executable process models may exist for a particular business process representing the different versions and the evolution of this business process over time. As a benefit of the described model-driven approach, it can be formally checked (e.g., model checking) whether a process model can be properly executed during runtime (e.g., guaranteeing for the absence of deadlocks and ensuring proper data flow). Finally, at runtime the PAIS orchestrates multiple instances of a process model according to the defined logic, also allowing for the integration of application services, users, and other resources.

2.4 Traditional Process Lifecycle Support

Traditional PAISs enable process lifecycle support as depicted in Fig. 1: At buildtime, an initial representation of the process to be supported is created either by

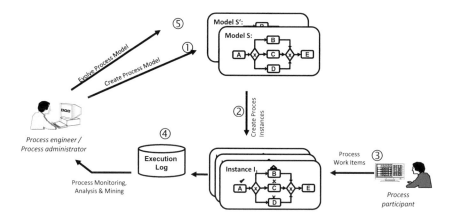

Fig. 1 Process lifecycle support in traditional PAIS

explicitly modeling the process based on process analysis results or by discovering its model through process mining [25] (1). At runtime, process instances are created from the executable process model (2), each representing a concrete business case. Process instances are executed based on the model they were originally derived from. While fully automated activities are immediately executed when they become enabled, nonautomated activities are assigned to the worklists of qualified actors (3). Execution logs record information about the start and completion of activity instances as well as their chronological order (4). The analysis of logs by a process engineer or process intelligence tools allows discovering malfunctions or bottlenecks. In turn, this triggers the evolutionary change of the process model (5).

2.5 Key Features of a Process-Aware Information System

In summary, a PAIS:

- Knows the logic of the supported processes; that is, processes are explicitly described in terms of executable process models.
- Ensures that activities are executed in the specified order or considering the specified constraints (i.e., the PAIS manages the flow of control during runtime).
- Controls the flow of data between the activities; that is, the output data of a particular activity can be consumed as input data by subsequent activities.
- Knows the application service to be invoked when an atomic activity is started.
- Assigns work items related to human activities to the worklists of authorized users and manages these worklists. Further, it reminds users to complete an activity before reaching its deadline.

- Enables end users to monitor the progress of process instances and to trace their previous execution.
- Comprises build- and runtime components that support different stages of the process lifecycle.

3 Enabling Process Flexibility at the Operational Level

The ability to efficiently deal with business process changes has been identified as one of the critical success factors for PAISs [11, 19, 23]. Although PAISs facilitate changes significantly through the separation of concerns, enterprises are reluctant to change PAIS implementations once they are running properly. High complexity and high costs of change are provided as major reasons for not fully leveraging the potential of PAISs. In particular, more flexible PAISs are needed, which enable enterprises to operationalize their processes in a way not causing any mismatch between the digital processes and those running in reality [19]. Moreover, a PAIS must not "freeze" the implementation of business processes [26], but allow authorized users to flexibly deviate from the prespecified processes whenever required (e.g., to deal with exceptions) as well as to evolve process implementations over time [20, 21]. Process changes should be enabled at a high level of abstraction [8, 9] without affecting consistency and robustness of the PAIS [17]. Finally, PAISs must allow users to cope with uncertainty by deferring decisions to the runtime if required [19].

Traditional PAISs do not support such advanced scenarios due to their inherent brittleness and inflexibility [26]. What is needed are PAISs that allow both business process implementations and process instances to be continually adapted and reformed to fit the actual needs and constraints of their environment and to fulfill the goals of the involved process participants in the best possible way—we denote such processes as *adaptive*. Traditional PAISs implicitly embrace the "engineer–use" dichotomy [26] as inherited from traditional approaches to software engineering. This dichotomy is based on the engineering principle that software systems are first *engineered* and then, once deemed fit for purpose, are *used* (i.e., *operated*). Maintenance and evolution tasks are not regarded as part of operation, but rather as interruptions to the "in use" state, which temporarily return the system to the "being engineered" state. In scenarios with dynamically emerging or disappearing requirements (e.g., healthcare [13, 16]), this "engineer–use" strategy is unworkable. The only feasible way to cope with dynamism is to dissolve the fundamental distinction between *engineering* and *use* and to seamlessly merge the entire service and process lifecycle into a single encompassing framework [25]. In turn, this leads to a new class of processes whose *engineering* and *use* are indistinguishable.

4   Adaptive Process-Aware Information Systems

This section reports on *adaptive PAISs*, a next generation technology enabling *adaptive processes* that abandon the "engineer–use" dichotomy. Adaptive PAISs must not be confused with *(self-)adaptive systems* as recognized by the adaptive systems research community [3]. Processes are adaptive in the sense that they are continually evolving and reshaping to fit to the situation at hand, but unlike classical adaptive systems (as understood in adaptive systems' research) they are not expected to do this themselves. On the contrary, the adaptation is performed with the help of the user/engineer. In other words, in *adaptive processes*, human engineers and users are part of the loop, and the use and adaptation of processes are seen as two sides of the same coin. In this sense, *adaptive processes* have more in common with agile software development methods, which focus on encouraging human developers to evolve software in a rapid and effective way. The following sections sketch how adaptive processes and, thus, process flexibility can be realized in PAISs. Note that we do not give detailed insights into formal or technical aspects of adaptive PAISs (see [12, 19, 21, 23, 24]), but want to emphasize the perspectives offered by them, illustrated along the AristaFlow BPM Suite we developed during the last decade.

4.1   The AristaFlow Process Management Technology

During the last decade, we developed the ADEPT2 next generation process management technology [17, 18, 21, 24] to tackle the flexibility challenges discussed in Sect. 3. ADEPT2 is an adaptive PAIS dissolving the "engineering–use" dichotomy and increasing ease of use for process implementers, application developers, system administrators, and end users. Further, robustness of process implementations and the robust support of dynamic process changes were fundamental project goals. To achieve them, a *correctness-by-construction* principle is applied during process modeling. Furthermore, it is ensured that ad hoc process instance changes do not introduce any errors or inconsistencies in the following. Due to the high interest of industry in the ADEPT2 technology, it was then transformed into an industrial-strength process management technology called *AristaFlow BPM Suite* [4, 22]. AristaFlow enables robust and flexible PAISs in the large scale. In particular, it ensures error-safe and robust process execution even at the presence of exceptions or dynamic process changes. AristaFlow was applied in a variety of application domains (e.g., healthcare, disaster management, and software engineering).

4.2   Support for Process Adaptation and Process Evolution

In general, process adaptations can be accomplished at two levels—the process type and the process instance level.

Ad Hoc Adaptations at the Process Instance Level Generally, it is not possible to anticipate all real-world exceptions and to capture their handling in an executable process model at buildtime. AristaFlow, therefore, enables users to situationally adapt single process instances (i.e., specific business cases) during runtime if required, for example, by inserting, deleting, or moving activities [17]. In a medical treatment process, for example, a patient's current medication may have to be discontinued due to an allergic reaction. In general, the effects of ad hoc changes are instance specific and must not affect other instances. Providing support for ad hoc deviations from a prespecified process model, however, must not shift the responsibility for ensuring PAIS robustness to end users. Exactly for this reason, AristaFlow provides comprehensive support for the correct, secure, and robust handling of runtime exceptions through ad hoc process instance changes. Reference [19] presents a taxonomy for ad hoc changes, discusses how the behavior of a process instance can be situationally adapted, and presents adaptation patterns that may be applied for this purpose. Moreover, Ref. [19] shows how PAIS robustness can be ensured when dynamically adapting process instances and how end users can be assisted in defining changes.

Process Model Evolution and Instance Migration Business processes evolve over time due to changes in their legal, technical, or business environment, or as a result of organizational learning [14, 15]. Consequently, PAIS implementations need to be adapted accordingly. We denote this as *process model evolution*, that is, the evolution of executable process models over time to accommodate changes of real-world processes. In general, process model evolution might require change propagation to already running process instances, particularly if the latter are long running. For example, let us assume that, due to a new legal requirement, patients have to be informed about potential risks before a surgery takes place. Let us further assume that this change is also relevant for patients for which the treatment has already been started. In such a scenario, stopping all ongoing treatments, aborting them, and restarting them is not a viable option. As a large number of treatment processes might be running at the same time, applying this change manually to all ongoing treatment processes is also not feasible. AristaFlow, therefore, provides efficient support to add this step to all patient treatments for which this is still feasible (e.g., if the surgery has not yet started). For this purpose, it offers techniques for dealing with already running process instances and their on-the-fly migration to the changed process model, without violating any correctness and soundness properties. In this context, well-known process adaptation patterns may be applied, which provide precise pre- and post-conditions for ensuring syntactical correctness and behavioral soundness of a process model; that is, a correctness-by-construction principle is applied [4, 17]. Deficiencies that cannot be prohibited by this approach (e.g., correctness of the data flow schema) are checked on the fly and are continuously reported to the user.

In general, process model evolution and instance-specific ad hoc changes have to be handled in combination with each other [21, 24, 25]. Moreover, AristaFlow provides built-in flexibility allowing process engineers to leave parts of the process model unspecified at buildtime and to add the missing information during runtime.

Especially, this approach is useful in case of uncertainty as it allows deferring decisions from build- to runtime.

4.3 Advanced Process Lifecycle Support in Adaptive PAIS

The described ability of AristaFlow for enabling ad hoc changes in a controlled, correct, and secure way as well as for the controlled evolution of process models (including process instance migrations) leads to a revised process lifecycle [25] (cf. Fig. 2): At buildtime, an initial representation of a business process is created, either by modeling the process or by discovering its model through process mining (1). New process instances can be derived at runtime from this executable process model (2). Instances are executed according to the original process model they were derived from, and activities are assigned to process participants to perform the respective activities (3). However, when unanticipated exceptional situations occur during runtime, process participants may deviate from the prespecified model by applying ad hoc changes (4). While execution logs record information about activities (3), process changes are recorded in change logs and may be semantically represented as cases (4). The latter enables the reuse of ad hoc changes in similar situations [25]. The analysis of these logs by process engineers or process intelligence tools allows for the discovery of malfunctions or bottlenecks, which often leads to an evolution of the process model (6). The latter is supported through versioning as well as the ability of dynamically migrating already running process instances.

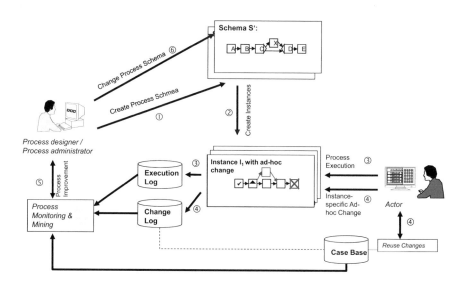

Fig. 2 Process lifecycle support in adaptive PAIS

4.4   Making Process Implementations Flexible and Robust

We now focus on a fundamental pillar of any robust process implementation, that is, *error handling*. In particular, we show how the presented process adaptation features can be utilized to make business process implementations flexible and robust.

4.4.1   Error Prevention

AristaFlow targets at *error prevention*, which is achieved by applying a *correctness-by-construction* principle during process modeling and service composition as well as by guaranteeing correctness and robustness in connection with dynamic process changes. The latter means that none of the PAIS correctness properties ensured by respective checks at buildtime may be violated due to a dynamic process change. This was probably the most influential challenge for our research. It also had significant impact on the development of the AristaFlow BPM Suite. In particular, we try to detect as many errors as possible at buildtime (e.g., flaws in the data flow or deadlocks) to exclude their occurrence during runtime. As discussed, however, errors cannot be always prevented. Therefore, another important aspect of PAIS robustness concerns its exception handling features. We will show that the AristaFlow BPM Suite provides an easy but yet powerful way to handle exceptions during runtime. In this context, the ability to support ad hoc process changes is very useful. By utilizing such dynamic changes, it becomes possible to even cope with severe process failures and to continue and complete respective process instances.

We will use an example to demonstrate how errors can be handled in the AristaFlow BPM Suite. Consider Fig. 3, which shows a simple process of an online book store. In the first step, a customer request is entered and required data is collected. Next the bookseller requests pricing offers from his suppliers. In the given scenario, he will request an offer from Amazon using a web service and another offer from another vendor using e-mail. After receiving the pricing offers from both suppliers, the bookseller checks whether he can find a special offer for the requested books in the Internet. Finally, he makes a corresponding offer to his customer.

The scenario contains several sources of potential errors. While some of them can be addressed at buildtime, others cannot. For example, assume that the process

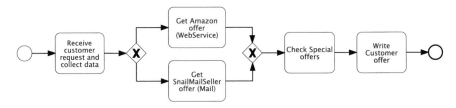

Fig. 3   Scenario: a simple process calling a web service (in BPMN notation)

implementer does not foresee a way to enter the offer from *SnailMailSeller* into the system. Then, the final activity might fail or produce an invalid output as its input parameters are not set properly. Another source of error might be the Amazon web service; for example, it might not be available when making the request and, therefore, activity *Get Amazon offer* might fail at runtime. Such errors can be foreseen and, hence, be considered at buildtime. However, unexpected errors might occur as well; for example, *Check Special offers* might fail due to troubles with the Internet connection.

The following requirements for error-safe and robust process execution exist: On one hand, errors should be avoided at buildtime, while on the other, PAIS should enable users to effectively deal with both expected and unexpected errors during runtime.

4.4.2   Error and Exception Handling in the AristaFlow BPM Suite

We consider the above example from the perspectives of the *process implementer* (i.e., the process engineer), the *system* (i.e., the PAIS), the *end user* (i.e., the process actor), and the *system supervisor* (i.e., the PAIS administrator). We discuss how each of these parties can contribute to the handling of errors.

Process Implementer Perspective

Figure 4 shows a part of the process from Fig. 3, as it can be modeled using the *AristaFlow Process Template Editor*. For process implementation, the idea of process composition in a *plug & play* style is pursued and supported by comprehensive correctness checks. The latter aims to exclude runtime errors during process execution. As a prerequisite, for example, the data flow dependencies among application services have to be made explicit to the PAIS.

AristaFlow provides an intuitive graphical editor and composition tool to process implementers (cf. Fig. 4). Further, it applies a *correctness-by-construction* principle by providing at any time only those change operations to the user which allow transforming a sound process model into another one; that is, change operations are enabled or disabled depending on which region in the process graph is marked for applying an operation. Deficiencies not prohibited by this approach (e.g., regarding data flow) are checked on the fly and are reported continuously in the problem window of the *Process Template Editor*. An example is depicted in Fig. 4, where AristaFlow detects that data element *Customer price per unit* is read by activity *Write Customer offer*, but not written by any preceding activity.

In general, one should not require detailed knowledge from process implementers about the internals of the application services they may assign to the activities of an executable process model. However, this should not be achieved by undermining the *correctness-by-construction* principle. In AristaFlow, all kinds of executables (e.g., web services, SQL procedures, Java Apps), which may be assigned to process

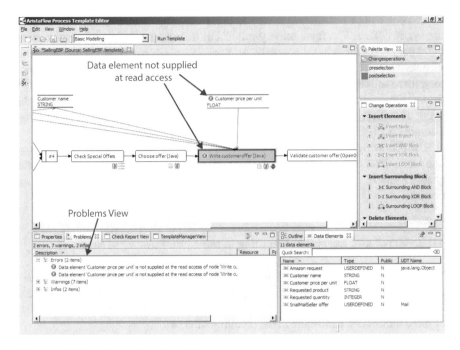

Fig. 4 AristaFlow Process Template Editor

activities, first have to be registered in the *Activity Repository* as activity templates. An activity template, in turn, provides all information to the *Process Template Editor*, for example, information about mandatory and optional input/output parameters of activities or data dependencies to other activity templates. The process implementer just drags and drops an activity template from the *Activity Repository Browser* window of the *Process Template Editor* onto the desired location in the process graph.

As a major advantage of this approach, common errors (e.g., missing data bindings) can be already detected at buildtime. Consequently, the time needed for testing and debugging process implementations can be significantly reduced; that is, AristaFlow guarantees that executable process models without any detected deficiencies are sound and complete with respect to the activity templates used.

System Perspective

The described approach ensures that, in principle, the process model is executable by the PAIS in an error-safe way. As always, this might not hold in practice. Again, consider the scenario from Fig. 3. The web service referred by activity *Get Amazon offer* (i.e., the service implementing this activity) might not be available when the process is executed, leading to an exception during runtime. Note that such errors neither can be detected in advance nor be completely prevented by the PAIS.

Failures of the Amazon web service might be anticipated by the process implementer. Thus, he may assign specific error handling procedures to the respective activity. Following a strict process paradigm, AristaFlow itself uses processes to coordinate exception handling; that is, a *reflective* approach is taken in which error handling is accomplished by a specific process executed in AristaFlow. A simple error handling process is depicted in Fig. 5. Depending on whether the failure of the activity was triggered by the user (e.g., through an *abort* button), either the system supervisor is notified accordingly or the process silently terminates. Generally, error handling processes can become arbitrarily complex and long running. Note that AristaFlow treats error handling processes the same way as any other process. Thus, they may refer to any activity registered in the repository. Note that this allows for error handling at a higher semantical level, involving users whenever required. If an activity fails, the respective error handling process is initiated and equipped with all the data necessary to identify and handle the error, for example, the ID of the failed activity instance, the actors responsible for the activity, or the cause of the error (cf. Fig. 5).

After creating an error handling process and deploying it to the *AristaFlow Server*, it can be assigned to an activity or process by simply selecting it from a list of processes. Whether or not a process is suitable as error handling process is decided based on its signature, that is, the input and output parameters of the process. Note that it is also possible to assign an error handling process to a complete process model instead of assigning it to a specific activity. Then, this general error handling

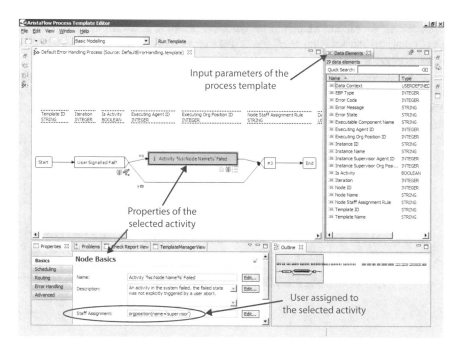

Fig. 5 A simple error handling process

process will be used if no other error handling process is associated with a failed activity. If no error handling process is assigned to the activity and process, in turn, a system default error handling process will be used instead.

As a considerable advantage of using processes for error handling, standard process modeling tools and techniques can be used for designing error handling strategies. Therefore, process implementers need not learn any new concept to provide sophisticated error handing procedures. As another important advantage, error handling at a higher semantical level becomes possible. For example, one may also realize more complex error handling strategies like compensation or apply ad hoc changes to replace parts of the failed process.

End User Perspective

The error handling process from Fig. 5 might not be always appropriate as it increases the workload of the system supervisor. Most standard errors can be handled in a (semi)automatic way by the actor executing the activity. Upon failure of the activity, the actor responsible for its execution could be provided with a set of possible error handling strategies among which he may choose. An example of such a more complex error handling process is shown in Fig. 6. Here, the user may choose between a variety of ways to handle the error, for example, retrying the failed activity, aborting the entire process instance, or applying prespecified ad hoc changes to fix or compensate the error. Moreover, the error handling strategies suggested in a particular context may depend on the background of the respective user, that is, on his knowledge, organizational position, and various other factors. Depending on the selected user, the respective strategy is chosen and applied to handle the error.

The described semiautomatic approach provides several advantages. As for each activity a predefined set of strategies can be offered to users, they need not have deep insights into the process of properly handling errors. This allows reducing waiting times for failed activity instances as users themselves can handle errors immediately without waiting for a busy helpdesk. In turn, this relieves the helpdesk from the tedious task of dealing with simple process errors.

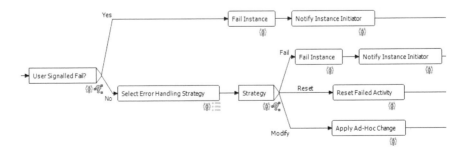

Fig. 6 A more complex error handling process involving the user

System Supervisor Perspective

Certain errors cannot be handled by the user. For example, errors might not have been foreseen at buildtime; that is, no appropriate error handling process exists, or it might be simply not possible to handle errors in an easy and generic way. In such cases, the system supervisor may use the *AristaFlow Process Monitor* as shown in Fig. 7 to take a look at this process instance, to analyze its execution log, and to decide for an appropriate error handling strategy. Additionally, the system supervisor may use the *AristaFlow Process Monitor* to keep track of failed instances; for example, he may intervene if a web service becomes unavailable permanently.

Reconsider the bookseller scenario from Fig. 3. Assume that a process instance wants to issue a request for a book using Amazon's web service facilities, but then fails in doing so. The system administrator detects that the process instance is in trouble and uses the *AristaFlow Process Monitor* to take a look at it (cf. Fig. 7). Analyzing the execution log of the failed activity, he detects that its execution failed because the connection to Amazon could not be established. Let us assume that he considers this as a temporary problem and just resets the activity such that it can be repeated once again. Being a friendly guy, he takes a short look at the process instance and its data dependencies and realizes that the result of this and the subsequent activity is only needed when executing the *Choose offer* activity.

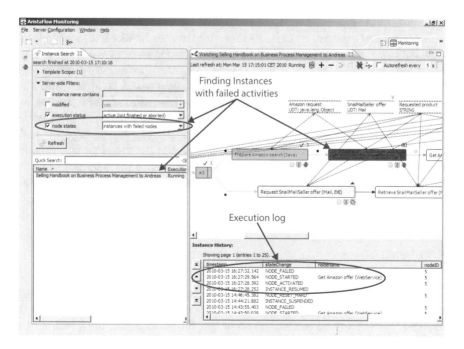

Fig. 7 AristaFlow Process Monitor: Monitoring Perspective

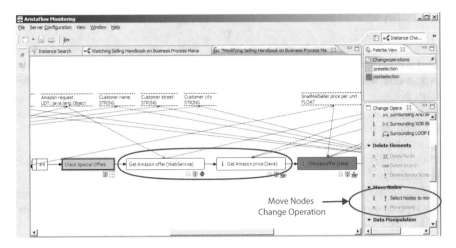

Fig. 8 AristaFlow Process Monitor: Instance Change Perspective

Therefore, he dynamically moves these two activities after activity *Check Special Offers*; that is, the user may continue working on this process instance before the PAIS tries to reconnect to Amazon (cf. Fig. 8).

To realize the described change, he can switch to the *Instance Change Perspective* of the *AristaFlow Process Monitor*, which provides the same set of change operations as the *Process Template Editor*. In fact, it is the *Process Template Editor* being aware that a process instance has been loaded and, therefore, instance-related state information is additionally taken into account when enabling/disabling change operations and applying correctness checks (e.g., the application of changes to already passed regions of the respective process model would be prohibited). The system administrator would now move the two activities to their new position by applying the respective change operation. The resulting instance is depicted in Fig. 8. Assume now that the web service problem lasts longer than expected and, therefore, the user wants to call Amazon by phone to get the price that way. In this case, he would ask the system administrator to delete the activities being in trouble and to replace them with a form-based activity allowing him to enter the price manually.

5 Conclusions

Adaptive processes fundamentally change the way in which human stakeholders interact and collaborate as they dissolve the distinction between process engineers and end users. To date, business process support technologies have focused on enhancing and automating the way in which process users collaborate and interact, but have not significantly changed the way in which the processes themselves are engineered (i.e., defined and maintained). It has been assumed that this is done by IT specialists in a distinct engineering phase with little or no connection to the execution of the processes or the normal operation of the enterprise. However, with adaptive processes, this distinction will blur (if not entirely disappear) and process engineers will become process users and vice versa. Stated differently, process engineering will be also regarded as a normal adaptive process involving the collaboration of multiple stakeholders.

References

1. Ayora, C., Torres, V., Weber, B., Reichert, M., Pelechano, V. VIVACE: A framework for the systematic evaluation of variability support in process-aware information systems. Inf. Softw. Technol. **57**, 248–276 (2015)
2. Buchwald, S., et al.: Bridging the gap between business process models and service composition specifications. In: Service Life Cycle Tools and Technologies, pp. 124–153 (2011)
3. Cheng, B., et al.: Software engineering for self-adaptive systems: a research roadmap. In: Software Engineering for Self-adaptive Systems, pp. 1–26. Springer, Berlin (2009)
4. Dadam, P., Reichert, M.: The ADEPT project: a decade of research and development for robust and flexible process support. Comput. Sci. Res. Dev. **23**(2), 81–97 (2009)
5. Fdhila, W., Indiono, C., Rinderle-Ma, S., Reichert, M.: Dealing with change in process choreographies: design and implementation of propagation algorithms. Inf. Sys. **49**, 1–24 (2015)
6. Haisjackl, C., Barba, I., Zugal, S., Soffer, P., Hadar, I., Reichert, M., Pinggera, J., Weber, B.: Understanding declare models: strategies, pitfalls, empirical results. Softw. Syst. Model. **15**(2), 325–352 (2016)
7. Hallerbach, A., Bauer, T., Reichert, M.: Capturing variability in business process models: the Provop approach. J. Softw. Maint. Evol. **22**(6–7), 519–546 (2010)
8. Kolb, J., Reichert, M.: A flexible approach for abstracting and personalizing large business process models. Appl. Comput. Rev. ACM SIGAPP **13**(1), 6–17 (2013)
9. Kolb, J., Kammerer, K., Reichert, M.: Updatable process views for user-centered adaption of large process models. In: Proceedings of the ICSOC'12. Lecture Notes in Computer Science, vol. 7636, pp. 484–498. Springer, Heidelberg (2012)
10. Künzle, V., Reichert, M.: PHILharmonicFlows: towards a framework for object-aware process management. J. Softw. Maint. Evol. **23**(4), 205–244 (2011)
11. Künzle, V., Weber, B., Reichert, M.: Object-aware business processes: fundamental requirements and their support in existing approaches. J. Inf. Syst. Model. Des. IGI **2**(2), 19–46 (2011)
12. Lanz, A., Weber, B., Reichert, M.: Time patterns for process-aware information systems. Req. Eng. **19**(2), 113–141 (2014)
13. Lenz, R., Reichert, M.: IT support for healthcare processes - premises, challenges, perspectives. Data Knowl. Eng. **61**(1), 39–58 (2007)
14. Li, C., Reichert, M., Wombacher, A.: Mining business process variants - challenges, scenarios, algorithms. Data Knowl. Eng. **70**(5), 409–434 (2011)
15. Lohrmann, M., Reichert, M.: Effective application of process improvement patterns to business processes. Softw. Syst. Model. **15**(2), 353–375 (2016)
16. Reichert, M.: What BPM technology can do for healthcare process support. In: Proceedings of the AIME'11. Lecture Notes in Artificial Intelligence, vol. 6747, pp. 2–13. Springer, Berlin (2011)
17. Reichert, M., Dadam, P.: ADEPTflex - supporting dynamic changes of workflows without losing control. J. Intell. Inf. Syst. **10**(2), 93–129 (1998)

18. Reichert, M., Dadam, P.: Enabling adaptive process-aware information systems with ADEPT2. In: Handbook of Research on Business Process Modeling, IGI, pp. 173–203 (2009)
19. Reichert, M., Weber, B.: Enabling Flexibility in Process-Aware Information Systems: Challenges, Methods, Technologies. Springer, Heidelberg (2012)
20. Reichert, M., Dadam, P., Bauer, T.: Dealing with forward and backward jumps in workflow management systems. Softw. Syst. Model. **2**(1), 37–58 (2003)
21. Reichert, M., Rinderle, S., Dadam, P.: On the common support of workflow type and instance changes under correctness constraints. In: Proceedings of the CoopIS '03. Lecture Notes in Computer Science, vol. 2888, pp. 407–425. Springer, Berlin (2003)
22. Reichert, M., et al.: Enabling Poka-Yoke workflows with the AristaFlow BPM Suite. In: Proceedings of the BPM '09 Demonstration Track, CEUR Workshop Proceedings, vol. 489 (2009)
23. Reichert, M., Rinderle-Ma, S., Dadam, P.: Flexibility in Process-Aware Information Systems. ToPNoC. Lecture Notes in Computer Science, vol. 5460, pp. 115–135. Springer, Heidelberg (2009)
24. Rinderle, S., Reichert, M., Dadam, P.: Disjoint and overlapping process changes: challenges, solutions, applications. In: Proceedings of the CoopIS '04, Lecture Notes in Computer Science, vol. 3290, pp. 101–121. Springer, Berlin (2004)
25. Weber, B., Reichert, M., Wild, W., Rinderle-Ma, S.: Providing integrated life cycle support in process-aware information systems. J. Coop. Inf. Syst. **18**(1), 115–165 (2009)
26. Weber, B., Mutschler, B., Reichert, M.: Investigating the effort of using business process management technology: results from a controlled experiment. Sci. Comput. Prog. **75**(5), 292–310 (2010)
27. Weske, M.: Business Process Management - Concepts, Languages, Architectures, 2nd edn. Springer, Berlin (2012)

Achievements, Failures, and the Future of Model-Based Software Engineering

Oliver Kautz, Alexander Roth, and Bernhard Rumpe

The borders of my language are the borders of my world.
L. Wittgenstein

1   Introduction

Using models is one of the primary techniques to understand and engineer the world. Modeling is by far not an invention of software engineering. All engineering disciplines use models to describe a system under development before actually building it. A model is used to get a shared understanding of the system and also to analyze whether the system will have the desired properties after building it. The term "model" dates back to the twelfth century, where a model meant to be a 1:10 version of a cathedral or dome, allowing a customer to "walk through" the building, to understand whether size, light effects, impressiveness, or other properties will be achieved, but also to understand whether the building will be statically save.

Models are not only used as a prescription of a system to be built. Models are also used in science to understand the existing world in a descriptive form. Already the ancient Greeks and Egyptians have built models of their worlds, including mathematical laws and a calendar system to predict the monsoon—it is barely imaginable that a pyramid could be built without extensive prior modeling. Archaeologists believe that cave paintings were used to teach younger tribal members hunting herds of wild animals. These paintings are models of hunting scenes. In social communities we learn role models for our behavior. We also get executable models in forms of recipes for preparing meals or construction manuals for assembling furniture.

Models appear in a plethora of forms. They can describe structural or behavioral aspects, interactions, and geometry, or they can be used as recipes for processes. Models can be quite informal and self-explanatory (e.g., cooking recipe, furniture

O. Kautz (✉) · A. Roth · B. Rumpe
Software Engineering, RWTH Aachen University, Aachen, Germany
e-mail: kautz@se-rwth.de; roth@se-rwth.de; rumpe@se-rwth.de

V. Gruhn, R. Striemer (eds.), *The Essence of Software Engineering*,
https://doi.org/10.1007/978-3-319-73897-0_13

construction manual) or have a rather formal appearance and a well-defined mathematical theory (e.g., differential equations for physics simulations).

With all this different forms of models in society, science, and engineering, it is not surprising that computer science developed its own idea of helpful models to design and understand software systems.

However, software is different from any other physical system that engineers would want to build. First of all, software per se has no physical manifestation. This leads to a number of characteristics for software itself as well as for software production and development processes. Obviously, production completely vanishes, when software can be downloaded and built on a push-button basis (or even automatically). There is no need for a physical manifestation of a factory for assembling individual software products during a rather expensive process. Therefore, software development is always a process of invention and stabilization until the final version is developed.

Because of its immaterial nature and the knowledge about its context, software itself is (or at least it embodies) a model of the elements that it deals with. A "Person" object is actually an abstraction of a real Person, containing only the relevant information about the person. But software is complex and thus needs engineering techniques. The two main classical techniques are "divide and conquer" in various forms: The software system is divided in subsystems and finally components. The development process is divided in phases, focusing on different artifacts, and iterations, allowing to start small and to improve the software in manageable steps. Early phases, such as understanding the problem (also called requirements elicitation), structuring the problem (also called requirements specification and high-level architecture definition), as well as precisely specifying the desired solution in smaller chunks (e.g., use case definition), do not result in programming artifacts but require various forms of models.

The Unified Modeling Language (UML) [39, 43, 44] was developed two decades ago to provide a standardized framework for this purpose. It includes and standard-izes preexisting modeling approaches and languages and adds new ones. The UML has 13 sublanguages in total that are applicable for a variety of purposes. However, it is difficult to say whether the UML, as a general-purpose modeling language, is the appropriate language for all use cases or where it should be improved or where language concepts should be removed or added.

The UML, its many predecessors, and its foundations in modeling techniques based on formal methods, such as finite automata [24], entity relationship mod-els [9], and others, demonstrate that computer science has not only invented its own forms of models but also made its forms of models explicit through defining modeling languages. Only if a modeling language is defined explicitly and precisely enough, which includes syntax, semantics, and the clarification about the pragmatic forms of use [22], then the language is usable for communication, shared understanding between humans, and also amenable for intensive tooling, such as checking semantic differences [30, 31] or consistency analysis [32].

In general, MBSE includes all development processes that use explicit models in artifacts, both for internal communication as well as for communication with a computer. The latter is intended for detailed analysis, simulation, productive or test code generation, interpretation, and configuration.

Subsequently, this chapter first clarifies in more detail what MBSE is and what the most popular modeling languages are in Sect. 2. Afterwards, we discuss its current failures and achievements in Sects. 3 and 4 to conclude with an outlook of the future of MBSE in Sect. 5.

2   Model-Based Software Engineering

MBSE is a software development process that aims to tackle increasing software development complexity by using abstraction and automation [5]. Abstraction is achieved by employing suitable models of (parts of) a software system. Automation systematically transforms these models into executable source code. The term model is considered as a high-level abstraction in textual or graphical notation. Even though its meaning is not clearly defined (cf. [45]), we understand a model that is used in MBSE as follows:

Definition 1 (Model [12]) A model is an abstraction of an aspect of reality (as-is or to-be) that is built for a given purpose.

In general, models can be distinguished into prescriptive and descriptive models depending on their purpose and use [17]. The primer describe an original that is created from the model. The latter describe an original to better understand it. Disregarding this classification, each model has to be written down in order to be useful for MBSE. This already implies that models in MBSE have finite representations, either in textual or graphical notation. Specifying models can either be done using a general-purpose modeling language (GPML) or a domain-specific language (DSL).

Definition 2 (Modeling Language [12]) A modeling language defines a set of models that can be used for modeling purposes. Its definition consists of (a) the syntax, (b) the semantics, and (c) its pragmatics.

While modeling languages are usually not tailored to a particular domain but rather address general-purpose concepts (e.g., the UML [39]), a DSL uses wording and concepts from the domain of interest. Hence, we understand a DSL as follows:

Definition 3 (Domain-Specific Language [11]) A DSL is a language that is specifically dedicated to a domain of interest, where a language is understood as a means for communication between stakeholders using a restricted amount of sentences.

A DSL targets at bridging the gap between problem and solution space [11] and is, generally, more restrictive than a GPML. DSLs usually drop Turing completeness and often allow fully automated formal verification of the (domain-specific) properties of interest. This is hardly feasible using Turing-complete general-purpose programming languages (GPLs).

2.1 Unified Modeling Language and Systems Modeling Language

A standardized language family for software development is the Unified Modeling Language, which is standardized by the Object Management Group [39]. The UML offers a wide portfolio of mainly graphical (but also textual) languages to model software systems [51]. An overview of all diagram types is shown in Fig. 1.

While the primary focus of the UML targets at software systems' design, another popular language (the Systems Modeling Language (SysML)) aims to provide a similar set of modeling languages for the design of systems [48]. It is based on the UML 2 and, hence, uses some diagrams with particular extensions for system design. In addition, the SysML provides the requirement diagram type, which is not part of the UML, to address requirements engineering. An overview of all supported diagram types is shown in Fig. 2.

2.2 Constructive Model Use: Interpreters and Code Generators

One major goal of MBSE is to model a software system or parts of the system by abstract models describing a subject of a particular problem domain. Models are

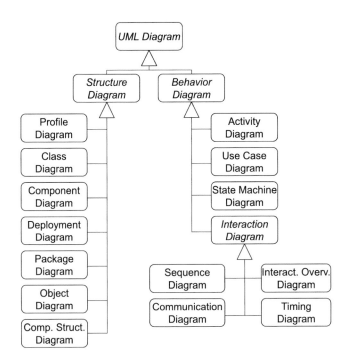

Fig. 1 Overview of UML diagram types

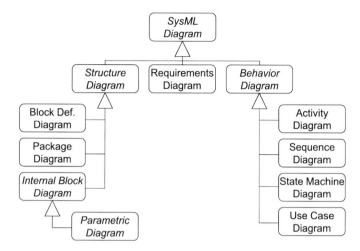

Fig. 2 Overview of SysML diagram types

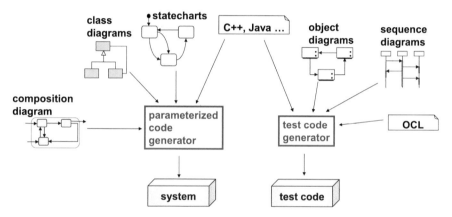

Fig. 3 Overview of different scenarios for using models in MBSE to generate system or test code

then used constructively for different aspects of a software system. This is achieved by developing and employing code generators as well as model interpreters to reflect the models' meanings in a system, which is potentially still under development.

A code generator takes models as input and produces (parts of) a software system [42]. Assuming code generator's correctness, the intended benefit is to reduce the costs for developing the system by hand. As models typically omit certain details, the generated code typically has to be complemented with handwritten code that the model abstracts from. This can either be done on the generated source code level (e.g., [21]) or on the input model level (e.g., UML/P [45]).

Figure 3 gives an overview of how UML models can be employed in MBSE. For example, UML class diagrams can be used to generate system code, which is source code used in production. Another example are UML object diagrams that can be used to define test cases and generate test code (cf. [44]). The main part of both examples is formed by a code generator to systematically transform a model into executable source code.

As an alternative to code generators, interpreters can be used to execute models. Interpreters are kinds of software systems that operate on models in context of a running system, that is, they interpret models based on a system's state. As the system state may change (possibly also during the interpretation of a model), the result from interpreting the same model may differ between successive interpretations. In contrast to code generation, model interpretation relies on a virtual machine that is aware of the semantics of the model. When executing a model by interpretation, a model interpreter evaluates the model and executes the corresponding virtual machine commands. Such approaches are known from scripting languages such as Python or Ruby, even though they do not conceptually differ from the underlying programming paradigm and are programming languages, too.

Some major benefits of code generation over interpretation are that (a) generated source code is easier to understand than interpreter logic, (b) generated source code can be optimized for different target platforms, and (c) code generators are easier to start with and to maintain because of existing code generator frameworks. In contrast to code generation, the major benefits of model interpretation are as follows: (a) changes in a model do not require code generation and, hence, allow higher agility in development, (b) changes to a model can be made at runtime and are directly reflected by the interpreter [10], and (c) it promises to be more flexible than code generation. Stated differently, code generation is typically performed at design time, before compile time, whereas model interpretation is typically done at runtime.

2.3 Benefits and Drawbacks of Using Models Constructively

Models explicitly describe a particular subject from the domain of interest and implicitly describe (parts of) a system for solving the problem the model describes. This implicit description is made explicit by code generators or interpreters.

Figure 4 illustrates the relations between models, the domain-specific problems they describe, and the solutions for solving the problems. Each model explicitly models (parts of) a domain-specific problem. When using the model constructively, it also implicitly relates the parts of the solution to the parts of the problem it describes. A code generator explicates this relation by defining the translation rules from the model to a representation in the solution space (typically GPL code) for solving the parts of the problem described by the model. Similarly, an interpreter explicates the description by defining the necessary steps for executing the model at runtime to solve the parts of the problem the model describes.

Fig. 4 Relation between domain-specific problems, models addressing the domain, and solutions to the problems

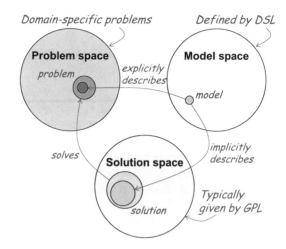

As models are intended to be more abstract than the subject they describe (problem space), models are also considerably easier to understand than the parts of the system they describe (solution space). They simultaneously serve as system documentation (solution space description) and primary development artifacts (problem space description). This avoids redundancies between system documentations and inconsistencies between documentations and implementations. Constructive use of models further significantly reduces the cost of system evolution: Adjusting a model can be carried out more effectively than adjusting the system it describes, which should be much more complex in comparison to the model. A model's syntax is typically expressed in the terminology of its application domain. With this understanding and assuming meaningful code generators, the impact of changing the content of a model is more coherent than to directly modify source code.

On the other hand, the initial cost for using models constructively is high: Designing a modeling language requires a detailed understanding of the problem domain (problem space) the language targets at. This understanding may be split among different stakeholders, which need to be intensively consulted to develop the modeling language as suitable as possible. Code generator or interpreter developers must additionally bring expertise in solving the problems described the modeling language. In summary, this requires a detailed understanding of the following aspects:

1. The parts of the problem domain that can be described using the modeling language (problem space)
2. The modeling language itself (model space)
3. How the models relate to the parts of the problem domain they describe (relation between model and problem, i.e., explicit description)

4. The solution space for solving the subjects described by models conforming to the language (solution space)
5. How to solve the problem described by a model using the provided solution space (relation between model and solution, i.e., realization of implicit description)

Thus, for applying constructive MBSE successfully, expertise in the solution space as well as the problem domain and knowledge about solving problems described by models is required prior to code generator or interpreter development. As models may describe nontrivial circumstances in complex domains, code generator or interpreter development may require highly skilled personnel.

On the contrary, in traditional software engineering projects, the model space and, therefore, the relations between models and problems as well as solutions do not exist. In such projects, it is easier to adapt to changing requirements (changes in the problem space) as these only require to adapt the solution. In MBSE projects, where models are used constructively, changes of the problem space may require costly adaptations of the model space as well as the relations between the model space and the other two spaces. With the increasing shift to agile development methodologies, dynamically changing requirements become a standard.

3   Failures of Model-Based Software Engineering

Even though MBSE promises to reduce complexity and decrease development time, there are pitfalls and challenges that may lead MSBE projects to fail. In the remainder of this section, we summarize these pitfalls and challenges.

Creating and Maintaining Code Generators An integral part of MBSE are code generators for translating models to source code. Current tool support (cf. [15, 36]) enables rapid and easy code generator development for arbitrary models. This might be true for relatively simple code generators that do not analyze the input models to adapt the generated source code. However, this situation is different when code generators become complex. This is often the case when complete software systems are generated, for example, [28]. In this situation, a code generator has to be regarded as a complex software system on its own. In some cases, it may also be a product line (cf. [42]) or needs to process modeling language product lines [36]. This demands for additional effort to develop and maintain the code generator because for every change in the input language or the generated source code, the code generator has to be adapted.

Design and Development of DSLs Each code generator relies on a model, which is an instance of a particular (or multiple) DSL. Each DSL is specifically tailored to a particular domain and potentially has to be adapted when reusing it for a different domain or a different scenario. However, designing and developing a DSL is, in general, a complex and time-consuming task, which is only partially supported by design guidelines [25]. This additional development effort has to be invested in order to effectively and efficiently employ MBSE. The state of the art in software language engineering only partially supports reusing parts of preexisting DSLs and corresponding tooling [36]. While language modularization scenarios for syntax definitions are widely covered by existing language workbenches [36], tool composition for processing models (e.g., code generator composition) seems to be still an open problem [37].

Modeling Needs Domain Knowledge In general, modeling requires a deep understanding of the modeling language and, more importantly, the domain itself. A modeler has to understand the requirements and demands of the domain and must be able to transform them into appropriate models (cf. Sect. 2.3). This task is, generally, (a) more complex than programming (sequential thinking versus specification-oriented thinking) and it involves (b) creating concise and possibly underspecified models, which demands an unconventional thinking process.

Compilers Are Highly Optimized; DSL Code Generators Just Do Their Work For GPLs, compilers are highly optimized to particular needs, for example, runtime performance. In contrast, models are processed by code generators or interpreters (cf. Sect. 2.2). Both are generally not highly optimized. Hence, for particular types of software systems, for example, high-performance algorithms, a MBSE approach fails if it does not make use of sophisticated adaptation mechanisms. Such mechanisms allow to adapt either the code generator, interpreter, or the generated source code to perform optimization tasks or handle underspecification. However, even if adaption is possible, the adaption process may still be more expensive (in terms of, e.g., development time, maintainability, etc.) than writing efficient code from scratch.

Project Setting Has to Fit MBSE A typical reason for MBSE project failure is rooted in the nature of the project itself. MBSE software projects are highly effective for software projects with repetitive and similar tasks. For example, imagine a software project that defines a REST interface for a particular domain model. In this project, the technology stack and the definition of a REST interface are clearly similar. Hence, suitable code generators can speed up development time by generating the REST interface from the domain model. However, for software projects without or with only little repetitive tasks—where every part of the source code is very individual—MBSE fails because it demands a code generator and a suitable DSL for each particular concern.

Model Tooling Is Not That Elaborated as for Programming (IDEs) The lack of tooling for model and code generator creation is a major challenge of MBSE. Even though there are language workbenches (cf. [15, 36]) that support generation or manual implementation of integrated development environments (IDEs) with syntax highlighting and auto completion, the resulting tools are not as supportive as well-established IDEs for GPLs. Furthermore, the tool support has to be maintained whenever the DSL evolves. A similar situation is also present in the development of code generators, where suitable adaptation concerns have to be addressed by additional infrastructures (cf. [21]).

MBSE and Agility Do Not Yet Work Well Together Agile software development has shown its effectiveness as a method to tackle complexity and ambiguity of software projects and to reduce the time to deliver software products. However, MBSE and agile software development methods are still not yet coalesced and demand for a combination of plan-driven and agile methods (cf. [27]). More importantly, the crucial role of model quality and tooling for creating, managing, and refactoring models is not yet resolved (cf. [8, 26]).

From the aforementioned pitfalls and failures of MBSE and from current research, the main questions to be answered are: *What kind of software systems can effectively be supported by MBSE? What needs to be improved to make MBSE suitable?* Clearly, software language engineering and code generator engineering needs to improve. This also holds for tooling supporting language reuse and composition as well as code generator and interpreter composition and creation. Hence, in the following, we present success stories of MBSE as well as the use cases' motivations and achievements with respect to MBSE. These examples are helpful to understand when MBSE is appropriate and why it is successful.

4 Where Model-Based Software Engineering Is Successful

Example domains where MBSE has proven successful are cyber-physical systems (CPS) [2] and component-based software engineering (CBSE) [38]. In these contexts, MBSE has been adopted by means of architecture description languages (ADLs) [35]. ADLs are special modeling languages providing syntax to describe the structure of a system under development. Academia and industry produced over 120 ADLs [29] in context of different domains such as automotive [13], avionics [16], consumer electronics [53], or robotics [46]. In context of ADLs, code generators take models describing the structure of a system under development as input and produce a runtime infrastructure for executing the system. Such models typically abstract away component implementation details and focus on the system's structure, that is, the system's components and their interconnections. The implementation of each individual component thus typically has to be implemented by hand. Some ADLs additionally enable to describe component behavior implementations. Where this possibility is available, it is even possible to generate complete software systems. Examples for graphical and textual CBSE-related DSLs are integrated into the AutoFocus [3], MontiArc [6], and Simulink [47] frameworks.

Other example domains successfully employing MBSE that use model interpretation are the domains of software build automation and web development. Makefiles, for example, are executed by command line interpreters. Web browsers interpret HTML models as text layout definitions and interpret JavaScript programs, for instance, to execute a reaction in response to user interaction events.

The neuroscience domain has successfully produced the NestML, which is a DSL used by neuroscientists for creating neuron models in a precise and concrete syntax familiar to domain experts [40]. A code generator translates NestML models into

C++ code that can be dynamically loaded into NEST [20], a simulator for networks of spiking point neurons. Before integrating NestML, domain experts created new neuron models for NEST by copy-and-paste from existing models. As neuroscientists are no programming experts, source code redundancy, suboptimal performance, improper documentation, and reduced maintainability are the consequences [40]. Investigations revealed cases where two different copy-and-paste models shared more than 90% of their contents [40]. The modeling language and its tools were well received by domain experts [40]. An evaluation revealing the increase in code reuse, performance, and documentation as well as the decrease in redundancy is currently not available.

MBSE has also been successfully applied in context of a customs information system to describe document verification rules and configuration files [18]. Such verification rules describe constraints that relate different fields of XML documents. A compiler translates verification rule models to Java byte code. A requirement on the verification rule DSL was that its models should be similar to rules expressed in natural language [18]. This indicates that verification rules are modeled by nontechnical users.

Another case study reports on successful application of MBSE in context of service robotics applications [1]. The goal is to achieve separation of concerns and to ease development of complex service robotics applications by applying models and code generators. Domain experts model the environment a robot operates in, robot and world abilities, as well as tasks and goals for the robot to achieve. The goal is to enable nontechnical domain experts to model the context of a service robotics application. From such models, generators produce scenario-specific source code. Robotics experts then complement the generated code with handcrafted implementations for the world and robot abilities at well-defined places. Thus, models capture the requirements of a particular instance in the service robotics domain (robot environment, robot/world abilities), and robotics experts complement the application with their robotics domain expertise. This ultimately reduces the costs for developing service robotics applications and enables separation of concerns.

JavaSM is a DSL that integrates state machines into Java to develop a command-and-control simulator [4]. The case study also relies on CBSE and product line architecture methodologies. The DSL is used for defining and refining state machines that specify component behavior. State machine-based implementations are frequently used in this case study. The motivation for developing the JavaSM is that state machine encodings in pure Java are extremely complex and thus hard to maintain and understand [4]. The achievement is a complexity reduction of component specifications: The case study's result is a more flexible way of implementing state machine-based simulators than is possible with pure Java implementations [4]. Hence, the case study is an example of where a DSL eases software development in a particular use case and hence increases productivity of developers.

Risla is a DSL for describing products developed in the financial engineering domain [52]. Financial engineering experts use Risla to model new products. The case study's motivation is to decrease the time needed for introducing new types of products and to ensure newly developed products are correctly implemented as intended [52]. The complexity of introducing a new product seems to be based on the case study's underlying software system, which is implemented in COBOL. The second motivation arises since it is only hardly, if even, possible to ensure a software engineer correctly implements the instructions given by a financial engineer. The goal is to employ models and code generators such that (1) new products can be added easily and (2) potential information loss during communication of domain experts and software engineers is avoided. This ultimately leads to a lower time to market for new products and eliminates a source for introducing incorrect behavior.

Other examples for well-known successful DSLs commonly used in (computer) science domains include, among many others, SQL for specifying database queries, LaTeX for writing documents, and MATLAB [33] for numerical computing and embedded systems. Other domains where DSLs have been used include artificial intelligence [34], graphics [14], model checking [23], operating systems [41], various protocols [7, 49], and video device drivers [50]. Most of these DSLs target at increasing productivity of software developers and ensuring program correctness.

5   Can We Draw Conclusions?

While MBSE has its drawbacks and failures, it still keeps its promises in some domains and software projects. In particular, summarizing the reasons for successful MBSE, we obtain the following indicators:

1. If a company is aware of its software needs to be available in many different versions and continuously evolves, and development continues for a long time, then MBSE is helpful. Models then act as abstract specifications for individual features as well as the overall architecture. Production code and test code generators are in place to decouple the application from the technology stack and to embrace variant management. This is achieved by using models as composable units (features) selected with respect to the needs of each individual product.
2. Domain experts are not necessarily classical software developers (programmers) but may also be nontechnical stakeholders without programming expertise. Such experts may prefer to use a DSL or a graphical modeling language rather than a GPL. In this case, models enable domain experts and users to actively participate in system development. Domain experts provide domain models to develop the system and users use models to configure it.
3. If a system is not only composed of software but also of complex hardware, then there is no alternative to using models for describing the overall system. Physical models are used by any engineering discipline, to understand a system under development before building it. If the system's software part is also to be understood early, then integrated physical and software models are helpful. The CPS and Industry 4.0 initiatives are shifting towards this direction.

4. If a system is grounded on a well-defined theory such as physics, chemistry, or biology, then scientists developing concrete models of their system under examination prefer to use models with syntax similar to the underlying mathematical theory. Such models are preferably used for simulation of real-world phenomena such as galaxies, climate, brain, chemical molecules, or physical particles.

In reverse conclusion, the overhead for initializing MBSE development processes often does not pay off compared to the benefits obtained from reusing models and generators in a modular way. This is the case, for instance, if a developing company is ensure whether an enhanced variant of an already existing software product needs to be delivered in a future project. This is often the case in purely software-based systems as, for example, enterprise information systems and software developed in web domains.

However, the use of models has still not yet been explored in all potentially possible domains. There are promising examples, such as nontechnical users writing Excel formulas without explicitly noticing they are actually programming. Supporting end users to program in a restricted and controlled fashion could be supported by appropriate modeling languages.

Like many other new and innovative technologies, MBSE has promised a lot and has not kept all of its promises. Fortunately, a lot of ideas and techniques from MBSE can be used for implicit modeling using GPLs. The encoding of state machines using the state design pattern [19] is such an example.

References

1. Adam, K., Butting, A., Heim, R., Kautz, O., Rumpe, B., Wortmann, A.: Model-driven separation of concerns for service robotics. In: International Workshop on Domain-Specific Modeling (DSM'16). ACM, New York (2016)
2. Alur, R.: Principles of Cyber-Physical Systems. The MIT Press, Cambridge (2015)
3. Aravantinos, V., Voss, S., Teufl, S., Hölzl, F., Schätz, B.: AutoFOCUS 3: tooling concepts for seamless, model-based development of embedded systems. In: Joint Proceedings of ACES-MB 2015 - Model-Based Architecting of Cyber-Physical and Embedded Systems and WUCOR 2015 - UML Consistency Rules (2015)
4. Batory, D., Johnson, C., MacDonald, B., von Heeder, D.: Achieving extensibility through product-lines and domain-specific languages: a case study. ACM Trans. Softw. Eng. Methodol. 11(2), 191–214 (2002)
5. Brambilla, M., Cabot, J., Wimmer, M.: Model-driven software engineering in practice. Synth. Lect. Softw. Eng. 1(1), 1–182 (2012)
6. Butting, A., Haber, A., Hermerschmidt, L., Kautz, O., Rumpe, B., Wortmann, A.: Systematic language extension mechanisms for the MontiArc architecture description language. In: Modelling Foundations and Applications (ECMFA'17), Held as Part of STAF 2017, pp. 53–70. Springer International Publishing, Cham (2017)
7. Chandra, S., Richards, B., Larus, J.R.: Teapot: language support for writing memory coherence protocols. In: Conference on Programming Language Design and Implementation. ACM, New York (1996)
8. Chaudron, M.R., Heijstek, W., Nugroho, A.: How effective is UML modeling? Softw. Syst. Model. 11(4) (2012)

9. Chen, P.P.S.: The entity-relationship model - toward a unified view of data. ACM Trans. Database Syst. **1**(1), 166–192 (1976)
10. Cheng, B., Eder, K., Gogolla, M., Grunske, L., Litoiu, M., Müller, H., Pelliccione, P., Perini, A., Qureshi, N., Rumpe, B., Schneider, D., Trollmann, F., Villegas, N.: Using models at runtime to address assurance for self-adaptive systems. In: Models@run.time. Lecture Notes in Computer Science, vol. 8378, pp. 101–136. Springer, Berlin (2014)
11. Cheng, B.H.C., Combemale, B., France, R.B., Jézéquel, J.M., Rumpe, B.: Globalizing domain-specific languages (Dagstuhl Seminar 14412). Dagstuhl Rep. **4**(10) (2015)
12. Combemale, B., France, R., Jézéquel, J.M., Rumpe, B., Steel, J., Vojtisek, D.: Engineering Modeling Languages: Turning Domain Knowledge into Tools. Innovations in Software Engineering and Software Development Series. Chapman & Hall/CRC, London/Boca Raton (2016)
13. Debruyne, V., Simonot-Lion, F., Trinquet, Y.: EAST-ADL - an architecture description language. In: Architecture Description Languages. Springer, New York (2005)
14. Elliott, C.: Modeling interactive 3D and multimedia animation with an embedded language. In: Proceedings of the Conference on Domain-Specific Languages on Conference on Domain-Specific Languages (DSL), 1997. USENIX Association, Berkeley (1997)
15. Erdweg, S., van der Storm, T., Völter, M., Tratt, L., Bosman, R., Cook, W.R., Gerritsen, A., Hulshout, A., Kelly, S., Loh, A., Konat, G., Molina, P.J., Palatnik, M., Pohjonen, R., Schindler, E., Schindler, K., Solmi, R., Vergu, V., Visser, E., van der Vlist, K., Wachsmuth, G., van der Woning, J.: Evaluating and comparing language workbenches. Comput. Lang. Syst. Struct. **44**, 24–47 (2015)
16. Feiler, P.H., Gluch, D.P.: Model-Based Engineering with AADL: An Introduction to the SAE Architecture Analysis & Design Language. Addison-Wesley Professional, Reading (2012)
17. Fieber, F., Huhn, M., Rumpe, B.: Modellqualität als Indikator für Softwarequalität: eine Taxonomie. Informatik-Spektrum **31**(5), 408–424 (2008)
18. Freudenthal, M.: Domain-specific languages in a customs information system. IEEE Softw. **27**(2), 65–71 (2010)
19. Gamma, E., Helm, R., Johnson, R., Vlissides, J.: Design Patterns: Elements of Reusable Object-Oriented Software. Addison-Wesley Longman Publishing Co., Inc., Boston (1995)
20. Gewaltig, M.O.: NEST (NEural Simulation Tool). Scholarpedia **2**(4), 1430 (2007)
21. Greifenberg, T., Hölldobler, K., Kolassa, C., Look, M., Mir Seyed Nazari, P., Müller, K., Navarro Perez, A., Plotnikov, D., Reiß, D., Roth, A., Rumpe, B., Schindler, M., Wortmann, A.: Integration of handwritten and generated object-oriented code. In: Model-Driven Engineering and Software Development. Communications in Computer and Information Science, vol. 580. Springer, New York (2015)
22. Harel, D., Rumpe, B.: Meaningful Modeling: What's the Semantics of "Semantics"? IEEE Comput. **37**(10), 64–72 (2004)
23. Holzmann, G.J.: The Spin Model Checker: Primer and Reference Manual. Addison-Wesley, Reading (2003)
24. Hopcroft, J.E., Motwani, R., Ullman, J.D.: Introduction to Automata Theory, Languages, and Computation, 3rd edn. Addison-Wesley Longman Publishing Co., Inc., Boston (2006)
25. Karsai, G., Krahn, H., Pinkernell, C., Rumpe, B., Schindler, M., Völkel, S.: Design guidelines for domain specific languages. In: Domain-Specific Modeling Workshop (DSM'09), Techreport B-108. Helsinki School of Economics (2009)
26. Kent, S.: Model Driven Engineering. In: Integrated Formal Methods. Lecture Notes in Computer Science, vol. 2335. Springer, Berlin (2002)
27. Kulkarni, V., Barat, S., Ramteerthkar, U.: Early experience with agile methodology in a model-driven approach. In: 14th International Conference on Model Driven Engineering Languages and Systems. MODELS'11. Springer, Berlin (2011)
28. Look, M.: Unterstützung modellgetriebener, agiler Entwicklung mehrbenutzerfähiger, ubiquitärer Enterprise Applikationen durch Generatoren. Ph.D. thesis, RWTH Aachen University, Aachen (2017)

29. Malavolta, I., Lago, P., Muccini, H., Pelliccione, P., Tang, A.: What industry needs from architectural languages: a survey. IEEE Trans. Softw. Eng. **39**(6), 869–891 (2013)
30. Maoz, S., Ringert, J.O., Rumpe, B.: A manifesto for semantic model differencing. In: Proceedings International Workshop on Models and Evolution (ME'10). Lecture Notes in Computer Science, vol. 6627, pp. 194–203. Springer, Berlin (2010)
31. Maoz, S., Ringert, J.O., Rumpe, B.: ADDiff: semantic differencing for activity diagrams. In: Conference on Foundations of Software Engineering (ESEC/FSE '11), pp. 179–189. ACM, New York (2011)
32. Maoz, S., Ringert, J.O., Rumpe, B.: Semantically configurable consistency analysis for class and object diagrams. In: Conference on Model Driven Engineering Languages and Systems (MODELS'11). Lecture Notes in Computer Science, vol. 6981, pp. 153–167. Springer, Berlin (2011)
33. Matlab Homepage (2017). https://de.mathworks.com/products/matlab.html. Accessed 09 May 2017
34. Mcdermott, D., Ghallab, M., Howe, A., Knoblock, C., Ram, A., Veloso, M., Weld, D., Wilkins, D.: PDDL - the planning domain definition language. Tech. Rep. TR-98-003, Yale Center for Computational Vision and Control (1998)
35. Medvidovic, N., Taylor, R.: A classification and comparison framework for software architecture description languages. IEEE Trans. Softw. Eng. **26**(1), 70–93 (2000)
36. Méndez-Acuña, D., Galindo Duarte, J.A., Degueule, T., Combemale, B., Baudry, B.: Leveraging software product lines engineering in the development of external DSLs: a systematic literature review. Comput. Lang. Syst. Struct. **46**, 206–235 (2016)
37. Mir Seyed Nazari, P., Roth, A., Rumpe, B.: An extended symbol table infrastructure to manage the composition of output-specific generator information. In: Modellierung 2016 Conference, vol. 254. Bonner Köllen Verlag, Bonn (2016)
38. Naur, P., Randell, B. (eds.): Software Engineering: Report of a Conference Sponsored by the NATO Science Committee (1969)
39. Object Management Group (2017). http://www.omg.org. Accessed 09 May 2017
40. Plotnikov, D., Blundell, I., Ippen, T., Eppler, J.M., Morrison, A., Rumpe, B.: NESTML: a modeling language for spiking neurons. In: Modellierung 2016 Conference. LNI, vol. 254. Bonner Köllen Verlag, Bonn (2016)
41. Pu, C., Black, A., Cowan, C., Walpole, J., Consel, C.: Microlanguages for operating system specialization. In: Workshop on Domain-Specific Languages (1997)
42. Roth, A., Rumpe, B.: Towards product lining model-driven development code generators. In: Model-Driven Engineering and Software Development Conference (MODELSWARD '15). SciTePress, Setúbal (2015)
43. Rumpe, B.: Modeling with UML: Language, Concepts, Methods. Springer International, Cham (2016)
44. Rumpe, B.: Agile Modeling with UML: Code Generation, Testing, Refactoring. Springer International, Cham (2017)
45. Schindler, M.: Eine Werkzeuginfrastruktur zur agilen Entwicklung mit der UML/P. Aachener Informatik-Berichte, Software Engineering, Band 11. Shaker Verlag, Herzogenrath (2012)
46. Schlegel, C., Steck, A., Lotz, A.: Model-driven software development in robotics: communication patterns as key for a robotics component model. In: Introduction to Modern Robotics. iConcept Press, Kowloon (2011)
47. Simulink Homepage (2017). https://de.mathworks.com/products/simulink.html. Accessed 09 May 2017
48. Systems Modeling Language (2017). http://www.omgsysml.org/. Accessed 09 May 2017
49. Thibault, S., Consel, C., Muller, G.: Safe and efficient active network programming. In: Proceedings Seventeenth IEEE Symposium on Reliable Distributed Systems (Cat. No.98CB36281) (1998)
50. Thibault, S.A., Marlet, R., Consel, C.: Domain-specific languages: from design to implementation application to video device drivers generation. IEEE Trans. Softw. Eng. **25**(3), 363–377 (1999)

51. Unified Modeling Language (2017). http://www.omg.org/spec/UML/. Accessed 09 May 2017
52. van Deursen, A., Klint, P.: Little languages: little maintenance. J. Softw. Maint. **10**(2), 75–92 (1998)
53. Van Ommering, R., Van Der Linden, F., Kramer, J., Magee, J.: The Koala component model for consumer electronics software. Computer **33**(3), 78–85 (2000)

Printed in the United States
By Bookmasters